Jonathan

He studied Psychology and
Needs teacher at Abbey Wood Secondary
His plays include *The Cherry Blossom Tree* (Liverpool
which won him the 1987 National Girobank Young Writer of the
Mohair (Royal Court Young Writers' Festival, London/International Festival of
Young Playwrights, Sydney, 1988); *Wildfire* (Royal Court Theatre Upstairs,
1992); *Beautiful Thing* (Bush Theatre, London, 1993 and Donmar Warehouse,
London/Duke of York's Theatre, London, 1994) winner of the John Whiting
Award 1994; *Babies* (Royal National Theatre Studio/Royal Court Theatre,
1994), winner George Devine Award 1993 and Evening Standard's Most
Promising Playwright Award 1994; *Boom Bang-A-Bang* (Bush Theatre, 1995);
Rupert Street Lonely Hearts Club (English Touring Theatre/Contact Theatre
Company, then Criterion Theatre 1995); *Swan Song* (Pleasance, Edinburgh/
Hampstead Theatre, London 1997). He is currently working on a sitcom, called
Gimme Gimme Gimme, for BBC2, transmission late 1998, two feature films *Gone
Shopping* and *The Hairdresser's Apprentice*, and a stage musical with Pet Shop Boys.
He has recently finished two new plays, *Hushabye Mountain* for English Touring
Theatre and *Guiding Star* for the Royal National Theatre.

JONATHAN HARVEY

Plays: 1

Beautiful Thing
Babies
Boom Bang-A-Bang
Rupert Street Lonely Hearts Club

introduced by the author

Methuen Drama

METHUEN CONTEMPORARY DRAMATISTS

1 3 5 7 9 10 8 6 4 2

This collection first published in Great Britain in 1999
by Methuen Drama
20 Vauxhall Bridge Road, London SW1 2SA

Random House Australia (Pty) Limited
20 Alfred Street, Milsons Point, Sydney, New South Wales 2061, Australia

Random House, New Zealand Limited
18 Poland Road, Glenfield, Auckland 10, New Zealand

Random House South Africa (Pty) Limited
Endulini, 5A Jubilee Road, Parktown 2193, South Africa

Beautiful Thing first published in *Gay Plays: Five* by Methuen Drama 1994.
Copyright © 1994 by Jonathan Harvey
Babies first published in the Royal Court Writers Series in 1994 by
Methuen Drama.
Copyright © 1994 by Jonathan Harvey
Boom-Bang-A-Bang first published in 1995 by Methuen Drama.
Copyright © 1995 by Jonathan Harvey
Rupert Street Lonely Hearts Club first published in 1995 by Methuen Drama.
Copyright © 1995 by Jonathan Harvey
Introduction copyright © 1999 by Jonathan Harvey
This collection copyright © 1999 by Methuen Drama

The right of Jonathan Harvey to be identified as the author of this
work has been asserted by him in accordance with the Copyright, Designs
and Patents Act, 1988.

ISBN 0–413–72450–6

Methuen Publishing Limited Reg. No 3543167

A CIP catalogue record for this book is available from the British Library

Typeset by Deltatype Ltd, Birkenhead, Merseyside
Printed and bound in Great Britain by Cox and Wyman Ltd,
Reading, Berkshire

Papers used by Methuen Publishing Limited are natural, recyclable products
made from wood grown in sustainable forests. The manufacturing processes
conform to the environmental regulations of the country of origin.

Contents

Jonathan Harvey:
A Chronology

1987   *The Cherry Blossom Tree*, winner of Liverpool Playhouse/National Girobank Young Writers' Award, produced at Liverpool Playhouse Studio, Liverpool.

1988   *Mohair*, produced at the Royal Court Theatre Upstairs, London, and represented the UK at the International Festival of Young Playwrights in Sydney, Australia.

1989   *Catch*, produced at Spring Street Theatre, Hull.

1990   *Tripping and Falling* produced by Glasshouse Theatre Company, Manchester.

1991   *Lady Snogs the Blues*, produced at Lincoln Theatre Festival.

1992   *Wildfire* produced at the Royal Court Theatre Upstairs.

1993   *Beautiful Thing* produced at the Bush Theatre, London.
West End Girls produced by Carlton Television

1994   *Beautiful Thing* on UK tour, then at the Donmar Warehouse, London, then Duke of York's Theatre, London. Winner of John Whiting Award, nominated for an Olivier Award and a Writers' Guild Award.
Babies produced at the Royal Court Theatre. Winner of the Evening Standard Award for Most Promising Playwright, nominated for Lloyds Bank Playwright of the Year Award. Winner of 1993 George Devine Award.

1995   Thames Television Writer-in-Residence, Bush
            Theatre.
            Boom Bang-A-Bang produced at the Bush Theatre.

1995/6   *Rupert Street Lonely Hearts Club* produced at Contact
            Theatre, Manchester, prior to UK, tour then
            Donmar Warehouse. Transferred to Criterion
            Theatre, London. Winner of Manchester Evening
            News Award, Best New Play.

1996   *Beautiful Thing* released as feature film, winner of
            Best Film at the London Lesbian and Gay Film
            Festival.

1997   *Swan Song* produced at Pleasance, Edinburgh, then
            Hampstead Theatre, London.

1998   *Guiding Star* produced at Liverpool Everyman
            Theatre and subsequently at Royal National
            Theatre in a co-production.
            Gimme Gimme Gimme, six-part sitcom for Tiger
            Aspect/BBC recorded.

For Richard

Introduction

I didn't always want to write plays. From an early age I foresaw a successful career for myself *on* the boards. I was an eager member of the Merseyside Youth Theatre during my primary school years, and perhaps my proudest moment was playing the Coroner of the Munchkins in *The Wizard of Oz* at the Neptune Theatre, Liverpool in 1978. In fact I was singled out at the dress rehearsal by the drama teacher as being the only cast member to attempt an American accent. And I only had one line, and that was sung. Because I was a 'featured' Munchkin, I got my own bow in the curtain call, but on opening night I ripped my satin bloomers and was too embarrassed to bow in case the people standing behind me (the Munchkins with no lines) caught a glimpse of my undies as I bent over to bow, so I ran away and bought an ice cream and went and watched the second half from the Gods. This was almost enough to deter me from my chosen path as an actor, but not quite. What finally put an end to my aspirations was a severe case of teenage acne several years later. I couldn't stand people looking at me, never mind paying good money to stare at me, because my face had taken on the aesthetics of a deep-pan pepperoni pizza – hold the chilli! My final acting part was as a jellyfish in a school production of *Robinson Crusoe*. In an underwater sequence I had to jump across the stage with a washing-up bowl on my head, which had old pairs of tights hanging off it. It was all done with ultra-violet light and special paints on the bowl and tights ... my grandmother said it was spectacular, she should know, she provided the tights.

I feel lucky to have grown up in Liverpool in the eighties. It never really crossed my mind that I couldn't be a writer. Everywhere you turned there seemed to be a renaissance of Liverpool-based drama, and I lapped it up. On television there was *Boys from the Blackstuff*, and the early days of *Brookside* (when the Patron Saint of writers, Jimmy McGovern, was a regular contributor). On the big screen there was *Letter to Brezhnev* and *Educating Rita*. And my local theatre was presenting plays in its Studio by local writers like Jim Hitchmough and Heidi Thomas. If you didn't know these writers personally, you always knew someone who was taught by Jimmy McGovern, or whose house was used as a location in *Boys from the Blackstuff*. It was an exciting time.

In 1987 the Playhouse ran a competition for young writers and I begged my parents for an electric typewriter and got scribbling. I came second originally, but when they discovered that the fella who'd come first had nicked someone else's play, ('That's *so* Liverpudlian!' I hear you say. Well let me tell you, he was from Burnley, Lancs.), I was promoted to first place. The play, *The Cherry Blossom Tree*, was a sell-out. I went to every performance. Mind you, it was only on for about a week.

Beautiful Thing was something like my seventh play. I hadn't done too badly with the previous six. Two of them had been on at the Royal Court in London, and one had been done in Australia. But in my heart of hearts I know that all those plays prior to the first one in this volume were part of my apprenticeship. They were done as part of young writers' festivals, or with youth theatres. *Beautiful Thing* was my first 'proper' play, performed in a 'proper' theatre, and not billed as being written by a 'young person'.

That's not to say that I wasn't young when I wrote it. I was twenty-four; though because I'd started so young I felt incredibly old and experienced. Ah, the naïveté of youth! But *Beautiful Thing* was also the first time I'd written anything with a gay theme. The timing felt right for me.

I wrote *Beautiful Thing* during the summer holiday from my teaching job in 1992. I was bored with teaching by then and wanted to be a full-time writer. However I'd just been got rid of by my agent and thought that I couldn't make the break without a new one. I sat on my bed and wrote it in about two weeks, then typed it up in two weeks. The last two weeks I spent using it to get a new agent and succeeded. I went back to school, handed in my notice and took frantic calls in the staff room from Alan, my new agent, arranging to meet various theatres who had liked the play. I met these people, but they kept turning the play down as they didn't like the ending. It was only later that I realised that Alan's assistant at the time was sending the scripts out with the last forty pages missing. She was fired, the pages were reinstated and before you know it The Bush was programming it for the following summer.

When writing the play I wanted to challenge the myth that if you're working class and a gay man, you get kicked out of the house and end up selling your body for twenty Woodbines down Piccadilly Circus. Yes it happens, but it never happened to me, and I suppose I wanted to tell my story. I'd seen several images of gay people on TV and film as I was growing up, and although I felt excited and empowered by them, I never fully identified with them. I also wanted to give young people who'd see the play some hope. I knew that in theatre you're usually preaching to the converted, so I was delighted that Channel Four then made it into a feature film. I was even more delighted that Hettie Macdonald was able to direct both the play and the film. She has a real knack of encouraging writers to knock their scripts into shape, and without her guidance the play would never have been the success that it was ... and the film would never have even been written, never mind made.

Before I left teaching I had been badgering away at John Burgess to give me a residency at the National Theatre Studio. At the time John was in charge of New Writing at the National and he'd got me into a writers' group there when my second play *Mohair* had been on at the Royal Court. I think he thought the play was quite melodramatic and immature, because everyone went around killing everyone else in it and getting quite worked up about it, but I think he thought that one day I'd write a good play. I sent him *Beautiful Thing*, which he thought was very rose-tinted (it is, so what?) but he'd made the mistake of telling me about the Studio's eight-week residencies for writers. They gave you an office, plays to read, a typewriter, access to the National's lovely canteen and £200 a week. I phoned him every week saying things like; 'I'm leaving teaching in three weeks' time and won't be able to get dole coz I've left of my own accord. Any vacancies?'. Finally he relented. I did my eight-week residency, and then got my dole because that job had run its course! During my eight weeks he encouraged me to write something based on my experiences as a teacher. I wrote *Babies*, mercilessly robbed from a particular night when I arrived at a pupil's birthday party to be entertained by a drag queen dressed as the Queen, where the mother had obviously taken a bit of a shine to me, and where the uncle of the pupil . . . oh read the play, it's far more interesting.

I heard nothing about *Babies*, and *Beautiful Thing* still hadn't been taken up by anyone so I took myself off to Brighton for a *Birds of a Feather* sitcom writers' course. I loved it. We were brainwashed from eight in the morning 'til midnight with all things sitcomy. I came away thinking my life would only be worth living if only I could write a fabulous script for those hilarious Birds. They must have liked me on the course because I was given a *Birds of a Feather* bible – i.e. 'Linda Robson has given up smoking so keep cigarettes to a minimum in scripts.' – and I read through it on the train on the way home. When I got indoors there was a message on my answer phone telling me I had won the George Devine Award with *Babies*, and The Bush had finally said yes to *Beautiful Thing*. The *Birds of a Feather Bible* went in the bin!

By the time *Babies* was produced at the Royal Court, *Beautiful Thing* had transferred to the West End. It was brilliant – I was never stuck for people to go drinking with. There were so many people in the Royal Court production, that I could go out with different actors each night, then go out with the gang from the other show, then start all over again with the *Babies* cast.

The next play I wrote was *Rupert Street Lonely Hearts Club*, which the National commissioned. It might have been all those hangovers from my time in the West End, but this is much more bittersweet in tone. All the characters are so lost, so lonely, and all of them looking for love. I was fed up that so many critics thought I could only write plays with happy endings, so I thought 'I'll show you!'. (Handy hint: If you can't be bothered to read the play, just turn to the last page, you'll understand what I'm talking about.) It was quite a depressing play to write, when your head's full of people on the verge of suicide all day it's quite hard to shake off.

I love the character of Marti. That gay man of a certain age, who can't believe that anyone might fancy him, but who covers it up with an outrageous sense of humour that is at once cutting and desperate. I've met many Martis in my time, and hope he's something of a warning. I certainly hope I don't turn into him. He's a warning about what you can become if you don't learn to love yourself. I'm also proud of Clarine. When I wrote the play I lived in a lovely flat on Streatham Common, and a couple of doors down there was a half-way house for people who were mentally ill. There was one particular woman who used to go to Sainsbury's in a midnight blue ball gown and tiara, and she had a heart of gold. She told me once that she loved Sainsbury's because there were so many people to talk to. I was quite shocked that audiences then found Clarine so funny on stage. Still, I think you laugh despite yourself, then feel guilty about it. And that sounds remarkably like a learning experience.

To shake off the depression of *Rupert Street* I decided to write something that was an out and out farce. I'd read a lot about a play called *An Evening with Gary Lineker*, where a group of friends get together to watch a football match on TV. I wondered what the gay equivalent would be. If I went on Mastermind my specialised subject would be The Eurovision Song Contest, so I soon had my answer. *Boom Bang-A-Bang* was quite an easy play to write, as I had no research to do. Again, I was blessed with another fantastic director in Kathy Burke, who told me which jokes weren't funny and which jokes were. I adored my second time at the Bush, with possibly the naughtiest bunch of actors I've ever worked with – many of whom are now firm friends. It was quite ironic that because *Rupert Street* was produced after this play the critics assumed that my writing was becoming darker. It's a good lesson for all writers, because it shows how much the critics know.

I'd like to thank all the actors, directors, designers and stage managers mentioned in this book, for giving me such happy memories and for making the written word really breathe on the stage. I'm as egotistical as the next writer, and will often be heard harping on about 'it'd be nothing without the writing' ... but of course theatre is such a collaborative experience, and without their knowledge and expertise these plays would never have been deemed good enough to publish.

I'd also like to say a special thank you to my agent Alan Radcliffe, the only heterosexual man I've ever met who throws fantastic Eurovision parties. He's always given me good advice, and along with his assistant Michael, has always been able to organise an advance for me just before my bills need paying.

And finally, I'd like to dedicate this volume of plays to my boyfriend Richard Foord. He's held my hand through all of these productions, and is my most loyal fan, and staunchest critic. He stops my head getting too big, and when I'm feeling down has the ability to make me feel I'm walking on air.

Jonathan Harvey
February 1998

Beautiful Thing

Beautiful Thing was first performed at the Bush Theatre, London, on 28 July 1993, with the following cast:

Jamie	Mark Letheren
Leah	Sophie Stanton
Sandra	Patricia Kerrigan
Ste	Johnny Lee Miller
Tony	Philip Glenister

Directed by Hettie Macdonald
Designed by Robin Don
Lighting by Johanna Town
Sound by Paul Bull

The play was revived and toured in 1994, ending with a run at the Donmar Warehouse, London. Sandra was played by Amelda Brown, Ste by Shaun Dingwall and Tony by Richard Bonneville. All other credits as above.

In September 1994, the play opened in the West End at the Duke of York's Theatre, with the following cast:

Jamie	Zubin Varla
Leah	Diane Parish
Sandra	Amelda Brown
Ste	Richard Dormer
Tony	Rhys Ifans

Characters

Jamie, *nearly sixteen, a plain looking lad.*
Leah, *Jamie's neighbour, sixteen. Attractive in a rough way.*
Sandra, *Jamie's mother, thirty-five.*
Ste, *another neighbour, also sixteen. Attractive in a scally way.*
Tony, *Sandra's young man, twenty-seven. Middle class trying to rough up.*

All the characters in the play except Tony have broad south-east London accents. Also heard, but not seen, is Ste's dad Ronnie, who is Irish. This part can be doubled by the actor playing Tony. Tony speaks with an irritating middle-class, trying to have street-cred, accent.

Setting

The play is set on the landing walkway in front of three flats in a low-rise block in Thamesmead, south-east London, May 1993.

This walkway is referred to in the script sometimes as balcony, landing or walkway. Ste's flat is on the left, facing us. Quite run-down. A clothes'-horse with dry washing hanging on it stands outside. Ste changes these clothes during Scene Four. There is a window with frosted glass in, beside the front door, which is Ste's bathroom. This is also a feature of Scene One. Sandra's flat sits in the middle, a rose between two thorns. Her door has recently been painted and there is a hanging basket next to it. Either side, on the ground, are two tubs, also of flowers. On her bathroom window hangs a net curtain which rises in the middle. Leah's flat is to the right of Sandra's facing us. It should be pretty nondescript. A child's rusty tricycle sits outside.

Also onstage we can see Jamie's bedroom, represented by a single bed and a bedside light. This could be located to the side of the flats. A *Hello!* magazine lies on the floor, along with a small Body Shop bottle.

When actors enter they either enter from a flat or from the right side of the flats, along the walkway. This should give the impression that Ste's flat is at the end of a row.

Act One

Scene One

'It's Getting Better' by Mama Cass blares out before the lights come up. As they do, the song fades. We find **Jamie** *and* **Leah** *sitting on their respective doorsteps in the sun.* **Jamie** *is wearing school uniform,* **Leah** *is not. Their front doors are open.* **Leah** *is smoking,* **Jamie** *has a can of coke. They are both looking out in front of them, up at the sky . . .*

Jamie   Richard of York gained battle in vain.

Leah *tuts.*

Jamie   Richard of York gained battle in vain.

Leah *tuts.*

Jamie   Oright, oright!

Leah   If you don't shut up I'm gonna get a brick and smash it right in your face.

Sandra *comes to the doorway of her and* **Jamie**'s *flat. She is holding a black bin bag full of rubbish, which she is taking out to the chute. She kicks* **Jamie** *out of the way and walks down the walkway and off.*

Jamie   What you thinkin'?

Leah *tuts.*

Jamie   Eh?

Leah   'Bout that brick.

Jamie   Nah go on.

Leah   Jamie!

Jamie (*tuts*)   Oright. (*Pause.*) Hot, innit?

Sandra *comes back empty-handed. She doesn't stop, but goes straight back into her flat, passing them an Exocet glance as she does.*

Leah   Oright, Sandra?

Sandra   Slag.

Jamie *shifts and she disappears inside.*

Leah   Who's Richard of York?

Jamie   Dunno. Gained battle in vain though, dinn'e?

Leah   He would, bloody toff.

Sandra *comes out with another bin bag. This time she stops.*

Sandra   You know what they'll do, don't you? They'll put you into care. They'll say, 'She's an unfit mother, bang 'im into one o'them 'omes. Coz I mean, she can't even get him to do his PE.' That's what they'll do.

She exits with the bag.

Leah   She's such a liar.

Jamie   I know.

Leah   You're sixteen, for God's sake.

Jamie   Fifteen.

Leah (*tuts*)   Shut up.

Sandra *enters again, from the chute, empty-handed.*

Sandra   I was a brilliant netball player when I was at school. 'Watch out for the girl in the plaits,' the other schools used to say. I could run as fast as anything.

Leah   Did you have plaits?!

Sandra   I'm talkina my son!

Leah   Did you?

Sandra   Yes! (*Exits to flat.*)

Jamie She's taking it out on the cupboard. Throwin' away everything I was saving for my kids. Books, toys. I don't want kids.

Leah Kids are cunts.

Jamie You're not looking.

Leah *tuts, then returns her gaze to the sky.* **Sandra** *comes to the door, brushing her hair.*

Sandra (*to* **Jamie**)   Anyone been calling you names?

Jamie Like what?

Sandra I dunno.

Jamie No.

Sandra Stumpy? Anyone called you that?

Jamie No.

Sandra I told you it'd stop.

Jamie I know.

Sandra I told you you'd grow. You never take the blindest bit o' notice to me.

Jamie I do.

Sandra Oh yeah?

Jamie Yeah!

Sandra Well, how comes every Wednesday afternoon without fail you're sittin' there?!

Jamie I've told you.

Sandra I'm gonna ring Miss Ellis.

Sandra *goes back in.*

Jamie Is your mum like this?

Leah I hate my mum.

Pause.

Jamie What d'you think?

Leah When?

Jamie When you're doing this?

Leah I sing. Helps me concentrate.

Jamie I can't hear ya.

Leah In me head, you stupid git.

Jamie What d'you sing? What sort o' songs?

Sandra (*off*) I'm just a girl who can't say no!! (*Laughs.*)

Leah You heard of Mama Cass?

Jamie Mighta done.

Leah It's by her, innit?

Jamie What's it called?

Leah 'It's Getting Better'.

Jamie Oh.

Leah You see. Mama Cass, helps me concentrate.

Jamie Fair enough. (*Pause.*) Sing it.

Leah What?

Jamie Go on.

Leah No.

Jamie I won't laugh.

Pause. **Leah** *looks up at the sky, then sings. She drops her south London accent and adopts the American tones of Mama Cass. She has quite a good voice.*

Leah (*sings*) I don't feel all turned on and starry-eyed.
I just feel a sweet contentment deep inside.
Holding you at night
Just seems kind of natural and right.

And it's not hard to see
That it isn't haff of what it's going to be.

Jamie   Haff?

Leah   Coz it's getting better
Growing stronger
Warm and wilder
Getting better every day
Better every day.

During the song **Sandra** *has come to the door. She watches* **Leah** *with a quizzical look.* **Leah** *stops.*

Sandra   Keep goin'. Might persuade him to go back to school.

Leah   Libs!

Sandra   It's not natural.

Jamie   What aint?

Sandra   For a girl of her age to be into Mama Cass.

Leah   She's got a really beautiful voice!

Sandra   Whassamatter with Madonna?

Leah   She's a slag!

Sandra   Hypocrite! (*Goes back in.*)

Jamie   Take no notice.

Leah   Fat chance.

Enter **Ste,** *in school uniform and carrying schoolbag.*

Jamie   Oright, Ste?!

Leah   Ste! Oright?

Ste   Yous two been bunkin' off together, have you?

Leah   Not together, no.

Jamie   We've been watching rainbows.

Leah   No we haven't. We haven't. I didn't even know there was a rainbow in the sky. I hate rainbows.

Sandra *comes out with another bin bag.*

Sandra   Hello, Ste.

Ste   Oright, Mrs Gangel?

Sandra   Well, it's nice to see someone can stay at school for the full day.

Ste   We done football today.

Sandra   It's the wrong season for football, innit?

Ste   Student teacher.

Sandra (*to* **Jamie**)   Is that the problem?

Jamie   No.

Leah   You get all dirty playing football, don't you?

Ste   Yeah.

Jamie   Muddy.

Sandra   Nothing wrong with a bit o' mud.

Leah   Did you win, Ste?

Ste   As always.

Leah   Ah.

Sandra   Hippopotamuses have baths in mud.

Jamie   Takes one to know one.

Sandra (*cuffs him round the earhole*)   You're just scared of a bit o' rain! That's all! Fifteen minutes o' bloody rain and you come running home! And look at it now! I'm bloody roastin'!

Jamie   I hate games.

Leah Well, that's the difference between you and me Jamie, see, coz I love games.

Jamie Well, why don't you go and bloody try it?!

Sandra Yeah, put your money where your mouth is, madam!

Ste See, I'm gonna use me sport when I'm older. Fancy workin' at the sports centre. So I gotta put the hours in, you know.

Sandra I know, Ste, I know. And it's a bloody good centre actually, coz I go step classes there. (*To* **Jamie**.) You don't!

Ste Swimming's my favourite sport.

Leah Yeah?

Ste Yeah.

Sandra (*to* **Jamie**) You can swim.

Leah I bet you look blindin' in your trunks Ste.

Sandra The pair o' you, you wanna get down them step classes, get a bit o' life into ya!

Leah You're not my mother!

Sandra Thank God for that!

Sandra *exits with bin bag in direction of the chute.*

Ste Anyway, gotta get in.

Leah Stay out here, Ste.

Ste I'm doin' the tea.

Leah Stick it on then come out here.

Ste Bubble and squeak, Leah. You can't leave bubble and squeak. Gotta watch it, like a hawk.

Leah Don't that make you fart. Bubble and squeak?

Jamie (*to* **Leah**) Only if you've got a fat arse.

Ste 'Ere, Jamie, you wanna do football, you know. It's all right. People'll talk to you then.

Leah   What you having for afters, Ste? (*Looks at* **Jamie**.) Spotted Dick?

Jamie (*to* **Ste**)   I don't like it.

Ste   You joined in in juniors.

Jamie   Juniors is different.

Ste   How is it?

Jamie   I dunno it just is.

Leah   People talked to you in juniors.

Jamie   What would you know? You aint been a' school in six months!

Leah   I'm psychic!

Jamie   Psychotic!

Ste   She's only tryina help.

Leah   Tell him, Ste!

Jamie   Yeah, well, I don't need fuckin' 'elp.

Enter **Sandra**, *empty-handed.*

Sandra   Language, Jamie! An' anyway, Leah, you couldn't go back to school if you wanted.

Jamie   Yeah, you're excluded.

Leah   Aint my fault.

Sandra   Whose fault is it then?

Leah   The system. Me mum said.

Ste   Oh, I'm goin' in.

Jamie   See you, Ste.

Ste   Yeah. Later, Jay.

Ste *lets himself into his flat.*

Sandra   Face facts, Leah, no bugger wants you.

Leah   That bloke from the telly wants me.

Sandra   Shut up.

Leah He does so there! He's doin' a documentary called 'Victims of the System'.

Sandra He's already made it, Leah. Your mother told me. He said he couldn't have you on it (**Jamie** *joins in.*) coz you were such a cow.

Leah He was a pervert anyway.

Sandra (*to* **Jamie**) I want you inside. She's a bad influence.

Leah (*to* **Jamie**) She's a bad influence.

Sandra Jamie!

Jamie I'm staying out here!

Sandra Right. I'm ringing your teacher.

Jamie (*tuts*) Leave Miss Ellis alone, she must hate you.

Sandra Shift your arse.

Jamie *shifts and* **Sandra** *goes indoors.*

Jamie (*tuts*) I wish I was on home tuition.

Leah I wish I was at school.

Jamie You only wanna go coz Ste goes.

Leah I don't.

Jamie D'you fancy him?

Leah *tuts*.

Jamie Everyone fancies Ste.

Leah No they don't.

Jamie Even Señorita Pilar de Moreno.

Leah Do what?

Jamie The new Spanish teacher. She run her fingers through his hair today and said untold things in fuckin' dago talk.

Leah I shoulda been Spanish.

Jamie You shoulda been somin'.

Leah When we used to watch that *Digame* programme with Miss Seale, I thought, 'That's me. Siestas, mini-faldas, discotecas'.

They adopt the husky Spanish tones of the programmes they have seen.

Jamie Me llamo Marcus, y me gusta ir al cine.

Leah Me gusta los platanos, me gusta los discotecas, y la musica pop.

Jamie Tengo diezinueve años.

Leah Mama Cass done a song about a Spanish garden. 'Ere!

Jamie What?

Leah There's someone in Ste's bathroom.

Jamie Yeah?

Leah *gets the rusty old trike.*

Jamie What you doin'?

Leah You hold it steady while I get up.

Jamie Leah!

Leah He's just won a game of football, he's covered in mud. Said so hisself. Well, what d'you do when you're covered in mud? Have a bath. Hold it. Steady, Jay.

He holds the tricycle steady while she climbs up and attempts to peer through the window and into Ste's bathroom.

Jamie Can you see anythin'?

Leah Yeah.

Ronnie (*off*) What the fuck?!

Leah Ooh, sorry, mate!

Laughing her head off, and trying to get down from the tricycle, she goes flying.

Ronnie (*off*)   Y'dirty slot!

Leah   It's his dad! Takin' a dump!

Ronnie (*off*)   Y'dirty slot!

Jamie   Oh no!

Sandra *comes out, dressed for work. She is buttoning up a light jacket as she speaks.*

Sandra   Miss Ellis has gone home. Secretary says I can speak to her in the morning. Now. There's a cheese salad in the fridge.

Jamie   I aint hungry.

Sandra   I can always throw it down the chute with the rest of your crap, Jamie Gangel.

Jamie   Salad's fine.

Sandra   It's good for ya. There was a phone-in on 'Richard and Judy' this mornin' about the bonus of a well-planned diet.

Jamie   I bet you rang in an' all. You can't keep off that bloody phone.

Leah (*to* **Sandra**)   D'you fancy that Richard Madeley, Sandra?

Sandra   Oooh no!

Jamie   She fancies the copper in *Crimewatch*.

Sandra   Don't you knock 'im!

Jamie   She phones in saying she recognises the photofits off the incident desk, only she don't, she just does it coz she thinks she'll get through to the copper.

Jamie *and* **Leah** *laugh.*

Sandra   Oh, you can laugh. I've only done it the once, don't exaggerate. And if you must know, Jamie, I only did it coz it looked like your dad.

Leah   What?

Sandra   The bloke who done the post office in Plumstead. I'm convinced.

Leah *laughs even more,* **Jamie** *is subdued.*

Sandra   And for your information, Jamie, love, I've gone off that copper.

Leah   My mum fancies Bill Beaumont off *Question of Sport.*

Sandra   He's cuddly.

Leah   That's not the word I'd use.

Sandra   Well, I don't know as many foul words as you. Now. The salad with the beetroot's for Tony.

Jamie   Tony?

Sandra   He'll be round in a bit.

Jamie   But you're goin' work.

Sandra   He's comina see you.

Jamie   Me?

Leah   This your new man, Sandra?

Sandra   So you're not on your own.

Jamie   I don't need a baby-sitter.

Sandra   I know.

Leah   I wouldn't mind meetin' him as it goes.

Sandra   Eh! Hands off!

Leah   I'm not into sloppy seconds, any more.

Sandra   What about the blokes we see knocking at your door? Very sloppy. (*To* **Jamie**.) And I shall be checking your homework when I get in, so be warned.

Leah Oh, and just when he was thinkin' of having a sex orgy.

Sandra My son's got taste, love. See you, Jay.

Jamie Yeah.

Sandra *exits. A toilet flushes in* **Ste**'s *flat.*

Leah (*sings*) Sing for your supper and you'll get breakfast
Dine with wine of choice,
If romance is in your voice.
I heard from a wise canary
Trillin' makes a fella willin'
So little swallow, swallow now.
Now is the time to sing for your luncheon and you'll get
   dinner
Dine with wine of your choice . . .
(*Spoken.*) Fancy liking that bloke off *Crimewatch*. He's ancient.

Jamie She's ancient.

Leah D'you reckon it was your dad what done the post office in Plumstead?

Jamie How should I know?

Leah I hate old people.

Jamie You like Mama Cass.

Leah It's allowed if they're dead. Oh, I dunno what to do.

Jamie Watch your rainbow.

Leah It's gone now. (*Pause.*) I dunno whether to go the park.

Jamie Don't look at me.

Leah I'll go in.

Jamie You do that.

Leah I will.

Jamie Give us all a break.

Leah   You and your mother. Two peas in a fuckin' pod, mate, I'm tellin' ya.

Jamie   See you, slagbag.

Leah *wallops him one.*

Leah   You asked for that!

Jamie   I know.

Leah *goes indoors.* **Jamie** *sits there. Presently Mama Cass's 'It's Getting Better' comes blaring out of* **Leah**'s *flat.* **Jamie** *winces. Shortly* **Ste**'s *front door comes flying open and* **Ste** *pops his head out. A dog starts to bark somewhere.*

Ste   Me dad's tryina get some kip!

Jamie   Knock her up, Ste, go on. Go on, Ste, knock her up.

Ste *goes to* **Leah**'s *front door and hammers it with his fist. It opens slowly and* **Leah** *appears, hairbrush in hand like a microphone, singing to the song.*

Ste   Turn it down, Leah, me ole man's tryina get some kip in there.

Jamie   Go on, Ste, tell 'er.

Leah *sings louder, raunchier, and waves two fingers in the air.*

Ste   Don't mess me about, Leah.

Leah   That's my idol!

Ste   I couldn't give a shit who it is.

Leah   You could learn a lot from 'er!

Ste   Leah!

Leah *sings even louder.*

Ste   Leah, I'm warning you!

Leah   Do I look scared?

Ste   Turn it down or I'll fuckin' brain ya!

Leah   Go back to your bubble an' squeak!

Ste   Not until you do that!

Leah Oh yeah? Gonna make me?

Jamie Leah . . .

Leah You can shut up an' all.

Jamie You know what his dad's like.

Ste (*to* **Jamie**) Oh, don't start.

Jamie Who's startin'?

Leah I like this bit.

Ste Leah, he'll kill you if he don't get his kip.

Leah God, it's only on volume six.

Jamie You know what happened the last time.

Ste (*to* **Jamie**) Shut up!

At this point **Tony** *enters. He carries a plastic bag.*

Leah Your dad might scare you, Ste, but he don't scare me.

Ste I'll fuckin' scare you in a minute.

Tony Afternoon, all!

Jamie (*tuts*) Oright?

Ste (*nods*) Afternoon.

Leah Evening.

Tony Okay, Jamie?

Jamie S'pose.

Ste Leah!

Tony (*to* **Leah**, *recognising the music*) Mamas and Papas?

Leah (*tuts*) Mama Cass, you thick git.

Leah *swings round and goes back in. The door slams. The music gets turned down.* **Ste** *looks at* **Tony**.

Ste   I owe you one, mate.

Jamie   Me mum ain' in.

Tony   Yeah. Just bumped into her. In the parking lot.

Ste   You got wheels?

Tony   Four.

Ste   Let's have a look?

They look over the edge of the balcony.

Jamie   Which one is it?

Tony   Volkswagen Camper. Gravy-brown. Left-hand drive. Picked it up at an auction. Four hundred notes.

Ste (*not impressed*)   See you, Jay.

Jamie   Mm.

Ste *makes his way back to his door.*

Tony (*to* **Jamie**)   Close your eyes.

Jamie   What?

Ste *stops on his step to watch.*

Tony   Close your eyes, Jamie, coz I got something.

Jamie, *closing them reluctantly, tuts.*

Tony *gets a brand-new football out of the plastic bag. He slips it into* **Jamie**'s *hands. He opens his eyes.*

Jamie   Oh.

Ste   Say thank you.

Jamie   Oh, thanks, Tony.

Ste   Thassa good one.

Ste *goes indoors.*

Tony   Your mum told me straight. You know. Problems. Been there. Mm. Walking through the park, game going on, my heart, you know, races. Scared, Jamie. Scared of the ball coming, you know, near me. Hey, we can fight this one together. Fancy a knockabout?

Jamie   Not really.

Tony   No, me neither. But some time, yeah?

Jamie   Yeah.

Tony (*looking at his watch*)   You watch *Grange Hill?*

Jamie   No.

Tony   Oh. Great.

Jamie   You can.

Tony   Oh. What you gonna do?

Jamie (*sighs*)   Homework.

Tony   Bit of a problem at the moment. New kid in the class. Think they're gonna follow a bullying storyline, you know? Don't quote me.

Jamie   Don't worry, I won't.

Tony   Great weather.

Jamie   Blindin' weather.

Tony   D'you mind if I go in? Only, I think, you know, something wrong with my retinas. Keep having to squint.

Jamie   You wanna get a pair o'sunglasses.

Tony   Shades, great.

Jamie *takes the football in.* **Tony** *follows him.*

Scene Two

Some sort of row is going on in **Ste**'s *flat. This is heard quite distantly throughout the scene.* **Tony** *sits on the step of* **Sandra**'s *flat later that* *night. It's still quite warm and he is topless. His shirt lies on the ground before him. He is smoking a joint. The door of the flat is ajar, and a faint murmur of a television can be heard.* **Jamie** *comes out holding a plate of salad.*

Jamie   Aren't you gonna eat this?

Tony   Sure. (**Jamie** *passes him the salad and he looks at it.*) Your mother, she's . . . she's amazing. She's, you know, something else. You joining me?

Jamie *comes out on the walkway.*

Jamie   I done me maths homework.

Tony   Yeah?

Jamie   Pythagoras' theorem. Wasn't Pythagoras a cunt?

Tony   Yeah.

Jamie   You're supposed to tell me off if I swear.

Tony   Right.

Jamie   I hate beetroot.

Tony   How d'you spell 'offensive vegetable', right?

Jamie   Where did you meet my mum?

Tony   Planet earth.

Jamie   Where?

Tony   Oh, you know, out and about, here and there. What's a place? It's somewhere where, you know, shit happens.

Jamie   Yeah, but where?

Tony   Gateways.

Jamie   You aint the first. She's not a slag or nothin', but you aint the first.

Tony   I'm the fourth, right? (*Chuckles, annoyed at* **Jamie**'s *choice of word.*) Slag?!

Jamie   There was Colin the barber, Alfie the long-distance lorry driver, and Richard the barman.

Tony   I just, you know, took a shine to her. She's got . . . charisma.

Jamie   She turn you on?

Tony (*gives a neurotic, what-sort-of-a-question-is-this? look to his left, then up at* **Jamie**)   Sure.

Jamie   She's thirty-five!

Tony   What's age? Age is just . . . just number. You know?

Pause.

Jamie   Mum said you was a painter.

Tony   Right.

Jamie   I know why she chose you. She wants the lounge doing. Only put the paper up last year and she already hates it. Bloke what sold it her said it got velvet in it, but it aint, it's imitation velvet. She feels gutted. Like that, my mum, goes off things fast. (**Tony** *laughs*.) What's so funny? She might go off you. You won't be laughing then, will ya?

Tony (*short pause*)   Jamie, how old are you?

Jamie   Fifteen. How old are you?

Tony   Twenty-seven. Not old enough to be your dad, right?

Jamie   What?

Tony   You know. (*Pause.*) Sure.

Jamie   What?

Tony   It's just shit, isn't it?

Jamie   What?

Tony The whole concept. Yeah. Anyway. I think we should, like, move towards getting away from that. Right?

Jamie Is that a spliff?

Pause. **Tony** *doesn't know how to reply.*

Give us some.

He passes him the joint. **Jamie** *has a big drag on it.*

(*Looks out to Canary Wharf.*)   When I was ten, me mum met this bloke called Richard. He was a barman like her. I used to . . . pretend he was my dad. Didn't realise he was only about eighteen. I used to tell people . . . and that.

Pause.

And then one night. I went in the kitchen for a glass of water. And there's me mum, sat on the floor, tears pouring down her face. Two black eyes. I never saw Richard again.

Pause.

I used to sit on his knee. He used to put his arm round me when we walked down the street and that. Called me trouble. And then . . . it's weird, innit? When somin' can just stop like that.

Tony That's cool.

Jamie Just . . .

Tony Hey . . .

Jamie What?

Tony Your mum's gonna be all right.

Jamie But things do, don't they? They just stop happening. Don't they? Feelings and that. The way . . . the way you feel.

Tony Some carry on.

Jamie She stopped crying. That's good, innit?

Tony   Good. You're sensitive. (**Jamie** *shrugs his shoulder and passes back the joint.*) I'm sensitive. Sometimes I just. Kind of. Cry. You ever done that?

Jamie   Yeah.

Tony   Yeah, it's called release. Famous people cry. Gazza.

Jamie   Anne Diamond.

Tony   Thatcher. (*Spits on floor.*)

Jamie   Princess Di.

Tony   Princess Di.

Sandra *enters from work.*

Sandra   This little princess is fuckin' knackered. 'Scuse language. Has he been behaving hisself?

Tony *stubs the joint out with his foot.*

Tony   Sandra! You look great.

Sandra   Oh, Tony!

Tony   What?

Sandra   You haven't eaten your little cheese salad.

Tony   Think I've got an ulcer. Or a gallstone. Right off my food.

Sandra   My feet. Someone's sticking swords in my feet.

Tony   I get that, it's got a name.

Jamie   It's them heels.

Sandra   It's your bedtime, Jamie.

Jamie   Aren't you gonna check me homework?

Sandra (*sitting on step, taking shoes off*)   Ooh, sod that, I'm knackered. All I fancy now is a cup o'tea and me bloody bed. Cor.

Jamie   I had maths and art.

Tony   Painting by numbers.

Sandra *sniggers, rubbing her weary feet.*

Jamie   Well. Night.

Tony   Night, kid.

Sandra   Night, Jay. Oi! (*Taps her cheek. He bends to kiss her.*)

Jamie   Night, then.

Sandra   Sweet dreams.

Jamie goes in. **Sandra** *inspects her legs.*

Sandra   Look at that. Varicose veins. Never work in a bar.

Tony *gets on the floor and kisses her legs.*

Sandra   Tony, I stink o' the pub. All booze an' fags. Oh, don't. I like it. Tony!

She hits him with a shoe.

Tony   He's a good kid.

Sandra   I've heard his mother aint that bad either.

Tony   I'll have to meet her, she sounds like quite a gal.

Sandra   The name's Gangel. That's Angel, with a G in front.

Tony (*puts his hand on her stomach*)   And that's magical.

Sandra   Oh, don't. I had some scampi fries. I feel a bit queazy.

Tony   Working tomorrow?

Sandra   Mm, I'm practically running that place.

Tony   I'll come and keep an eye on him.

Sandra (*tuts*)   You don't have to.

Tony   I know. I'm an individual. (*Leans over to kiss her.*)

Sandra   You can say that again.

They have a kiss. **Sandra** *still has her shoes in her hand, and runs the heels down his back. Mid-kiss,* **Ste**'s *door flies open and* **Ste** *runs out in a bit of a state.*

Sandra *and* **Tony** *keep kissing, till* **Sandra** *spots* **Ste**, *then breaks away.*

Sandra   Ste!! (*Laughs.*)

Ste   All right?

Sandra   What's the matter with you, eh?

Ste   Can I stay over, Mrs Gangel?

Sandra   You know my name, Ste!

Ste   Can I?

Sandra   Is it your dad again?

Ste   Our Trevor.

Sandra   You'll be top to tail with Jamie, I'm afraid.

Ste   I'd rather that than be in there.

Sandra (*to* **Tony**)   Inn'e a lovely lad, eh, Tony?

Tony   Great.

Sandra (*to* **Ste**)   Well, you get yourself in then, Ste. Go on, you get yourself to bed.

Ste   Thanks, Mrs Gangel.

Sandra   Ere, Ste.

Ste   What?

Sandra   D'you wanna little cheese salad?

Ste   Can I?

Sandra   D'you mind beetroot?

Ste   No.

Sandra   Go on, take it, good for you, salad. Go on!

Ste   Thanks.

Sandra *passes* **Ste** *the salad. He steps over them and into her flat.*

Sandra (*calls after him*)   Mind you don't get crumbs in the bed! (*Laughs to* **Tony**.) Don't want stains on my sheets! (*Laughs.*)

Tony   What sort?

Sandra   What sort d'you think? (*Laughs.*) Beetroot! (*Laughs.*)

Tony *tries to kiss her again. She's having none of it.*

Sandra   His bloody family. Wait up. I gotta do somin'.

She goes to **Ste**'*s door and bangs on it. We hear* **Ste**'*s dad,* **Ronnie**, *shout from inside.*

Ronnie? Trevor? It's me, Sandra! (*To* **Tony**.) You go in, love.

Tony *gets up and goes indoors.* **Sandra** *opens the letter-box and calls through.*

Sandra   Your little Steven's round at our place tonight. I've every mind to report you! Ronnie? Ronnie, are you listening to me? This is Sandra here! I am NOT happy!

Ronnie (*off*)   Ah, fuck off, y'arl nacker!

Sandra   This has got to stop!

She lets the letter-box drop. She goes to go indoors. She stops at her plants and picks off a few dead leaves.

You look parched love.

She goes indoors.

Scene Three

Jamie *sits up in his bed wearing a pair of reading glasses.* **Ste** *stands by the bed, holding the plate of salad.* **Jamie** *has his mother's* Hello! *magazine out in front of him.*

Ste   You don't mind?

Jamie   No.

Ste   You sure?

Jamie Course.

Ste I could sleep on the floor.

Jamie You hate the floor.

Ste And you don't mind?

Jamie No. I don't.

Ste Great.

Ste lays the salad on the bed and sits on the bed to undress. During the following he begins to undress for bed.

Jamie Haven't you eaten?

Ste No. It's not yours, is it?

Jamie No. Do you want the light off?

Ste Do you?

Jamie Don't care.

Ste D'you mind it on?

Jamie No.

Ste Coz o'the salad.

Jamie Fine.

Ste is taking his shirt off now. Then his trousers follow.

Jamie Mum went really mad at me today. This games business. She threw a load of me old stuff out I was hangin' on to.

Ste Yeah?

Jamie Yeah.

Pause. Ste now has his boxer shorts on.

Jamie D'you want another T-shirt?

Ste Nah, I'm all right, Jay.

Jamie Are you sure?

Ste Sure.

Jamie Well, if you do.

Ste Cheers. I'm getting in now.

Jamie Right.

Ste *gets into bed. His head the opposite end to* **Jamie**. **Jamie** *passes him a pillow.*

Jamie Have this.

Ste Cheers.

He puts the pillow behind him and sits up. He makes a start on the salad.

D'you mind me eating this?

Jamie Nah. I was gonna read anyway.

Ste What you readin' then?

Jamie Er . . . it's me mum's. (*Holds magazine up.*)

Ste Oh yeah? I've seen that in the shop. (*Notices it's called Hello!*) Hello!

Jamie Hello!

They have a bit of a giggle about this.

'Ere, d'you wanna fork?

Ste Nah, eat it with me fingers.

Jamie Want some bread?

Ste This is great.

Jamie Right. (*Pause.*) I'm gonna read now.

Ste Okay.

Silence. **Jamie** *casually reads the magazine,* **Ste** *munches on the salad.*

Cor, I'm starving.

Jamie Can't have you goin' hungry, can we?

Ste What bit you reading?

Jamie It's about Sally from *Coronation Street*.

Ste What, the blonde one?

Jamie Yeah.

Ste What's it say then?

Jamie (*reads*) Although Sally spends her working week filming in Manchester, she likes nothing better than to spend her weekends at her London penthouse flat. Weekends are busy for Sally, juggling a hectic social life with time for that special man in her life. Her partner is another actor, but she is coy about revealing his name. Saturdays are spent shopping and eating out, and Sundays are set aside for catching up with old friends or taking long strolls on Hampstead Heath which her flat overlooks.

Pause.

Ste That's north of the river, innit?

Jamie Mm.

Ste So she's called Sally? In real life as well as on the telly?

Jamie Yeah, I hate that name.

Ste It's not her fault I s'pose.

Jamie I blame the parents.

Ste Mm. D'you always wear glasses when you read?

Jamie Supposed to.

Ste You don't in school.

Jamie Hardly fetching, is it?

Ste Nah, looks all right.

Jamie Yeah?

Ste Yeah, I'm telling ya.

Jamie How's your salad?

Ste Bang on food.

Jamie Good for your sports.

Ste That's right. Good for your spots an' all.

Jamie You haven't got any spots.

Ste   Yours are clearing up.

Jamie   Tar.

Ste   D'you fancy that Sally?

Jamie   Not really. Do you?

Ste   Nah. Haven't given it much thought.

Jamie   D'you fancy her next door?

Ste   Fancy Leah?

Jamie   She fancies you.

Ste   Don't.

Jamie   I'm only saying.

Ste   Jamie.

Jamie   What time should I set the alarm for?

Ste   Quarter to eight.

Jamie   Right. (*He gets alarm clock off the floor. Whilst setting it.*)
If you wanna bath in the morning I can put the water on.

Ste   Nah, I'll get home.

Jamie   Right.

Ste   Jamie?

Jamie   What?

Ste   Will your mum mind if I leave this beetroot?

Jamie   No.

Ste   Only she asked if I liked it.

Jamie   Leave it if you don't wannit.

Ste   She won't mind?

Jamie   No. She's not a very good cook, my mum.

Ste   She is.

Jamie   Hmm, that's a matter of opinion.

Ste puts the plate on the floor and starts to settle down in the bed.

Jamie You goin' sleep?

Ste Yeah, I'm knackered.

Jamie I'll turn the light off.

He puts the magazine on the floor and turns off the bedside lamp. He settles down. Silence.

Ste?

Ste Mm?

Jamie You all right?

Ste Yeah.

Jamie Right. (*Pause.*) Ste?

Ste What?

Jamie I thought you were making the tea tonight?

Ste I burnt it.

Jamie Oh.

Ste Mm.

Jamie What was it?

Ste Bubble and squeak.

Jamie Oh yeah. (*Pause.*) Ste?

Ste What?

Jamie Night.

Ste Night, Jamie.

Silence.

In the blackout 'California Earthquake' by Mama Cass plays, leading us into the next scene.

Scene Four

A few days later and it's still hot. Out on the walkway **Leah** *is sunning herself in swimming costume and baggy T-shirt, lying on a towel. She is reading a geography text book.* **Tony** *sits doing a* *newspaper crossword in one of two white patio chairs outside* **Sandra**'s *flat.* **Leah**'s *and* **Sandra**'s *doors are open.*

'California Earthquake' floats out from **Leah**'s *flat.*

Leah D'you think I'm tall for my age?

Tony Come again?

Leah I said 'D'you think I'm tall . . . for my age?'

Tony Depends how old you are. If you were three, yeah. Forty-eight, no. Yeah? (*Pause.* **Leah** *returns to her book.*) Revising?

Leah I am tall.

Tony (*in reference to her book*) Any good?

Leah (*reads chapter headings from book*) The rock formations of Wookey Hole. Sedimentary Discharge of the Gaping Gill. A day in the life of Jean: A girl who lives on the San Andreas Fault. Bully for her. 'It's scary,' says Jean, 'but you learn to live with it.' Silly bitch.

Tony Oh, but think about it. Living on the edge of a big slit of earth that could open up, and like, swallow you whole.

Leah No, you should just look where you're going. Or move house. No use moaning about it and going in books.

Tony Right.

Leah (*looking at book*) She don't look very tall, does she? They wanna write it next to her picture. 'Jean's a bloody midget'.

Tony You know why you're so tall, don't you? Coz you're mature.

Leah Wassat?

Tony Grown up.

Leah You wanna tell her that.

Tony Who?

Leah Your bird.

Tony Sandra?

Leah She talks to me like I got cunt written on my forehead.

Tony You shouldn't use words like bird.

Leah (*pause*) You wanna watch yourself.

Tony Why?

Leah She's got a reputation.

Tony Yeah?

Leah I'm saying nothing. (*Pause.*) But I wouldn't tell anyone round here you were seeing her. If they read the crap I do, they'd say Sandra was the San Andreas Fault and the Gaping Gill rolled into one. The way she walks she couldn't stop a bull in an alleyway. (*Laughs.*)

Tony I'll tell her that.

Leah (*still laughing*) She already knows!

Jamie *comes out and goes and knocks on* **Ste***'s door during the last line.*

Leah He aint back yet.

Jamie In'e?

Jamie *makes to go back in but* **Sandra** *comes to the door. She's wearing summery gear. In one hand she holds an unlit cigarette. In the other, the end of a green garden hose.*

Sandra (*holding cigarette up*) Anyone got a match?

Leah Yeah, my arse your face.

Jamie Your arse aint that nice, love.

Sandra Pump me up, Jay.

Jamie *goes in. Soon we hear him manually pumping water inside the flat. Water splashes out of the hose.*

Sandra I like getting pumped up. D'ya know what I mean?

Leah (*to* **Tony**) What did I tell you?

Tony (*to* **Leah**) Hey, remember feminism, yeah? Sisters together, sisters strong!

Leah My sister lives in Crayford. I aint seen her in six months.

Sandra (*holding the hose between her legs like a man having a wee*) 'Ere, Tony, you when you've had ten too many.

Leah (*as* **Tony** *laughs*) You're funny.

Sandra *turns and squirts* **Leah** *with water.* **Leah** *jumps up.*

Leah Oh, bloody 'ell!

Sandra Oh, sorry, Leah, didn't see you there!

Leah Grow up!

Ste *comes in from school.*

Ste (*to* **Leah**) Oright?

Leah Do I look it?

Sandra Had a wash today, Ste? (*Laughs.* **Ste** *makes a dash for his flat and she squirts water at him.*) You have now. Okay, Jamie.

Ste *lets himself into his flat.*

Leah You've soaked me, Sandra!

Sandra Oh, stop moaning, you're young, intya?

The water goes off. **Jamie** *comes to the door.*

Jamie Was that Ste then?

Sandra Yeah. Little surprise for us in the fridge, Jay, go and get 'em.

Jamie *goes in.* **Ste** *comes out to take the drying off the clothes'-horse.*

Tony Yo Ste! Blinding day for drying.

Ste Blinding, yeah.

Leah Blinding. (*She applies suntan lotion to her legs.*)

Tony (*to* **Leah**) What factor's that?

Leah Four.

Sandra S'probably nicked. Youth of today.

Leah (*tuts*) Shut up, is it nicked!

Tony (*to* **Leah**) Could I use that after you?

Leah What, borrow it?

Tony Aha.

Leah No.

Jamie (*coming out with arms full of lager cans*) Who wants a lager? Get pissed!

Leah Go on then.

Tony (*to* **Jamie**) Great specs.

Jamie Want a lager, Ste?

Ste Er . . .

Sandra Go on, Ste, it's just what you need on a day like this.

Ste Stick it there I'll be out in a sec. (*Takes drying in.*)

Sandra (*to* **Jamie**) Give Tony one please. (*To* **Tony**.) It's genital, bar work.

Jamie Genetical mother.

Sandra That an' all, you humourless git. Crack one open for me while you're at it, Tony. I fancy somin' wet dribbling down the back o'me gullet. What d'you say?

Tony I say ditto, right?

Sandra You say whatever you want, Tony. Better in than out, d'you know what I mean?

Leah (*lager*) This is beautiful.

Sandra (*shouts like a barmaid*)   Can I have your glasses, gentlemen please! Drink up now, let's be having you! (*Own voice.*) Born to brewery, it's in me water. (**Ste** *comes out with a new pile of drying.*) See that? That's women's lib, that is.

Leah   There's no women in his flat to lib.

Jamie   You're gonna get smoke all over Ste's clothes now.

Ste   Don't matter, s'only me dad's.

Sandra   You okay today, Ste?

Ste   Yeah.

Jamie   Mum!

Tony   Jamie!

Leah   I went to have a look at a new school today. Up in Greenwich. Might have a space for me next month. There's only twenny kids in the whole school.

Ste   There'll be twenny-two if you go. You and Mama Cass. (*Laughter.*)

Sandra   Is it residential?

Leah   No.

Sandra   Shame. Coulda given you an 'and packing.

Leah   That's a cuss.

Sandra   And I could've packed that fat bitch an'er music an'all.

Jamie   You shouldn't speak ill of the dead.

Sandra   Aw, I know. Shame how she died. (*Giggles.*) Oh, shouldn't laugh.

Leah   How did she die?

Sandra   Tell her, Tony.

Tony   Bread and margarine. Not the typical ingredients of a Molotov Cocktail.

Ste   Do what?

Sandra What you on about, Tony? She died choking on a sandwich.

Ste No!

Leah Did she?

Sandra (*to* **Jamie**) Now you know why I tell you not to gobble your chips down.

Leah What sort o'sandwich?

Sandra I dunno.

Tony Wasn't she heavily into the drugs scene?

Leah Was she?

Ste They all are them pop stars, int they? Bloody head-cases the lot of 'em.

Sandra Oswald Mosley eat your heart out.

Leah No, Ste. East 17 aint into drugs, and they're all pop stars.

Sandra Yeah, but, Leah, what you gotta remember is, East 17 are healthy lads. Mama Cass was obese.

Jamie So?

Sandra So she was probably very unhappy, and prone to, you know, dabbling.

Jamie She mighta been happy being fat!

Leah Yeah!

Jamie Just coz she's different to you, doesn't make her a weirdo!

Sandra Well, answer me this then, Jamie. If she was so happy being fat, why was it she died choking on a sandwich, eh? Why wasn't it a walloping great fry-up or somin'?

Tony You got a point there.

Jamie Bollocks.

Ste Mighta been a bacon and egg sandwich.

Jamie/Leah Yeah.

Sandra   No! No. It's all coming back to me now, it was chicken . . .

Tony   Or beef or something . . .

Sandra   Yeah, it was definitely somin' low in cholesterol.

Sandra *takes the hose indoors.*

Leah   She's full o'shit.

Tony (*to* **Leah**)   Hey, watch it.

Leah   Shut up!

Jamie   My mother's the fountain of all knowledge. You should know that by now.

Sandra *hears this as she re-enters with her Vileda Supermop. She continues mopping up the water that has splashed on the walkway.*

Sandra (*to* **Jamie**, *entering*)   Yeah, well, when you can keep up with the questions on *Bob's Full House*, you get back to me. All right?

Jamie   *Bob's Full House*? I'm more of a *Mastermind* man.

Leah   Liar!

Tony   Remember *University Challenge*? (*Beat.*) Crap show.

Sandra (*accentuating her mop movements in time with her speech*)   'If You Sprinkle When You Tinkle, Please Be Sweet And Wipe The Seat'. (*Chuckles.*) Got that on the door of the Gents' loo at work. (*To* **Jamie**.) You could learn a lot from that.

Jamie   And you could learn a lot from keeping your mouth shut.

Sandra (*to* **Ste**)   Ooooh, I bet you don't speak like that to your ole man, eh, Ste?

Ste   I don't speak. Full stop.

Sandra Oh yeah. No offence, Ste, d'you know what I mean?

Jamie Mum!

Leah It's disgustin', innit? When men dribble. You wanna use a cloth, Jamie.

Sandra (*to* **Leah**) First decent thing you've said all day, girl.

Jamie Shut up.

Tony Men of the cloth. (*Sniggers.*)

Jamie (*tuts*) Oh, shut up!

Sandra Oi! Manners!

Jamie Me mother never taught me none!

Sandra Er, she taught you please and thank you and respect God's creatures, so keep your trap shut.

Jamie Shut up.

Sandra Shut up? Shut up? You're killing the art o'conversation you are.

Jamie What conversation? No one gets a word in edgeways with you around.

Sandra Inn'e a wit, eh? Inn'e a laugh? Eh? Makes me die he does.

Jamie That IS the intention.

Sandra And that from the same boy who used to send me Valentines.

Jamie Oh, don't start.

Sandra I've started so I'll finish! (*Laughs.*) He wouldn't leave my side when I took him to nursery, you know. Kept getting phone calls. 'Mrs Gangel, he won't settle without ya. Pines for you he does. Pines for you at the drop of an 'at.'

Jamie No I never.

Sandra They thought you was being abused you was such a quiet bugger. Huh, they should see you now. They'd get a right shock. Had me down as a bad mother coz you told them you slept in a drawer.

Jamie   I did!

Sandra   Only coz I couldn't afford a cot! If they could see me now, they'd think I was bleedin' marvellous. Show me another woman on this estate who can say she goes with an artist, and I'll show you a bloody liar.

Tony   Great music.

Leah   Artist?

Sandra   (*poses*)   Quick, Tony! Paint me picture, I feel gorgeous!

Ste   Are you an artist, Tony?

Sandra   Come on, Tony, get your brush out and give us a few strokes.

Leah   Are you, Tony?

Tony   Mm.

Ste   And you paint pictures and that?

Tony   Sometimes.

Ste   Blindin'!

Leah   He's a dark horse.

Tony   I used to work in a factory actually, six months.

Sandra   Ignore 'im, he's an artist.

Tony   I'm not an intellectual, right?

Jamie   I thought you was a painter and decorator.

Tony   I could be . . .

Jamie   Well, what you doin' with her then?

Sandra   I'm artistic!

Leah   How are you artistic?

Jamie   Yeah!

Sandra   I got good colour sense. Tony said so. You've seen my lounge diner.

Jamie   Hardly makes you Van Gogh though, does it?

Ste   I'm going in.

Sandra   You do that, Ste. I'm just about to chop me ear off.

Jamie   Stay out here, Ste.

Ste   Nah, I'm going boxing with me dad later.

Sandra   Can't get enough of it, eh? (*Laughs.*)

Leah   That's a cuss!

Ste (*to* **Sandra**)   Spectating.

Sandra   Oh, you kids today, there's no life in ya.

Ste   See ya.

Ste *goes in,* **Sandra** *carries on with no break.*

Sandra   When I was your age we made our own fun.

Leah   What? Set fire to dinosaurs and watch 'em burn?

Sandra (*laughs uproariously*)   Cheeky cow!

Jamie (*to* **Sandra**)   Oh, why can't you just shut up?

Sandra   What?

Jamie   That's bang out of order what you said to Ste.

Sandra   Oh, we all know his dad leathers him, I'm only having a laugh.

Jamie   What 'bout when that bloke o'yours beat you up? Weren't laughing then, were ya?

Tony   I think now's the time to change the subject.

Jamie   Well, change it then.

Tony   Did anyone see that documentary last week? About . . .

Sandra No, Tony. He's a clever bastard. And don't we just know it, eh? (*To* **Jamie**.) Just remember, you, I give you them brains so think on.

Jamie (*making to go indoors*) I always thought you'd had a lobotomy.

Sandra (*laughs*) What did you say?

Jamie Explain it to her someone. (*Exits.*)

Tony Lobotomy, it's when . . .

Sandra I know what it means, Tony. (*To door.*) Cheeky little barstool! (*She goes to the door and calls through.*) You're not too old to be taken over my knee, young man! D'you hear me?

Jamie (*off*) I hear you, the whole o'bloody Thamesmead can hear you!

Sandra Get a life! Get a sense o'humour!

Jamie (*comes to door*) Well, maybe if you say something funny for once in your life, I'll start laughing.

Sandra I AM funny!

Jamie Funny in the head.

Sandra You spotty little wimp, how dare you say that to me?

Tony Sandra . . .

Sandra (*to* **Jamie**) Look at you, butter wouldn't melt. I've got your number, Jamie, and if anyone needs help it's you. You're fuckin' weird.

Tony Hey, cool it, guys . . .

Leah I'm goin' indoors.

Sandra You do that, lady!

Leah (*gathering her stuff up*)   I'm gonna go somewhere where I can get some peace and bloody quiet.

Sandra   Try Uranus.

Tony   Sandra.

Sandra   You! In!

Tony and Leah both disappear inside.

Sandra   I work all the hours God sends to keep you in insults. If this was my pub I'd have you barred.

Jamie   Well, go on then. Bar me. Kick me out. (*Sniggers.*) You wouldn't dare. I'm all you've got. Me and your fucking plants. Coz he ain't gonna be around much longer.

Sandra   What would you know? You don't know nothing!

Jamie   You've got my number? Well, I've got yours, Sandra. So. Why don't you try and be a little more like a mother to me?

Sandra   Oh, yeah, pull that one on me. I'm a terrible mother who don't know her arse from her elbow. I never had a mum so sometimes I'm gonna make mistakes.

Jamie   I'm not surprised she abandoned ya.

Sandra   You cheeky little bastard.

She slaps him across the face. He slaps her back. She lays into him, fists flying. He holds his hands up to his face, protecting himself. She's not giving up so he hits back. They fight like cat and dog, knocking Ste's washing over in the process. Finally **Sandra** *is sitting on* **Jamie**'*s chest, a fierce look in her eyes. This dissolves to tears. She weakens her grip.* **Jamie** *pushes her off. He goes and sits in one of the patio chairs.*

Jamie   Am I like my dad?

Sandra   No. You're like me.

Jamie   How am I weird?

Sandra   Oh, give it a rest, Jamie. Christ.

Jamie   You said it.

Sandra   You're all right. Okay, so you got me for a mother, but who said life was easy? You are. You're all right.

Sandra *gets up and goes indoors.* **Jamie** *starts to cry. The door to* **Ste**'*s flat opens and* **Ste** *stands on the step.*

Ste   D'you wanna come the boxing?

Jamie   Shut up.

Ste   Got a spare ticket.

Jamie   Leave me alone.

Ste   You all right?

Jamie   Apparently.

Ste *sheepishly goes back indoors.* **Jamie** *wipes his face.*

Scene Five

That night **Jamie** *and* **Ste** *sit up in* **Jamie**'*s bed, sharing a bottle of lemonade,* **Ste** *opposite* **Jamie**. **Sandra** *calls off.*

Sandra (*off*)   Jamie?! D'you wanna watch *The Sound of Music*?!

Jamie *to* **Ste**, *tuts.*

Sandra (*off*)   It's on Sky, Jamie!

Jamie   Who does she think I am?

Sandra (*off*)   D'you want me to tape it?

Jamie (*calls*)   Yeah!

Sandra (*off*)   Okay!

Jamie (*to* **Ste**)   Anything for a quiet life.

Ste   I wish I had a mum.

Jamie   What happened, Ste?

Ste Come in from the boxin', this ole mate o'me dad's turns up. Pissed. Kept goin' on about West Ham drawin'. 'Fucking draw,' he kept saying, 'Fucking draw!' And me dad starts joining in, and our Vinnie, and our Trevor. Going on and on about it.

Jamie So why?

Ste I never joined in.

Jamie You're okay here.

Ste They don't even ask where I've been.

Sandra (*off*) D'you want some toast, lads?

Jamie (*calls*) We're goin' asleep.

Sandra (*off*) Oh. Sorry, lads.

Jamie (*to Ste*) Can I see?

Pause. **Ste** *turns his back on* **Jamie** *and lifts up his T-shirt.*

Sandra (*off*) Jamie? Sorry, love. Who played the Baroness?

Jamie Eleanor Parker.

Sandra (*off*) Oh, that's it, I wanna show off to Tony. Sorry, lads. Won't happen again.

Ste Have I got any on me back?

Jamie Couple.

Ste Never looked.

Ste *pulls his T-shirt down. He takes a swig of lemonade.* **Jamie** *gets a small Body Shop bottle from the floor.*

Jamie I got this stuff. It's me mum's. It's from the Body Shop. Peppermint foot lotion. It soothes your feet. I use it coz I like the smell. (*Pause.*) Lie down and I'll rub it into your back. If you want.

Slowly **Ste** *lies down.* **Jamie** *pulls* **Ste**'s *T-shirt up.* **Ste** *lifts his head up, he holds the lemonade bottle out in front of him.* **Jamie** *pours a little lotion onto* **Ste**'s *back.*

Jamie Cold init?

Ste Yeah.

Jamie *slowly massages it into* **Ste**'s *back.*

Ste They think I'm a wimp.

Jamie My mum thinks I am an' all.

Ste But I aint.

Jamie Neither am I.

Ste A wimp wouldn'a come round here. I done somin'. Wimps don't do nothin'. (*Pause.*) I'm gonna work at the sports centre. Do me shifts in the fitness pool, do me shifts in the leisure pool. I know I can do it.

Jamie Swimming's your favourite.

Ste You're on your own when you're swimming. You can't think about nothing else. Just the strokes, and where you are in the pool. Up and down. Up and down. (*Pause.*) I'm gonna stink of mint.

Jamie Peppermint.

Ste Peppermint.

Pause.

Jamie Have you ever kissed anyone? And stuck your tongue in?

Ste Looking like this?

Jamie You ain' ugly.

Ste They've made me ugly.

Jamie I don't think you're ugly.

Jamie *rests his head in the small of* **Ste**'s *back. They stay like this for a while.*

Ste   Carry on doin' me back.

Jamie   Dunnit hurt?

Ste   Only a little bit.

Jamie   Turn over I'll do your front.

Ste   I can't. (*Pause.*) I'm too sore. I'd make too much noise and then your mum'd come in.

Jamie   She's watching telly.

Ste   No, Jay.

Jamie   I won't hurt you.

Ste   I think we better get to sleep.

Jamie *pulls the T-shirt down.*

Ste   Turn the light off.

Jamie   No.

Ste   Please.

Jamie   I don't wanna.

Ste *gets under the covers.*

Jamie   Can I come up that end with you?

Ste   No.

Jamie   Please.

Ste   You stay where you are.

He gets the pillow and moves round to lie next to **Jamie**, *head to head.* Satisfied?

Jamie   Mm. Night. (*Leans over and kisses* **Ste** *once on the lips.*)

Ste   D'you think I'm queer?

Jamie   Don't matter what I think.

He switches off the bedside light.

Can I touch you?

Ste　I'm a bit sore.

Jamie　Yeah.

In the darkness, 'Sixteen Going on Seventeen' from **The Sound Of Music** *plays.*

Act Two

Scene One

A week later, mid-afternoon. It is still hot. **Jamie** *is sitting on the step of his flat, with the front door open. He is cleaning his glasses.* **Ste** *comes on from the street. They both wear school uniform.*

Jamie Hiya.

Ste Oright?

Jamie Bunkin' off?

Ste No, I'm at school, what's it look like?

Jamie Not like you.

Ste It's only Sports Day.

Jamie Not like you to miss a race.

Ste First time for everything.

Jamie You're in the relay team.

Ste Yeah, well . . . don't wanna put . . . put strain on me ankle. It's . . . injured in training.

Jamie Oh.

Ste S'not the end of the world.

Jamie I was gonna stay and watch you, then Miss Penrose said you'd pulled out so I came back here. Told me mum it wan't compulsory. Sports Day.

Ste Thassa big word, innit?

Jamie Compulsory? I know.

Ste I been down Tavy Bridge.

Jamie Get anything?

Ste Nah, skint.

Jamie I aint seen ya. Where you been hiding?

Ste Nowhere.

Jamie Knocked for you a few times.

Ste I aint been hiding.

Jamie Thought you mighta come round.

Ste I aint been hiding, all right? It's hot, bloody heat wave, Jamie, and you expect me to be indoors?

Jamie No, it's just, you know, just a bit weird.

Ste I was out. All right? What's weird about that? I wan' hiding. I was just, you know, out.

Jamie Been worried about ya.

Ste Don't be.

Jamie Well, I was.

Ste Well, don't be!

Jamie Have they. . . ?

Ste No.

Jamie What?

Ste Nothing's happened. Yeah? I'm all right. I'm pucker. Everything . . . everything's pucker.

Jamie You aint running coz you're black and blue. That's why, innit? I know. I've seen. That's why you aint in the relay team.

Ste Give it a rest, Jamie.

Jamie Oh, things getting better then, are they? Life a bowl o'cherries in the end flat? Daddy laid off the fist work? Or haven't you burnt the tea lately?

Ste I said, leave it out.

Jamie You're scared.

Ste I aint scared o'nothin'!

Jamie Yeah?

Ste Yeah! Last week, right. I went Woolwich. Comin' out of a shop and there's this geezer in the gutter, pissed out of his skull, lying there. And everyone was just walking past him. I had to step over him. (*Pause.*) And it was my old man. (*Pause.*) Got me thinking on the bus. Why be scared of a bloke who's dead to the world?

Jamie When he knocks ten different types o'shite outa ya.

Ste He's an embarrassment. Nothing more, nothing less. Why be scared o'that?

Jamie Scared o'being called queer?

Ste (*pause*)   Are you?

Jamie (*pause*)   Dunno. Maybe. Maybe not.

Ste And are you?

Jamie Queer?

Ste Gay.

Jamie I'm very happy. (*Pause.*) I'm happy when I'm with you. (*Pause.*) There, I've said it now, haven't I? Go on, piss yourself.

Ste No.

Jamie Why not? Don't you think it's funny?

Ste I don't wanna.

Jamie I think it's hilarious.

Ste Yeah?

Jamie Too right.

Ste Well, why aren't you laughin' then?

Jamie (*pause*)   D'you wanna come round tonight? (*Pause.*) 'No, Jamie, I don't!'

Ste I got a tongue in me head!

Jamie Well, say somin' then.

Ste Can't.

Jamie   Well, say no then.

Ste   Let's do somin'.

Jamie   What?

Ste   Let's go the park and have a kick-about.

Jamie   Football?

Ste   Yeah, go and get your new ball.

Jamie   What?

Ste   Come on, Jamie, I can't hang around here all day, it does me head in.

Jamie *disappears inside. He returns quickly with the football* **Tony** *bought him earlier. He stands in the doorway holding it.*

Ste   Come on then, on the head, son!

Ste *angles to do a header,* **Jamie** *keeps the ball.*

Jamie   I can't.

Ste   Jay . . .

Jamie   I'm crap.

Ste   That's coz you never try.

Jamie   I hate football.

Ste   Just kick it. (**Jamie** *tuts and kicks the ball to* **Ste**.) No, you're doing it wrong. Like this. (*Kicks it back to* **Jamie**, *demonstrating a proper kick.* **Jamie** *kicks it back again.*) Yeah, that's more like it. Keep your foot like this, it's all in the angle.

They kick the ball between them.

Jamie   Are you gonna come round then?

Ste   I don't know.

Jamie   Go on. Come round.

Ste   Jamie.

They carry on kicking as they speak.

Jamie Is this how Gary Lineker started, d'you think?

Ste What? Like you?

Jamie Yeah?

Ste If I remember rightly, Jamie, whenever we had football in juniors, you ran up and down the field playing *Cagney and Lacey*.

Jamie Shut up.

Ste You used to row with Neil Robinson over who was gonna play the blonde.

Jamie You mean Cagney, Chris Cagney. (*Adopts an American accent, in imitation of Chris Cagney.*) My name's Christine Cagney and . . . and I'm an alcoholic.

Ste You never went near the ball.

Jamie Gary Lineker was just the same!

Ste Yeah?

Jamie Yeah.

Ste Which one was he then?

Jamie Lacey, the fat one.

Ste (*laughs*) He aint fat.

Jamie I know.

Ste He's pucker.

Jamie I know, he's all right, inn'e? (*Giggles, keeps the ball and reverts to his Cagney impersonation.*) I dunno, Mary Beth . . . I . . . I just don't seem to be able to find the right kinda guy. They take one look at me, a cop in a pink fluffy jumper, and just . . . back off.

Ste Oh, Christine Cagney, you make me heart bleed!

They have a bit of a laugh, **Jamie** *kicks the ball over and they carry on. Just then,* **Leah** *pops her head out of her door.*

Leah   Oi!! You got any lead piping? (*The lads laugh.*)

Ste   No!

Leah   Jamie?

Jamie   No!

Leah   Well, any sort o'piping?

Ste   No, why?

Leah   Oh, have a look round your flat, Ste. Your Trevor has all sorts knockin' about in there. Please, Steven, it's really important.

Jamie   What d'you need lead piping for?

Leah   An experiment. Ste?!

Ste (*going in*)   I'm telling ya now, he won't have any.

Leah   Cheers, Ste. (**Ste** *goes in, she comes out.*) Are you sure you haven't got any pipes?

Jamie   Positive.

Leah   Go and ask your mum.

Jamie   What's this experiment? (**Leah** *taps her nose.*) Oh, oright.

Jamie *goes indoors.* **Leah** *fidgets for a bit, then her gaze comes to rest on* **Sandra**'s *hanging basket. She moves towards it and headbutts it.*

Leah   Ow!! (*Sings a note.*) La-a!! (*She headbutts it again then sings a note.*) La-aa!!

Sandra *rushes out.*

Sandra   Get off o'there, you little cow. I won that basket in the South-East Thames Barmaid of the Year Award. Look, it's engraved. Sandra Gangel, 1985. You know that coz me picture was in the *New Shopper*.

Leah (*tuts*)   Sorry.

Ste (*coming out empty-handed*)   Can't see none.

Leah   You sure?

Sandra   What on earth do you want lead piping for?

Leah   Mind your own business.

Sandra   You're bloody warped, you are, don't you know lead's poisonous?

Leah   Look who's talking.

Sandra   Yeah and I talk sense, which is more than you do, madam.

Leah   I talk plenty o'sense!

Jamie *comes out at this point with the garden hose.*

Sandra   You wouldn't know sense if it came up to you, slapped you round the face and said 'I'm sense'.

Leah   Oh, stand on your head and let your arse do the talking.

Jamie   Will this do?

Leah   Blinding.

Jamie   D'you want me to turn it on?

Sandra   I'm having no water fights, missis!

Leah   No, don't turn it on. Just hit me over the head with it.

Jamie   Eh?

Ste   What?

Leah   I'll look away. Yous keep talkin'. Then as a surprise, hit me over the head with the hose.

Sandra   It won't be a surprise then, will it, you thick git!

Leah   Don't tell me when you're gonna do it!

Jamie   I don't understand this, d'you want me to hit you hard?

Leah   Yeah. Ste, you do it, you're stronger than him.

Ste   No!!

Sandra   I'll do it!

Jamie   I'll do it!

Leah   Talk!

Leah *turns away, her back to the three of them.*

Ste   What d'you want us to talk about?

Leah   Anything, just talk, will ya?

Jamie   The weather?

Leah   You aint talking. Oh, here read this. (*She gets a cassette cover out of her pocket.*) Read that. The underlined bit. (*Passes it to* **Ste**. **Jamie** *hovers with hose as* **Leah** *turns her back again.*)

Sandra   Steven?

Ste (*reads*)   Cass Elliot followed them there, but the group initially resisted her repeated requests to join them, arguing that her range wasn't high enough for Phillips' new-styled compositions.

As **Ste** *reads,* **Jamie** *approaches* **Leah** *slowly, from behind, hose in hand.* **Sandra** *stops him by grabbing his arm and takes control of the hose.* **Jamie** *steps back.* **Sandra** *now approaches* **Leah** *slowly.*

However, a lead pipe struck Cass on the head during a bout of interior decorating and having recovered from the resultant concussion, she discovered that her voice had changed.

Leah (*bewitched*)   She discovered that her voice had changed.

Sandra *pulls the hose over* **Leah**'s *head and pulls it round her neck, strangling her.*

Sandra   So!! I'm a slapper, am I? I'm the Gaping Gill and the San Andreas Fault rolled into one?! You twisted little bitch! How dare you say all that to my fella? You venomous little cow, what are ya?

She releases the pressure of the hose and pushes **Leah** *to the ground.* **Leah** *chokes and coughs.* **Sandra** *slaps her round the head briskly.*

I dunno what that home tutor teaches you Leah, but it certainly aint respect!

Leah (*sings a note*) La-aa!!

Ste Should I phone an ambulance?

Sandra Call a vet, have it put down.

Leah (*another note*) La-aa!!

Sandra You could never turn Tony's mind against me, Leah, d'you hear me? Coz he sees you for the interfering little slapper that you are.

Leah (*tearful*) I wanted it to change.

Sandra Yeah, well, some things never change.

Leah I wanted it to change!

Sandra The leopard never changes its spots, and the slapper never changes her knickers! Be told!

Sandra, *brandishing the hose, goes inside as* **Jamie** *steps aside for her.*

Jamie My mum aint a slag!

Ste You shouldn't have said that to Tony!

Leah Don't you start. (*Still crawling round, coughing.*)

Ste Come on, Jamie, let's go the park.

Leah (*grabs football*) I'm coming!

Jamie There's enough dog crap in that park as it is without you adding to it an' all.

Leah Let me come!

Jamie No way!

Ste Grow up, Leah!

Leah   Let me come or I'll spread it round where you slept every night last week.

Jamie   What?

Ste   Dunno what you're talkin' about.

Leah   Let me come.

Jamie   He slept on the couch..

Leah   Not what I heard. Top to tail, your mum said. Very nice.

Ste   Give us the ball.

Jamie   Take no notice, Ste

Leah   I'm seeing your Trevor later for a drink.

Ste   Give it to me!

Leah   You know how alcohol loosens the tongue!

Ste   Leah!

Leah   Try it.

Ste   I don't like hitting girls.

Leah   Hit me then, go on, hit me, you stupid queer. (*She throws the ball at* **Ste** *and gets up.*) He already knows! You know what these flats are like, walls are paper thin. Why d'you think he's twatting the face offa you, eh? He knows!

Ste   There's nothing to know!

Leah   Top to tail?

Jamie   You know fuck all.

Leah   Oh, really?

Jamie   Yes, really.

Leah   I know this much. I've been sticking up for you. For the pair o'ya. Told him I knew you'd slept on the couch. Told him I'd been in and seen. (*Pause, while this registers.*) You think I'm such a loser, don't ya? You think you can say what you like to me coz at the end of the day I'll still be at the bottom of the slag-heap. Just coz I was kicked outa school. Just coz . . . you think it's all just gonna wash over me!

Jamie   Leah.

Leah   All I wanted was a bloody kick-about, in the park. I was only bored for Christ's sake! (*Changes tack.*) I goes, 'You shouldn't say things like that about Jamie and Ste. About your own brother. They're just mates.'

Ste   Nothing happened.

Leah   I was only thinking of you.

Jamie   Nothing's happened.

Leah (*to* **Ste**)   When was the last time your Trevor hit you?

Jamie   What's it to you?

Leah   When? I bet it was Thursday.

Ste   So?

Leah   That's when I told him. That's when I lied.

Jamie (*pause*)   Let's all go the park. You can come with us, Leah.

Leah (*shakes her head*)   It's all right. I int after sympathy.

Leah *goes into her flat.* **Jamie** *kicks the ball to* **Ste**, *half-heartedly.* **Ste** *kicks it straight at him.*

Ste   Come round tonight?! Come round tonight?! How the fuck can I come round tonight?!

Jamie   I thought you wanted to go the park?

Ste   Oh, and play *Cagney and Lacey*?

Jamie   Have a knockabout.

Ste   You don't like football!

Jamie   I don't feel confident with it.

Ste   Yeah, well, neither do I, son, neither do I!

Ste *makes to go in his door. From* **Leah***'s flat comes the sound of 'I Can Dream Can't I?' by Mama Cass.*

Jamie   Ste!

Ste   What now?

Jamie (*pause. He walks over to* **Ste** *with the ball*)   You may as well have this.

Ste (*knocks it out of* **Jamie***'s hands*)   You wanna feel confident? You go and practise! Go and kick it against a wall. Go on! Let's see how good you get. Go and kick it against a brick bloody wall!

Ste *goes in and slams the door.* **Jamie***, left on his own, bounces the ball on the ground, over and over again. As the lights dim, 'I Can Dream' gets louder, linking to the next scene.*

Scene Two

The next morning, about eight o'clock. **Sandra** *comes out in her dressing gown with a clipboard and biro. She is working out the staff rota for work. She obviously wants to get out of the house. She stands there filling in the rota chart.* **Jamie** *comes out, off to school, without his reading glasses. He hands his mother a cup of tea.*

Jamie   From Tony with love. Says it's nectar from the Gods for a very special angel.

Sandra   Has he put sugar in it?

Jamie   Dunno. See ya.

Sandra (*takes a swig*)   He hasn't. (*As* **Jamie** *goes.*) Oi!

She taps the side of her cheek for a goodbye kiss. **Jamie** *comes back and kisses her. As he does,* **Ste** *comes out of his flat to go to school. But seeing* **Jamie***, he goes back inside.*

Jamie *tuts.*

Sandra   What's his problem?

Jamie   He's in love, that's all.

Sandra No!

Jamie Mm. See ya.

Sandra Yeah. Tatafilata. B.Y.E.

Jamie *exits.* **Tony** *comes to the door with his own tea. He's wearing* **Sandra***'s spare dressing-gown.*

Tony Did you get my message?

Sandra Very nice. Shame about the sugar though.

Tony Oh. I'll . . .

Sandra No. It's all right . . .

Tony Need a hand?

Sandra No, I'm all right.

Tony (*moving to her*) Come on. Two brains, get the job done quicker.

Sandra . No, Tony, it's all right.

Tony I thought we could go to Greenwich, the park. Legs astride the Meridian as they say.

Sandra Who?

Tony What?

Sandra Who says that?

Tony Oh, you know, folk. (*Northern.*) There's nowt so queer as folk.

Sandra Mm, well, I got too many things to sort out in there. (*Indicates flat.*) You go if you want.

Tony (*looking over her shoulder at chart*) Sharon can do Thursday lunch. Stick Warren up there, gives you the night off.

Sandra Tony . . .

Tony You need a window in your diary.

Sandra Listen, I'm not seventeen and doing a Friday night at the Bargepole for pin money any more. This is my living, and I'm bloody good at it.

Tony Sure. You're right. I'll do some hoovering. Or whatever.

Sandra I thought you wanted to go to the park?

Tony No problem.

Sandra Oh, it's a lovely day. Take your sketch pad and doodle.

Tony You're addicted to that pub, addict!

Sandra Hey, don't knock it, there's money in booze!

Tony Is that all you want from life? Big bucks?

Sandra Oh, Tony, I'm not talking about swanning off to Monaco and bonking Grace Kelly's widower. I'm talking about having enough handbag to get a decent pair o'shoes that don't let the rain in.

Tony I can get you shoes.

Sandra No, it's all right.

Tony I can make you shoes.

Tony Get your sketch pad and go the park. Draw a few trees for me.

Tony All my gear's at the studio.

Sandra Right. (*Gets a fiver out of her dressing-gown pocket.*) Here's a fiver. Buy a sketch pad.

Tony You can't afford that.

Sandra It was a good night for tips last night, go on.

Tony I'm not a charity.

Sandra And I'm not Minister for the Arts.

Tony I wish you were. You'd be knockout. (*Takes the money.*) I'll get dressed.

Sandra Good idea.

Tony (*goes to the door, turns to* **Sandra**.) Hey and Sandra . . .

Sandra What?

Tony (*winks and clicks his teeth, very Hollywood schmaltz*) Thanks.

Sandra *cringes.* **Tony** *goes in. She gets on with her rota.* **Ste** *comes out.*

Ste Oright?

Sandra Well, hello there, Casanova.

Ste What?

Sandra A little bird tells me you're in love.

Ste No.

Sandra Oooh, four-letter word, love. Don't look so worried. Jamie's told me all about it.

Ste What?

Sandra Yeah, well, about time too. You deserve a bit o'luck. You're all right, you are.

Ste What?!

Sandra I'm jealous. Twenny years younger, coulda bin me!

Ste Oh yeah?

Sandra Come on, what's she like?

Ste Sandra . . .

Sandra Well, what's her name then?

Ste No . . .

Sandra Short for Nolene, is it? Very *Home and Away*! Well, I hope it works out for ya, Stevie. 'Ere, buy Nolene a present wi'that. (*Gets another fiver out of her pocket.*) Sign of affection, a present.

Ste No I couldn't.

Sandra Go on, I don't need it. Get her some flowers!

Ste No, Sandra, really . . .

Sandra (*chucks the money onto the walkway*) Well, I'm not picking it up. (*She goes to her door.*) Is she like me? (*Does a little wiggle and laughs.*)

Ste I can't take your money, Sandra.

Sandra Don't look a gift horse up his wotsit. D'you know what I mean?

Sandra *goes indoors.* **Ste** *stares at the fiver, struggling for a bit. Then he grabs the fiver and runs.*

Scene Three

Jamie*'s bedroom that night.* **Jamie** *sits fully clothed on the bed.* **Ste** *stands beside him holding a plastic bag.*

Jamie You wasn't in school.

Ste I'm aware of that.

Jamie I musta really pissed you off.

Ste No.

Jamie If you want, I could write you an absence note.

Ste I went up Woolwich, had a ride on the ferry. Got you this. (*He hands* **Jamie** *the bag.* **Jamie** *unwraps a shaggy hat.*) Had a bit o' money like.

Jamie Is this for me?

Ste I'll have it if you don't wannit.

Jamie No, I'm having it.

Ste You like it, yeah?

Jamie Yeah, I do.

Ste Well, put it on then. (**Jamie** *puts the hat on.* **Ste** *sits on the bed.*) It just don't feel right, I'm sorry, Jay. Here. Your mum and Tony the other side o'that wall, my ole man and Trevor that side. I've got an aunty in Gravesend. She's dead old.

Thought we could go and stay there one night coz she's deaf. But that wouldn't feel right either.

Jamie   Look what I got. (*Moves his pillow and pulls out a copy of* Gay Times, *hands it to* Ste.)

Ste (*flicks through then reads a bit*)   Dear Brian, can you transmit the HIV virus via frottage? What's that?

Jamie (*tuts*)   Yoghurt. It's French.

Ste   Cor, thick git! (*Reads some more.*) Dear Brian, I am twenty-three, black and gay. The problem is that although I'm happy being with a man and have a strong desire to live with a lover, I get that horrible feeling that people are going to talk about me behind my back, and that they won't accept me as I am. Also, my family don't know. Unhappy, North London.

Jamie   Get over that river mate, I'll make you happy! (**Ste** *whacks him on the head with the magazine.*) See Ste, you're not the only one in the world.

Ste   I know, there's whatsisname out of Erasure.

Jamie   Find page ninety-two.

Ste   What? (*Leafs through.*)

Jamie   Column four, ten down from the top.

Ste (*reads*)   The Gloucester Pub. King William Walk. Opposite Greenwich Park Gates.

Jamie   One-eighty bus'll take us right to it.

Ste   So?

Jamie   So d'you fancy it?

Ste   I dunno. Someone might see us.

Jamie   We'll go in disguise. Wear sunglasses.

Ste   Bagsy your hat.

Jamie   Are you gonna come then?

Ste   I think I can squeeze you in somewhere.

*As **Jamie** says the next speech, he gets up off the bed and runs his fingers over the hat, very much the temptress.*

Jamie   I've never had a hat for a present before. It's a nice hat. You gave it to me. And now, I'm gonna give you somin' to say thank you that you'll never forget.

Ste   Jay?!

Jamie   On your back!!

Ste   (*lying back*)   What you doin', Jamie?

Jamie   Close your eyes.

*Ste closes his eyes then opens them again. **Jamie** coughs a reproach. Ste shuts them. **Jamie** whips out a pad and pen from under the bed. Writes.*

Jamie   Dear Miss Ellis. Sorry Steven wasn't in school today, only he was feeling a little queer. Lots o'love, Ste's Dad!

They collapse laughing.

'Make Your Own Kind of Music' by Mama Cass links us into the next scene.

Scene Four

*Jamie's bedroom. The early hours of the morning, a few nights later. Complete blackness. **Jamie** is in bed. **Sandra** comes in, in the dark.*

Sandra   Jamie? You awake? Jamie I know you are.

Jamie   What?

Sandra   Where've you been please?

Jamie   Nowhere.

Sandra   Oh yeah? It's half-one in the morning actually. (*Pause.*) Where did you go?

Jamie   Out.

Sandra Jamie! (*She bends and switches on his bedside light.* **Jamie** *doesn't move, lying with his back to her.*) You went the Gloucester, din't ya? Look at me. (**Jamie** *rolls over.*)

Jamie Only went for a drink.

Sandra That's where gay people go. They go there and they go Macmillans in Deptford.

Jamie It's not just gay people who go. Other people go.

Sandra People like you?

Jamie Yeah?

Sandra It's no time for lying, Jamie.

Jamie It's not a lie.

Sandra I had a phone call tonight.

Jamie Oh, you're lucky.

Sandra From your tutor.

Jamie Miss Ellis?

Sandra She's worried about ya.

Jamie God, coz I bunk off games does it mean I'm gay?

Sandra No. Coz someone hit you.

Jamie Everyone gets hit.

Sandra And called you queer. And it aint the first time. She's worried about what it's doing to ya.

Jamie I'm all right.

Sandra Are you, Jamie? Coz I'm not sure you are. I mean, what am I supposed to think? When you're . . . you're going out drinking and coming home at half-one. Getting hit, getting moody, I don't think you are.

Jamie Well, I am, so go back to bed!

Sandra Er, I'll go when I'm good and ready if you don't mind.

Jamie I'm tired.

Sandra You're pissed.

Jamie No I'm not.

Sandra Pissed from a bloody gay bar!

Jamie How d'you know it's gay anyway?

Sandra Coz it's got a bloody great big pink neon arse outside of it. Jamie, I'm in the business, I get to know these things!

Jamie You been spying on me?

Sandra No. Someone at work seen you go in . . .

Jamie Don't mean I'm gay . . .

Sandra Going in with another boy, so who was that?

Jamie (*beat*) Ste.

Sandra Ste? Right.

Jamie Still don't mean I'm gay. They wanna mind their own business.

Sandra That's what I said.

Jamie Well then, what you goin' on at me for?

Sandra Because sometimes, Jamie, I can put two and two together and make bloody four, I'm not stupid, you know.

Jamie I never said you were!

Sandra So I think I deserve an explanation.

Jamie I went for a drink. Big deal. Everyone in my class goes drinking.

Sandra   Yeah, but they don't all go the bloody Gloucester though, do they!

Jamie   Some of 'em take drugs, at least I'm not doing that!

Sandra   I bloody hope you're not!

Jamie   Ah, well, thanks a lot. Thanks a bundle. Go back to bed!

Sandra   I can't sleep, Jamie!

Jamie   Well, don't take it out on me.

Sandra   Jamie. Will you just talk to me?!

Jamie   I'm knackered.

Sandra   Please, Jamie. Talk to me.

Jamie · What about?

Sandra (*sitting on bed*)   I'm your mother.

Pause.

Jamie   Some things are hard to say.

Sandra   I know. I know that, Jamie . . .

Jamie (*crying now*)   I'm not weird if that's what you're thinking!

Sandra   I know you're not, love.

Jamie   You think I'm too young. You think it's just a phase. You think I'm . . . I'm gonna catch AIDS and . . . and everything!

Sandra   You know a lot about me, don't ya? Jesus, you wanna get on that *Mastermind*. Specialised subject – Your Mother. Don't cry. I'm not gonna put you out like an empty bottle in the morning. Jesus, I thought you knew me well enough to know that. Why couldn't you talk to me, eh? Going behind my back like that, getting up to allsorts. There's me going to bed of a night feeling sorry for ya, coz you had to share a bed with Ste. And . . . and all the time you were . . . you were doing a seventy minus one . . .

Jamie   What?

Sandra   Think about it.

Jamie *tuts*.

Sandra   Do you talk to him?

Jamie   Me and him's the same.

Sandra   He's sixteen years of age, Jamie. What pearls of wisdom can he throw your way? He aint seen life. He's never even had a holiday.

Jamie   It's difficult, innit?

Sandra   Am I that much of a monster?

Jamie   No!

Sandra   Don't get me wrong. I like the lad. Always have. All I'm saying is he's young.

Jamie   He's good to me.

Sandra   Is he?

Jamie   Yeah.

Sandra *is bottling up the tears. She can't bring herself to cry in front of* **Jamie**. *She gets up quickly and runs out of the room. She comes on to the walkway and starts to cry.* **Jamie** *bawls.* **Tony** *comes into* **Jamie**'*s room.*

Tony   What's up?

Jamie   Go away.

Tony   What have you done now?

Jamie   Nothing!

Tony   Then why's she so upset?

Jamie   I'm a queer! A bender! A pufter! A knobshiner! Brownhatter! Shirtflaplifter!

Tony   I get the picture.

Jamie   Leave me alone.

Tony   And she knows this.

Jamie   No, I thought I'd tell you first.

Tony   This is . . . it's . . . it's okay. Night, kidder.

Jamie   Yeah.

Tony *leaves the room and comes out onto the walkway where* **Sandra** *stands crying. It is dark on the walkway, except for a thin shaft of light which creeps across from* **Sandra**'s *open door.*

Tony   There's no need to cry.

Sandra   Oh, isn't there?!

Tony   It's okay, I know. It's natural. (*Pause.*) You like tomatoes. I like beetroot.

Sandra   Shut up.

Tony   Hey, I'm not saying it's easy, yeah? No way. (*Tries to cuddle her.*)

Sandra (*wriggling free*)   Off of me.

Tony   I know. That's cool.

Sandra *gets some fags out of her pocket and a lighter. She lights up, her hands shaking. She wipes her face as she speaks.*

Sandra   He was . . . he was the most beautiful baby in Bermondsey you know. Pushed him round. In his little frilly hat. In a big blue pram called Queen o'the Road. Oh, fuckin'ell.

Tony   None of that's changed.

Sandra   State o'me.

Tony   Just let it out, Sandra.

Sandra   Shut up.

Tony   You're fighting it, hon.

Sandra   Fighting? I've been fighting all me life. Kids pickin' on 'im – I was there. Council saying bollocks to benefit, I was there. When I had three pee in me purse and an empty fridge I went robbin' for that boy. And you talk to me about fighting? You! What have you ever had to fight for in your life?!

Tony   Come here.

Sandra   I'm all right.

Tony   Sandra . . .

Sandra   Go back to bed, Tony.

Tony   You need support.

Sandra   I wanna be on me own.

Tony   No.

Sandra   Yes.

Tony   If you're sure.

Sandra   I'm sure.

Tony   Well . . . I'll be waiting.

Tony *submits. He's ready to go back in when* **Leah***'s door swings open and* **Leah** *steps out, her door swinging shut behind her. She holds an egg whisk to her chest. She steps forward. When she speaks she does so in a deep South American drawl. She is tripping on acid.* **Tony** *is waylaid by her.*

Leah (*to* **Tony**)   Not so fast! This is my big speech.

Sandra   Oh, for crying out loud.

Tony   Huh?

Leah   I've never won anything in my life before. Certainly not Slimmer of the Year.

Leah *clears her throat.* **Sandra** *and* **Tony** *look to each other, then to* **Leah***.*

Leah   Thank you to all members of the Academy. This means so much. I'd like to thank my manager, the wonderful Ted Bow-Locks. And my band, they're all here . . . (*Waves to* **Tony**.) Hi, guys! I'd like to thank Jesus Christ for coming to earth. I'd like to thank the President for being great . . . but most of all I'd like to thank one very special person . . .

Sandra   What the . . .

Leah   The woman from whom all energy flows. This award is as much hers as mine. The woman who gives me so much . . . inspiration. Let's hear it for . . . Mama San!

Sandra   Leah?

Leah   People say to me, they say . . .

Sandra   Leah, are you drunk?

Leah   'Where do you get your energy from?'

Sandra   Leah, it's half-one in the morning.

Tony   Has she taken something?

Leah   And I say, 'Hey! Mama San!'

Sandra (*to* **Leah**)   Is your mother in?

Leah   Mama San! Git down honey! Your vibes are shootin' right through of me!

Sandra   Is she working nights?

Leah   Don't let the light leave you, Mama San.

Sandra (*goes to* **Leah**'s *door and bangs on it*)   Rose?! (*To* **Leah**.)   Get your keys out. Hurry up.

Tony (*to* **Leah**)   Have you taken, like, a trip, you know?

Sandra (*tuts. Calls through to her flat*)   Jamie?! Leah, have you got your key please?!

Tony   Don't shout at her!

Leah   You're giving me bad vibes, Mama!

Tony   She's on something.

Sandra   Jamie!!

Leah (*to* **Tony**)   You're an old, old man. And I don't like old men.

Tony   That's cool. That's no problem.

Sandra   It is a problem actually, Tony. Don't pander to her.

Tony   I'm not pandering to her.

Leah   Panda? Where's the panda.

Jamie *comes to the door.*

Jamie   What now?

Leah (*spies an imaginary panda*)   Oh, there he is! Hello!

Sandra   Jamie, does she take anything?

Jamie   What like?

Tony   Look, we're not talking aspirin here, right?

Jamie   Drugs?

Sandra   Jesus.

Jamie   Dunno.

Sandra   Get her key off her, Tony.

Leah *is caught up in looking closely at* **Sandra**'s *hanging basket.*

Tony   We mustn't touch her.

Sandra   Get her away from my special basket, Tony! You're being too easy on her!

Tony   No, we'll freak her out!

Sandra   She's freaking me out, Tony!

Jamie   What you taken, Leah?

Sandra   I've never seen anything so ridiculous in all me life. (*Grabs* **Leah**.) Leah! Give us your bloody key!

Leah *whimpers and fights for breath.* **Tony** *grabs* **Sandra**'s *arm.*

Tony   Sandra!

Sandra   Er, body language, Tony! (*Struggles with him.*)

Jamie Look at her!

Leah (*slipping to floor*) I'm dead. Dead and buried. (*Flops to floor.*)

Tony Look what you've done now.

Sandra I don't believe you just did that, Tony.

Jamie What's she doing?

Sandra I'll have a nice bruise in the morning thanks to you.

Tony Christ, er, I saw a video about Woodstock once. What do we do?

Sandra I've got a nice suggestion, but there's children present.

Tony We can't leave her there all night!

Sandra/Jamie Why not?!

Ste *comes out of his flat in his bed gear, the light from his flat brightening the walkway.*

Ste What's the noise?

Sandra Oh, let's make a party of it, shall we?

Jamie You don't know anything that's good for drug addicts, do ya?

Ste What?

Tony She's not a drug addict!

Sandra And my name's Wincey Willis! (*To* **Ste**.) Tony thinks she's taken acid. And Tony knows these sorts o'things coz he's that way inclined hisself I wouldn't wonder.

Ste Orange juice. (*Everyone looks to* **Ste**.) Me brother says if you have a bad trip on acid, drink orange juice.

Jamie   'Ere, it might be that Ecstasy! Everyone takes that round here.

Tony   It's not Ecstasy.

Sandra   Oh really?

Tony   No, the symptoms are all wrong.

Jamie   Have you got any orange?

Sandra   No.

Ste   We have.

Tony   Will you get it?

Ste   Yeah. (*Exits.*)

Sandra (*to* **Tony**)   Proper little Doctor Dolittle, intya?

Tony   I don't need this right now, Sandra.

Sandra   Oh, and I do? I'm telling ya, I'll be glad to get outa this bloody place.

Tony   Can we just keep the noise down?

Jamie   What d'you mean, Mum?

Sandra   Oh, and I suppose you like standing out on the landing at two in the morning? Surrounded by drug experts and the like.

Tony   Oh, loosen up Sandra.

Sandra   Oh, you can shut up, Tony, if you don't mind.

Tony (*to* **Jamie**)   Your mother's tired.

Sandra   I said shut up, didn't I?

Ste *comes out with a carton of fresh orange. He hands it to* **Tony**. **Tony** *leans over* **Leah**. *The others watch, fascinated.*

Tony   Leah? (*Pause.*) Leah? (*Still no response.*) Mama Cass?

Leah (*immediately lifts her head. Conspiratorially*)   I know they're all talking about me. I know it. But what do you expect? This is the price of fame. Ask any of the greats, they'll tell you: Betty, Joan, Marilyn.

Tony (*holding carton out*) I've got a beautiful drink here. And if you drink it, you'll have the time of your life.

Leah Really?

Tony It's the best.

Leah You see the problem is . . . you have seventeen heads. And my mother made me swear that I'd never take a drink off a guy with seventeen heads.

Sandra (*to* **Jamie**) I'm sorry, this is knocking me sick now.

Tony Right. Ste, you try.

Ste No.

Jamie Go on, Ste, give it a try.

Ste (*steps forward. To* **Jamie**) Wish me luck.

Jamie At a boy, Ste.

Sandra *watches this exchange with interest.* **Tony** *hands* **Ste** *the drink.* **Sandra** *stares at* **Jamie**, *then round to* **Leah**.

Leah Mm. Pretty boy.

Ste (*to* **Leah**) Right . . . see this right . . . you know if you drink it, you'll feel better. D'you know what I mean?

Leah (*giggles to* **Tony**) Is he a fan or something?

Tony Yes.

Leah Mmh!

Tony (*to* **Ste**) Call her Mama Cass!

Jamie (*laughs*) Gutted!

Ste No.

Tony (*grabs carton*) Mama Cass?

Leah (*takes carton and drinks some*)   Why, sir! Your juice tastes mighty fine to me!

Tony   Have some more.

They all watch as **Leah** *drinks. As she does,* **Sandra** *speaks.*

Sandra   There's a pub up in Rotherhithe. The Anchor. The brewery want me to be temporary licensee. (*They all, bar* **Leah**, *look to* **Sandra**.) It's got a little beer garden, and a piano. And you can watch the boats go up and down on the Thames. And it's got a nice little flat above it. Room for a family.

Leah (*to* **Tony**)   Are you in the band?

Tony   No.

Leah   Yes you are.

Tony   Yes. I am.

Jamie   Why didn't you tell me?

Leah   You know, you're very good.

Sandra   You were out.

Tony   Cheers.

Leah   You're a very beautiful person.

Jamie   But . . .

Leah   Am I a beautiful person?

Tony   Yes. You're immensely beautiful.

Jamie   You coulda told me before.

Sandra   Snap! Tony, how long's this gonna take?

Ste   Ten hours.

Sandra   What?!

Jamie   Blimey!

Sandra   Ten hours?

Ste   I think so. I dunno. That's what I've been told. I don't do it. Respect meself too much.

Sandra   Her mother won't be back till breakfast.

Tony   We'll have to take her inside.

Sandra   Oh, brilliant.

Jamie   She's not getting in with me!

Sandra   I hope you don't think I'm sitting up with her Tony, coz I'm telling you now . . .

Tony   I'll sit up with her. It'll be all right. I'm good with kids.

Leah   What's happening?

Tony   Why don't you come into this nice house with me?

Leah   Mama!

Tony   Mama . . .

Leah   Mm. I don't know.

Tony   You'll love the wallpaper.

Sandra   Oh, thanks.

Tony   Here. (*Holds out his hand so she can take it. The others stand aside so* **Tony** *can lead* **Leah** *in. She looks at them.*)

Leah   Please . . . no autographs. (**Tony** *and* **Leah** *step inside.*)

Tony (*off*)   Isn't it nice?

Leah (*off*)   Groovy patterns, wow!

Sandra   Right, the show's over. We can all get in now.

Jamie   You played a blinder there, Ste.

Sandra   Jamie. I want you indoors.

Jamie   I'm just talking to Ste.

Sandra   You got school in the morning.

Jamie   No I haven't. Tomorrow's Saturday.

Ste Time for my beauty sleep anyway.

Jamie Ste, she knows.

Sandra Who's she? The cat's mother?

Jamie Me mum knows.

Pause. **Ste** *looks horrified. His lower lip starts to tremble.*

Ste You gonna tell my dad? (*Cries.*)

Sandra No.

Ste Oh my God . . .

Sandra Oh, don't you start, I said no, didn't I?

Jamie Ste, it's all right. (*Attempts to put his arm around* **Ste**, *who shrugs him off.*)

Ste Jamie . . .

Sandra Jamie . . .

Jamie Ste . . .

Sandra Steven, stop crying please. I am not going to tell your dad.

Ste (*to* **Jamie**) Why d'you have to go and grass?

Sandra Please, Steven.

Jamie I never!

Ste Yeah, well, how come she knows?

Sandra Coz SHE never come down with the last shower! Jamie, get 'im an 'anky. There's a box of autumnal shades by my bed. (**Jamie** *goes inside.*) Jesus, Ste, will you stop crying? I don't believe in secrets. I like people to be straight up and honest. But I'm no fool. D'you think I want these flats to be infamous for child murder? No. So I won't be telling your dad.

Ste He'd kill me!

Sandra Yes. I've just said that.

Ste No, he would.

Sandra I think we've established that already actually, Ste.

Ste They all would, all of 'em.

Sandra I'LL bloody kill you in a minute if you don't stop snivelling and shut up! You're a good lad. That's what counts. And . . . somewhere you'll find people what won't kill you.

Ste No I won't.

Sandra Well, you've found the Gloucester.

Ste I hate it.

Sandra Yeah, well, somewhere else then, shut up.

Ste There aint nowhere else.

Sandra There is actually, Steven, coz there's an island in the Mediterranean called 'Lesbian', and all its inhabitants are dykes. So I think you got your eye wiped there. (**Jamie** *comes out with a box of hankies.*) Now. Wipe 'em properly.

Jamie There.

Ste Tar. I'm sorry.

Jamie Don't be a dickhead.

Ste Fuck me.

Sandra Er, there'll be none o'that out here, thank you. (*To* **Jamie**.) Are you gonna be long out here?

Jamie No.

Ste No, Sandra.

Sandra Well . . .

Ste We won't, Sandra. I'm going to bed. Honest, Sandra.

Sandra That's me name, Ste, don't wear it out. Night, Steven. (*Goes in.*)

Ste Night.

Sandra *exits*.

Jamie   What's Leah like, eh?

Ste   I know.

Jamie   Jees!

Ste   She's blinding, your mum.

Jamie   She's all right.

Ste   Innit? Who else knows?

Jamie   Only Tony. (*Pause.*) Give us a kiss.

Ste   No!

Jamie   Let's go the stairs, no one can see there.

Ste   There's no such thing as just a kiss. I'll knock you up in the morning, yeah?

Jamie (*Christine Cagney*)   Knock away, Mary Beth, knock away!

Ste   See you, Christine.

Ste *goes to his door.* **Jamie** *stays where he is and watches.* **Ste** *turns round.*

Ste   What?

Jamie   Watching.

Ste   What?!

Jamie   You!

Ste (*points to* **Jamie***'s door and orders him to move*)   Now!

Reluctantly **Jamie** *goes. Both doors close.*

Scene Five

The next evening, about seven-thirty. **Ste** *is out taking his drying back in.* **Leah***'s door is open. She comes to the door and watches him quietly.*

Leah   I wished I was the one that was going away. (*Pause.*) I wished. I hate it round here, don't you?

Ste   S'all right.

Leah   These flats. Them pubs.

Ste   Done it all, intya?

Leah   I gets up in the morning, bake me face in half a ton o'slap. Tong me hair wi'yesterday's lacquer . . . and that's it. Same every bleedin' day. Fuck all to look forward to except Mama Bloody Cass. Nothing ever happens. Nothing ever changes.

Ste   What about your new school?

Leah   Fell through.

Ste   D'you wanna come the Gloucester?

Leah   The what?

Ste   Gay pub.

Leah   I don't know any gay blokes.

Ste   Yes you do.

Leah (*smiles*)   Yeah.

Ste   Me and Jay are going in half an hour. Come on, plenty o'men.

Leah   Yeah and they all dance backwards and never get married.

Pause.

Sandra's *door opens, unseen by* **Leah**.

Leah   D'you think Jamie's mum'd give me a job in her new pub?

Sandra *appears, dolled up to the nines. She looks gorgeous. She is carrying a full bag of rubbish to take to the chute.*

Sandra   Doubt it.

Ste   You look nice, Sandra.

Sandra (*stopping*)   Cheers, Ste.

Leah   Goin' out wi' your bloke?

Sandra   No. Girls from work.

Ste   Have a nice time.

Sandra   Thanks, love. (**Ste** *goes in.* **Sandra** *puts her bin bag down.*) No licensee in their right mind'd have you pulling pints, Leah.

Leah   I can't help it. I'm a Gemini. I got a split personality.

Sandra   Bollocks, you know when you're being a little cow.

Leah   Everyone hates me.

Sandra   We despair of you. That's different. You can't wrap yourself up in a dead fat American git for the rest of your life you know.

Leah   I know.

Sandra   Well then. (*Picks up bin bag.*)

Leah   I gotta go in. Get ready. I'm going out wi' Ste and Jamie.

Sandra   The Gloucester?

Leah   Yeah. I intend to find meself a nice dyke tonight, Sandra, coz I'm tellin' ya, I'm through with men.

Sandra *chuckles.* **Leah** *goes in.* **Sandra** *turns to go to the chute. But* **Tony** *enters from the stairs. Leather jacket on, pretty swish. They stare at each other.*

Tony   If I had a camera now . . .

Sandra (*beat*)   What?

Tony   Well . . . I'd take your picture.

Sandra   I don't like having my picture took. Camera don't like me.

Tony   My camera would love you.

Sandra   No it wouldn't, Tony.

Tony It would. It'd be like that . . . (*Blows a kiss. Laughs.*)

Sandra Tony, what you doing?

Tony Can't keep away from you, babes.

Sandra Tony, I told you I was going out with the girls from work.

Tony Thought I could tag along.

Sandra Girls night out. You'd only be bored.

Tony I wanna celebrate too.

Sandra I know. But . . .

Tony They'd mind.

Sandra I mind.

Tony Right. Well, how about one little kiss? Send me on my way. Something to think of till tomorrow. (*Goes to kiss her. She pushes him away.*)

Sandra You're drowning me, Tony.

Tony Well. I'll ring you.

Sandra Tony . . .

Tony What's your next night off?

Sandra I dunno yet.

Tony Well, you make the decisions.

Sandra I'm sorry, Tony, but . . . I think you better go.

Tony I'm not in a rush . . .

Sandra No. No. (*Beat.*) Put that down the chute for us, will ya?

Tony *stares at her. She turns to go in and freezes.* **Tony** *waits a while longer, then picks up the bin bag and walks away.* **Sandra** *swings round, looking like she is going to call him back. Stops herself.*

Jamie *comes out wearing a jumper. He has two glasses of wine. He hands one to* **Sandra**.

Jamie   Mum? Have this. Get you in the mood.

Sandra   Tar.

Jamie   You're going Woolwich, intya?

Sandra   What? Yeah. Pub crawl then Stars Nightclub.

Jamie   You'll pull dressed like that. (**Sandra** *sighs a laugh, looking at floor.*) Why don't you come with us? (*Beat.*) Ring the girls and tell them you'll see 'em later. (**Sandra** *shakes her head.*) You don't know how to enjoy yourself, do ya?

Sandra   Bloody cheek.

Jamie   There's a male stripper on tonight as well.

Pause. **Sandra** *considers it.*

Sandra   Give me five minutes!

Sandra *runs indoors.* **Jamie** *sits on the step, sipping his wine. From* **Leah**'s *flat 'Dream a Little Dream of Me' by Mama Cass comes floating across the balcony.* **Ste** *comes out, freshened up.*

Ste   In't you gonna be hot in that jumper?

Jamie   Well, you bought it me.

Ste   Yeah, for up Rotherhithe. It's on the River. You'll freeze.

Jamie   We're on the River here. (*Tuts.*) Anyone about?

Ste (*nods to his flat*)   In there? (**Jamie** *nods.*) No.

Jamie (*beat*)   Dance with me.

Tentatively they take each other's hands and start to slow dance to the music. They are lost in each other.

Leah *comes out, ready for the off. She stands on her doorstep and watches the lads. She hasn't got any pockets, so she holds her purse, fags, lighter and keys in her hand till the end of the scene. She takes a fag out and lights up.*

Sandra *comes out with her wine. She watches* **Jamie** *and* **Ste** *dancing and then looks to* **Leah**.

Sandra   'Ere, Leah, gizza little drag o' that.

Leah *passes her the fag.* **Sandra** *takes a big drag.* **Leah** *goes indoors and turns the music up. She comes back out again.*

Leah   Sandra.

Sandra   What?

Leah   Come on.

Sandra *and* **Leah** *start to slowdance as well. They chat intermittently.*

Sandra   'Ere, Ste!

Ste   What?

Sandra   Imagine your dad's face!

Pause.

'Ere, Leah.

Leah   What?

Sandra   What's this dyke gonna be like?

Leah   Oooh, big and butch!

Sandra   What colour eyes?

Leah   Green.

Sandra   Yeah?

Leah   Yeah.

Sandra   Tall?

Leah   I'll have to look up.

Sandra   Nice.

Leah   Yeah.

Sandra   Yeah.

The music turns up of its own accord, blasting out. A glitterball spins above the stage, casting millions of dance hall lights. **Ste** *and* **Jamie** *are dancing.* **Leah** *and* **Sandra** *are dancing.*

The lights fade.

Babies

Characters

Joe Casey, *a Learning Support teacher and tutor of 9CY, aged 24*
Woody, *his boyfriend, aged 26*
Vivian Williams, *aged 32*
Manda Williams, *Viv's daughter, aged 16*
Tammy Williams, *Viv's daughter, a member of 9CY, aged 13*
Kenny Figaro, *Viv's brother, aged 30*
Ivy Williams, *Viv's mother-in-law, aged 65*
Sonia Sweeney, *Viv's next door neighbour and best friend, aged 40*
Ernie Sweeney, *Sonia's husband, aged 43*
Gemma Sweeney, *their daughter, aged 14*
Kelly, *a member of 9CY, aged 14*
David, *a member of 9CY, aged 14*
Richard, *a member of 9CY, aged 14*
Simone, *a member of 9CY, aged 14*
Valerie Pinkney, *Viv's neighbour over the road, aged 42*
Drag Queen, *a friend of Kenny's, aged 50*

Setting

The play is set in south east London, 1994. All the characters who live on the estate speak with South East London accents, whereas Joe and Woody are both from Liverpool. The Drag Queen is from North London. When the party is in full swing, the music should reflect the taste of the kids, 1994 summer chart music, except when Vivian is playing her Dolly Parton tape.

Babies was first performed at the Royal Court Theatre on 5th September 1994 with the following cast:

Vivian Williams	Lorraine Ashbourne
Ivy Williams/Valerie Pinkney	Helen Blatch
Drag Queen	Reginald S. Bundy
Gemma Sweeney	Joann Condon
Woody/Kenny	Karl Draper
Kelly	Sharon Duncan Brewster
Joe Casey	Ian Dunn
Sonia Sweeney	Elizabeth Estensen
David	Ricci Harnett
Manda	Louise Heaney
Ernie Sweeney	Kenneth MacDonald
Richard	Simon Sherlock
Tammy	Melissa Wilson
Director	Polly Teale
Designer	Bunny Christie

Act One

Scene One

Classroom

9CY's tutor base, in a modern south east London comprehensive school. There is a teacher's desk and the front row of four students' desks and chairs. At these desks sit **Kelly**, **Simone**, **David** *and* **Richard**. *Their backs are to the audience. Supposedly the rest of the class are where the audience are, so when a character talks or looks to the audience, they are in fact addressing another classmate.*

On the teacher's desk sits **Joe Casey**, *taking the register. He is the form tutor.*

The kids are dressed in modern school uniform: navy blue trousers, sweatshirt and trainers. They each have a 'Head' bag, in different colours, except **Kelly**, *who has a plastic bag.* **David** *also has an oboe case. They are all about thirteen/fourteen.*

Joe Casey *wears jeans and a leather jacket, he is twenty-four. Whereas the kids all speak in broad south east London accents,* **Joe** *speaks with a broad Liverpool twang.*

As **Joe** *takes the register there are various replies of 'here', 'yeah', and 'yo Sir' from the class.* **Simone** *swings round in her chair and chats with her mate* **Angel**, *behind her.*

Joe	Kelly	*At the same time.*
	Lee	
	Donna	**Simone** (*whisper*) Angel! Angel!
	Kellie	Did you see him? . . .
	Lee	What d'he say?
	Simon	Did you tell him? Was he gutted?
	Angel	Are you? . . .
	Lee-Anne	Sit on our bench in science. I
	Terry	wanna know everything. Yeah . . .

Osman	Oh no he didn't! . . .
David	Have you seen Lee-Anne Bennet's
Richard	culottes? . . .
Kelly-Ann	I know! . . .
Sukhvinder	Mark One or what?
Balvinder	(*Laughs*.)
Simone. Simone?	Who give you that black eye?

Simone What? Oh here Sir.

Joe Face the front Simone.

Simone (*tuts*) Tell me in science. (*Turning*.) Yeah Sir.

Joe Kaylee
Justin
Leah
Gurjit
Vicki
Robert
Wayne
and Tammy. Oh yeah. (*Closes register*.) Actually, eyes front 9CY. You too, Balvinder. Right, a word, please. (*Burps*.) Pardon me.

Simone Better out than in.

Joe Thanks Simone. Now. I want yous all to cast your minds back, if you will, to the end of last term. Yeah? Remember that day I sent Tammy on the errand with the staple gun? And I told you all her dad was really ill with cancer? Mm? Well you've probably noticed, but Tammy's not been in school this week.

Kelly (*to* **Simone**) Her dad's died.

Simone Has he?

Joe Well most of you probably know by now, but Tammy's dad died at the weekend.

Kelly Sir. Simone's crying.

Joe Okay.

Kelly (*to* **Simone**) Do it louder. (**Simone***'s crying gets louder*.)

Joe Now when Tammy comes back to school, how d'you think we should all behave? Bearing in mind that her dad's just died.

David Sir, be dead nice and that.

Richard Shut up Simone!

Joe Yeah. Be supportive to her. That's a really important word, yeah? Support. I mean just imagine how you'd feel if your dad had just died, or your mum . . . or your guardian . . . I know I'd be dead sad. So. (*Beat.*) No Balvinder, you wouldn't be over the moon. Balvinder! (*Class giggles.*) Now look here, if I catch any of yous taking the mickey, I'll send you straight to Miss Sterry and we'll see what she's got to say shall we?

Richard She's a lesbian!

Joe Thank you Richard.

Kelly Is she Sir?

Richard She's a moany old cow!

Joe Er excuse me! We don't, and I repeat *don't* talk like that about members of staff in this room, do we?

Richard *tuts.*

Joe Do we?

Richard No Sir.

Joe Thank you. Sexuality is a private and personal thing. Okay? Now a word about your homeworks please, that was the worksheet: 'Cinderella Fights Back'.

Kelly Sir can I take Simone to the toilet?

Joe Er . . .

Kelly Her mascara's run.

Joe Give us your diary.

Simone *goes in her bag for her school diary. She takes out twenty Bensons and a lighter and slips them in her pocket. She then finds her* *diary.* **Kelly** *has jumped out of her seat. She goes and links arms with* **Joe**.

Kelly Ah cheers Sir. In'e a blinding teacher eh?

Joe (*releasing her arm*) What's the rule on physical contact?

Kelly (*tuts*) Ah but you are Sir. I'm glad we never got that Mr Burgess as a tutor, he's real moany.

David It was sad about Freddy Mercury, wannit Sir?

Joe Very, David. Now . . .

David He was gay, wann'e Sir.

Joe I think he was bisexual actually David.

Richard What's that then?

Simone (*getting up with diary*) AC/DC, swings both ways.

Kelly That one out of Erasure's a gayboy, and he's gorgeous!

Simone (*handing diary to* **Joe**) Oh don't Kell! He wears girls' clothes.

Richard I hate fucking poufters!

David Oh Rich!

Kelly You're probably one yourself Rich, tell him Sir.

Joe I'm telling no one nothing. Richard? Would you like to get my magic pen and go and rub out one of your red squares on the merit mark chart? We don't have language or homophobia like that in these four walls. Okay?

Richard Oh that's out of order!

David Haha! Gutted Rich!

Kelly Blinding. Sir!

Joe If you think it's out of order Richard, perhaps you better go and tell Miss Sterry that.

Richard (*as class laughs*) What, that lesbian? (*More laughter.*)

Joe Right. Outside now!

Richard She wears men's clothes!

Joe I said outside!

Richard (*going*) Aw, this school's an arsehole.

Joe You can only judge an arsehole by the turds that pass through it Richard. Get out! (*He goes.*) Right. Now can I talk about your homeworks, which I might add was the most disastrous pile o'crap I've read in me life.

He opens **Simone***'s diary. Just then seven warning pips sound, heralding the end of registration. Sounds of pandemonium breaking out.*

Joe Oh why are there never enough minutes in the day? Okay, pack your things up and get off to science. I'll have that chat this afternoon.

Simone Sir, me diary Sir.

Joe Pop to the loo on your way to science Simone.

Kelly Oh write us a note to say we'll be late Sir!

Joe I'll do no such thing, now go on.

Kelly God!

Simone I'm changing tutors!

Kelly So am I!

Kelly *and* **Simone** *grab their stuff and go.* **David** *gathers up his bag and oboe case and hangs about until the rest of the class has gone.*

David Sir? I've been picked to be Chelsea's mascot on the thirteenth of June.

Joe Goway have yer?

David Yeah! And guess where we're going!

Joe Where?

David It's an away game, go on, guess!

Joe I . . .

David Liverpool!

Joe Oh well look out for me mother then, she goes to all the home games.

David I'm too old to be mascot really, so me dad told em I was only twelve. He only got away with it coz I'm small.

Joe Good things come in little packages.

David I just hope I don't grow too much before then. I'll be in the shit well and truly. Oh sorry Sir.

Joe What?

David I swore.

Joe Oh yeah, well don't.

David Should I take the register back for ya?

Joe D'you mind?

David No. I gotta put me oboe back in the school safe, it's on the way. See ya Sir.

Joe Cheers David.

David *takes the register and goes to the door. He stops.*

David You aint forgot you still got Richard outside have you Sir?

Joe Er no.

David Should I tell him to come in? Or d'you wanna leave it 'til break time?

Joe Erm . . . break time.

David Staff room? Or are you doing a break duty?

Joe Er . . .

David It's Wednesday Sir, break duty. I'll tell him to see you by the special-needs huts shall I?

Joe Okay.

David Right. Later Sir. (*Going.*) Ere Rich!

David *exits.* **Joe** *packs up his stuff and follows suit.*

Scene Two

Crematorium

*It starts to snow. 'You'll Never Walk Alone' sung by a squeaky
soprano with electric organ plays out over a tannoy in the grounds of
the crematorium. A line of wreaths stands alongside a gravel path.
Each wreath has a card with message attached to it. One wreath spells
'Scottie'. Another forms a neck-high bottle of vodka. Another forms a
huge packet of 'Marlboro' with a cigarette jutting out.*

Viv Williams *and her two daughters* **Manda** *and* **Tammy** *slowly
process out of the crematorium. The girls are crying and* **Viv** *walks
between them hugging them.* **Viv** *is an attractive thirty-two, young-
looking enough to pass for the girls' elder sister.* **Manda** *is sixteen and*
Tammy *thirteen. They are wrapped up warm to brave the elements.*

Following closely behind them are their next door neighbours **Sonia**
and **Ernie Sweeney**. *They are all dressed in funeral clothes.* **Sonia**
tries to act and speak a bit classier than **Viv**.

They stop by the wreaths. **Sonia** *and* **Ernie** *stand apart from the
others.* **Ernie** *gets a packet of cigarettes out and offers one to* **Viv**.

Ernie Viv?

Viv *shakes her head.* **Sonia** *stands admiring the bottle of vodka
wreath.*

Sonia Isn't that beautiful?

She leans over to read the card attached to it.

Sonia (*reads*) Up in heaven a star is shining
      Down on earth my heart is whining
      Save a place at Jesu's table
      I'll be with you when I'm able.

Tammy I wrote that.

Sonia (*still reading*) Enjoy the vodka, all my love. Tammy.

Manda Read my one Sonia, the packet o'Marlboro.

Sonia (*bends down and reads*) Simply the best
      Better than all the rest

Better than anyone else
Anyone I've ever met.
That's you dad. Love Manda.

Viv His favourite song.

Ernie That's touching that is.

Sonia (*to* **Tammy** *and* **Manda**) Your daddy will be a very proud man.

Viv Right, they've got your nan in the car. You be okay in the second car Son?

Sonia (*nods*) See you back at the house.

Viv (*to girls*) Come on.

She leads off. **Tammy** *wants to stay.* **Manda** *goes back to her, puts her arms round her, hugs her then they go off.* **Sonia** *and* **Ernie** *watch.*

Ernie Automatic.

Sonia What?

Ernie Them cars.

Sonia Where's Gemma?

Ernie Over there reading the tombs.

Sonia Go and get her.

Ernie Shout her.

Sonia Decorum Ernie.

Ernie *goes off to fetch their daughter.* **Valerie Pinkney** *comes along the gravel path with a small arrangement of flowers. She adds it to the line of wreaths.*

Sonia Valerie, I didn't realise you were here.

Valerie Didn't cry did she?

Sonia Vivian?

Valerie When my Norman passed on I was inconsolable.

Sonia She'd had half a tranquiliser off Doctor Nayar.

Valerie Them cars is a bit common. It's the girls I feel sorry for.

Ernie *returns.*

Ernie Says she's staying here.

Valerie I'm expected at the washeteria.

Valerie *goes off.*

Sonia What's she staying here for?

Ernie Says she likes it.

Sonia Oh I've got some cherry lips in my pocket. You go and stall the car. I'll go and coax her.

Ernie *goes off one way,* **Sonia** *the other.*

Sonia Gemma?

'Simply the Best' by Tina Turner, starting at the chorus, bursts out leading us into the next scene.

Scene Three

Street

On the same estate as the school, six months later.

Vivian Williams *and her two daughters,* **Manda** *and* **Tammy,** *career down the pavement.* **Viv** *is smoking, and pushing a Kwik-Save trolley piled high with bags of food. They carry shopping bags.* **Tammy** *jumps on the side of the trolley to try and have a ride on it. They are now all dressed in summery gear.*

Viv (*slapping her off*) Oi, get down from there Tammy!

Manda Act your age, Camel tits.

Tammy *comes off, but almost immediately jumps on again.* **Viv** *slaps her across the hands, forcing her down.*

Viv Get down Tammy! How many times d'you need telling? It'll buckle under your weight.

Manda Fat slag!

Tammy Piss off!

Viv *stops the trolley, slaps* **Tammy** *across the bum and then points at her in the face, intimidatingly, all three actions well rehearsed, and very fast.*

Viv Oi!! You've got a fat arse! I've told you. (*Points to trolley.*) Now push!

Tammy (*tuts*) God.

They move off again. **Tammy** *pushes the trolley a lot slower than her mum.*

Viv Hurry up girl, we haven't got all day!

Viv *and* **Manda** *laugh.* **Viv** *passes the ciggie over the trolley to a grateful* **Manda**, *who has a few drags.*

Tammy It's heavy.

Viv Well use your bloody elbow grease.

Tammy I'm pushing as hard as I can!

Manda Well push harder! (*Passes ciggie back to* **Viv**.)

Tammy Carry some more bags Manda.

Manda Libs!

Tammy Shut up.

Manda (*putting her own bags in the trolley*) Haha gutted! Wait 'til the Pinkneys see you!

Tammy The Pinkneys are a bunch of slags!

Viv Watch out for that dog crap Tam.

Tammy Me arm hurts.

Viv It's your birthday Tammy. You gotta do something towards it.

Tammy I'll do the hoover.

Viv Manda's doing that.

Manda Oh libs!

Viv Shut up and talk properly Manda. You're as bad as her.

Manda Well none of my mates are coming to this bloody party. Not even me own bloody boyfriend.

Viv Yeah well when your bloody boyfriend can see his way clear to being bloody civil to me he can step back inside our house. I don't like him.

Tammy Gutted! Haha!

Manda Fat arse!

Viv Oi! Don't start.

Tammy What time's Kenny coming then?

Viv He's bringing your nan round about eight.

Manda Oh God.

Tammy Is she still coming?

Viv She's still your nan, Tammy, even if your dad has died.

Tammy And is Kenny staying?

Viv No. He's gotto open the pub up ann'e? But he'll be back later on.

Manda He is coming though?

Viv Yes! Any more questions?

They slow down as they reach the Pinkneys' house. They stop and stare in the direction of the audience, standing in front of the trolley so that it is hidden from view.

Viv Aye aye. The Pinkneys are in.

Manda State of their windows. You'd think they could see 'emselves clear to getting 'em mended.

Tammy (*sings, like a football chant*) Trampo-os! Trampo-os!

Viv Who's she looking at?

Manda Gozzy bitch.

Viv (*shouts*) Yeah you can stare Valerie Pinkney! Oh yeah? Yeah? (*To girls.*) Look at her shaking her head. (*Shouts.*) It's

only shopping, Valerie! (*They step aside to reveal the trolley.*) No
law against that. It's bloody paid for! (*To girls.*) Over the
road and in.

The three of them retreat to the back of the stage. **Viv** *gets a key out
of her pocket and hands it to* **Manda**. **Manda** *and* **Tammy** *start
unloading the trolley and exit.*

Viv Everything straight in the kitchen.

Viv *hasn't taken her eyes off* **Valerie Pinkney**'s *house.* **Tammy**
and **Manda** *exit.* **Manda** *comes back with an envelope.*

Manda There's another letter here mum.

Viv Give it here.

Manda *hands her mum the letter and looks to* **Valerie Pinkney**.
Viv *holds the letter up and rips it for* **Valerie** *to see. She then sticks
a finger up and exits with some shopping bags.* **Manda** *follows.*

Scene Four

Joe Casey's *lounge*

*An old wooden ironing board with an iron on it stands next to a comfy
chair. Sprawled across the chair is* **Joe Casey**'s *fella* **Woody**. *He
flicks through the channels on TV with a remote control and settles on
watching 'Blind Date'.* **Joe** *comes in holding two shirts on coat
hangers.* **Woody** *has a Liverpool accent too.*

Joe Which d'you think? (*Pause.*) I'm talking to you.

Pause. **Woody** *shifts round in his seat to look at* **Joe**.

Woody What?

Joe Which d'you think?

Woody Well it depends, doesn't it?

Joe On what?

Woody On whether you wanna be the Butch Skal or the
Camp Queen.

Joe Oh the Butch Skal, definitely the Butch Skal.

Woody Well neither then, you'll have to take something of mine.

Joe (*not giving up*) Woody, which one?

Woody I don't want anything to do with this and you know that.

Joe I'll wear this.

He drapes one shirt over the back of the easy chair and sets about ironing the other.

Joe Are you going out tonight?

Pause. **Woody** *pretends not to hear.*

Joe (*to himself, but for* **Woody** *to hear*) Oh! I'm having a relationship with Helen Keller.

Woody Might go to the Fridge.

Joe Oh might yer?

Woody Yeah I might, coz Paul rang and he's going.

Joe Oh that's nice for yer.

Woody Yeah and it'll be nice for all the other Liverpool queens who are going an' all.

Joe Oh you'll have a ball then.

Woody Yeah, I will. If I go.

Joe God, what's to do with this iron? Have you been ironing your shell suit bottoms again?

Woody I'd be justified.

Joe It's just one night Woody. All the nights I've sat in here, staring at Cilla Black, knowing you're on a bender and won't be back 'til Sunday tea-time . . . how d'you think that makes me feel?

Woody You don't like E.

Joe I don't like relying on it to make me feel everything's okay.

Woody Oh and I do?

Joe There must be some reason why you do it.

Pause. **Joe** *carries on ironing.* **Woody** *starts emptying his pockets out, looking for something.*

Woody Where's me Rizlas? Have you moved me Rizlas?

Joe Oh, starting early tonight aren't we? What's it to be then? A little later on . . . eh? Two Es? Three Es? Six?

Woody Twenty-five the way you're making me feel!

Joe Yeah well not on my wages, mate! If you can't sort your head out Woody, and I know I can't, don't run away to drugs to help yer.

Woody I haven't for the past three weekends!

Joe So why go back now?

Woody All I want is a joint. You've never batted an eyelid about a joint before.

Joe It's not the joints I'm worried about Woody, it's you.

Woody Well don't go to this fucking kid's party then. That wasn't part o'the deal.

Joe Woody, we've been through all this. I've got to know the family, haven't I? Since the dad died. Show some respect for God's sake.

Woody I wouldn't've been seen dead inviting one o'my teachers to a party. That girl must be seriously off her chunk!

Joe Ah well you never had a teacher like me did yer?

Woody Can't I come with yer?

Joe You're the one who kept going on about space.

Woody *turns the TV off with the remote. He fingers the shirt on the back of the chair a while.*

Woody What are you like eh? Six months ago you were moaning on at me to tell me ma and da . . . an' all that . . . and now look at you. Going round there and pretending you're straight.

Joe You were so far back in the closet you were in fucking Narnia.

Woody I told them didn't I?

Joe I know lad.

Woody D'you just not mention it or what?

Joe Yeah.

Woody Well . . . what if they say have you got a bird?

Joe Can't keep pets in this flat, simple as that.

Woody (*correcting himself*) Girlfriend.

Joe I don't know.

Woody Ah you're doing me head in Joey.

Joe Oh and what d'you want me to say? Well actually I live with an electrician called Woody who gooses me twice nightly?

Woody Twice nightly? Don't flatter yourself.

Joe Can you imagine the sort of stick you'da given your teachers if you'd known they were gay?

Pause. **Woody** *switches the TV back on.* **Joe**'*s still ironing.*

Woody You're gonna kill me if I do E tonight aren't yer?

Joe No.

Pause.

Joe Just don't expect me to go traipsing halfway round London tomorrow trying to find you. If you forget where you live again Woody then go and chill out at Paul's. (*Beat.*) And fucking stay there.

Woody *gets up out of the chair and makes for the door.* **Joe** *puts the iron down.*

Joe Where are you goin'?

Woody I'm goin' out!

Joe I didn't mean it Wood!

Woody Well why say it then? (*Makes to go again.*)

Joe Woody!

Woody (*stops*) What?

Joe You haven't even changed!

Woody Doesn't matter what I'm wearing! Three hours from now these rags'll be fucking silk mate I'm telling yer! Fucking silk!

Woody *runs out. A door bangs.* **Joe** *slowly makes his way back to the iron and recommences ironing.*

Scene Five

Street

Valerie Pinkney *is out sweeping her path. She's early forties, hair up in a pineapple effect and wearing an England football club tracksuit and Scholls. She sweeps fiercely at the letter which* **Viv** *ripped up earlier, every so often having a look at* **Viv***'s house.*

Outside **Viv***'s house stands the empty shopping trolley. Suddenly* **Viv***'s front door opens and* **Tammy** *comes out. She gets the trolley and begins crossing the street, pushing the empty trolley back to the supermarket.*

Valerie Child labour's illegal in Britain!

Tammy Stop writing letters to my mum!

Valerie Your mother oughta be ashamed of herself!

Tammy Stop putting them through our door.

Valerie I saw the drink in that trolley. Street smells like a brewery thanks to her!

Tammy Dad died six months ago now!

Valerie Six months is nothing!

Tammy She's entitled to enjoy herself!

Valerie Your dad'd turn in his grave if he knew how she carries on. In at all hours, carrying on . . .

Tammy You didn't know my dad like . . .

Valerie He was my bus driver! An upstanding pillar he was. Sixteen years he took me to work!

Tammy Shame he never crashed!

Valerie Ooh the conker dunt fall far from the tree.

Tammy Piss off.

Valerie (*holds brush like a spear*) Come here and say that, lady!

Tammy It's all right.

Tammy *moves off.* **Valerie** *shakes the brush after her.*

Valerie Go on!

Tammy I'm going!

Valerie Go on!

Tammy *goes off with the trolley.* **Valerie** *attacks her path with gusto. Just then,* **Viv**'s *next door neighbour* **Sonia** *pops her head out of an upstairs window.*

Sonia Tammy!?!

Tammy *stops and looks up. So does* **Valerie**.

Sonia Evening Valerie.

Valerie *grunts and goes back indoors with her brush.*

Tammy What?

Sonia Can you give my front door a good push? Only it's stuck and I gotta get round to do your mum's hair. You give it a push and I'll come down and try pulling. Don't go away.

Sonia's *head disappears.*

Scene Six

Viv's *bedroom*

There is a double bed and a dressing table stool. **Viv** *sits on the dressing table stool while her mate from next door,* **Sonia**, *tongs her hair with a Braun Independent.* **Sonia** *is forty, and carries specs on a chain round her neck.* **Manda** *sits on the bed, holding a letter from* **Valerie Pinkney** *open in her hand.*

Manda How d'you spell prostitute?

Sonia P.R.O.S.

Viv T.I.T.

Sonia U.T.E. init?

Viv Mmh.

Manda Cor her spelling's diabolical.

Sonia Takes one to know one I say. D'you know what I mean Vivian?

Viv I do Sonia. Carry on Mand.

Manda (*reads letter*) 'Your Scottie was a decent man. If he wasn't dead now, he'd have topped himself with the shame you're making of his good name.'

Sonia Ooh!

Manda 'The thing that makes me most angry . . .'

Viv Listen to this bit . . .

Manda 'Is what it's doing to your poor girls. Your Manda and your Tammy.'

Sonia As if you didn't know what their names were. D'you know what I mean Vivian?

Viv Mmh!

Manda 'A little bird tells me they've both been seen down the Sewage.'

Viv I hope you haven't, Missis!

Manda (*tuts*) No! She's a lying old cow.

Sonia Carry on love.

Manda (*reading*) 'You're a tramp, a whore and a hussy Vivian Williams and your dress sense leaves a lot to be desired. You're not fit to be a mother. And I won't stop 'til the pair of them are put in a home.'

Sonia Write a letter to the council. That's harassment that is. Give her a taste of her own medicine, I say. Get her transferred.

Viv If I don't deck her first.

Sonia Where does violence get you Viv? Fourteen Nowhere Street, that's where. You wanna keep every letter she writes as evidence.

Viv You get ready now Mand.

Manda I'm talking wi'yous two.

Viv No you're not, get ready.

Manda (*tuts, gets up*) I hate living here.

Viv Well move out then. I could do with the space.

Manda (*tuts*) I will.

Sonia Hard life, init Manda?

Manda No. (*Exits.*)

Sonia She's at that age, isn't she?

Viv What, when they're a little bitch all the time?

Sonia Mm.

Viv She's always been that age.

Sonia *continues to tong* **Viv***'s hair. Her hand starts to shake.*

Sonia I'm getting a flashback Viv!

Viv What? On the bed. Sit on the bed.

Sonia Ooh! (*Sits.*)

Viv Describe it to me Sonia. I'll get me pad. Hang on.

Sonia It's her. Oh God! She's come for me again. I don't want to go.

Viv What's she saying Sonia? I'm right there with you babes.

Sonia I can't hear. It's too noisy.

Viv Try Sonia.

Sonia She's saying 'Come, little girl, come with me.'

Viv No!

Sonia Yeah!

Viv *has a notepad out from under the bed. She scribbles in it as* **Sonia** *speaks.*

Viv Keep going Sonia.

Sonia It's dark. Who turned the light out?

Viv Brilliant!

Sonia No . . . no . . .

Viv Concentrate Sonia.

Sonia No . . . it's going.

Viv Concentrate!

Sonia (*tuts*) No. (*The flashback has ended.*)

Viv Oh that was short, wannit?

Sonia Mm. Ooh I feel all dirty.

Viv Few more like that and the *News of the World* are gonna love you!

Sonia Why does it always happen when I'm not feeling hundred percent?

Viv That's when you're susceptible Sonia. (*Puts pad under bed.*) That's when the spirit world strikes.

Sonia Oh I coulda done without that.

Viv Come on. Finish me off then I'll do you.

Sonia (*tuts*) I dunno.

Sonia *gets up and starts tonging* **Viv**'s *hair again.*

Viv So what's wrong? Your back again?

Sonia I'll be on edge all night. In case any of them kids bash into me.

Viv I'll warn 'em Sonia.

Sonia I wanna come, don't get me wrong. It's just . . . well we couldn't afford a party this year for our Gemma. She was ever so upset.

Viv Well what's a birthday without a party?

Sonia That's what I say.

Viv But you're working now. You can give her a blinding one at Christmas.

Sonia I know. I know. She's going round with such a face on her. It gets me down.

Viv Has she started?

Sonia No it's not that. They took her support teacher off of her.

Viv What?

Sonia Last week. I had to go to an appeal.

Viv She needs that support teacher.

Sonia Well they say she don't.

Viv She can't read, Sonia!

Sonia Oh you try telling them that. It's Greenwich Education init? Buggered in my book.

Viv She was nice that support teacher.

Sonia I know.

Viv Had a look of Moira Stuart.

Sonia I told her.

Viv You wanna tell Joe. See if he can sort something out.

Sonia Joe?

Viv Tammy's teacher. He's coming tonight.

Sonia Oh.

Viv Tammy thinks the world of him.

Sonia I think it's too late.

Viv No! He can work wonders that Joe. When Tammy flooded the school toilets playing silly buggers with her mates, he got us off paying the bill.

Sonia Oh?

Viv Yeah. Told that Miss Sterry one we were in unfortunate circumstances, what with Scottie and that.

Sonia Oh they wanna have more teachers like that, I say.

Viv Have a chat with him. You never know. He's quite tasty as it happens.

Sonia Viv!

Viv What?

Sonia You're awful you are.

Viv I'm a single woman.

Sonia Oh I'm saying nothing.

Viv Sing my praises to him Sonia. That's all.

Sonia You wanna be careful?

Viv Since when have I ever been careful?

Sonia He might be a married man.

Viv No. He's young. Healthy.

Sonia Well, a bird in the hand's worth two in the bush, I say. That's you done. Give it a brush.

Viv *steps up and brushes her hair through.*

Viv Brilliant Sonia. You're an angel.

Sonia Dunno bout that. (*Sits on stool.*) Make it simple, I gotta feed the dog.

Viv *takes the tongs to* **Sonia**'s hair.

Scene Seven

Viv's lounge

A music centre blares out 'All That She Wants' by Ace of Base. In a cosy armchair in the corner sits **Manda**, *having a fag. She is now dressed for the party, wearing a blue blazer of her mother's with the sleeves rolled back, a bra top, cycling shorts and high heels. Her hair is lacquered and frizzed to high heaven, and she has slapped the make-up on. Her legs are crossed and she gyrates her foot in time to the music.*

Elsewhere in the room is a low coffee table and a trolley, both piled high with food. A sheepskin rug lies on the floor. Next to **Manda**'s *armchair stands an occasional table with a photo of her late father on it. Finally, three high bar stools are placed around the room.*

Tammy *enters with a tray of sausage rolls. She too is dicky-dolled-up for the party, in a short, dusty pink PVC raincoat, humungous gold ear-rings and spanking new trainers. On her hands she wears fingerless lace gloves. Her hair is gelled close to her head in a ballerina bun at the back.*

Manda What are they?

Tammy Sausage rolls.

Manda Coffee table.

Tammy *puts the tray down on the trolley.*

Manda I said coffee table!

Tammy Shut up!

Manda If you put 'em on the trolley it'll fuckin' break won't it? You stupid cow.

Tammy *takes the tray and puts it on the coffee table instead.*

Manda Hurry up, people are gonna start arriving soon.

Tammy *tuts and exits.* **Manda** *flicks her ash extravagantly onto the carpet, still gyrating to the music. Presently* **Tammy** *comes back in with a second tray.* **Tammy** *puts it on the coffee table.*

Manda What you doin' now?

Tammy What's it look like?

Manda Put 'em on the trolley, now!

Tammy Why?!

Manda Just do it will ya?

Tammy You told me to put the sausage rolls on the coffee table!

Manda Yeah, but they're not sausage rolls, they're sandwiches. Sandwiches int as heavy as sausage rolls. Wor! Was you born a moron?!

Tammy (*tuts*) God!

Tammy *does as she is told then makes her way out of the room as* **Viv** *enters, boogieing. She wears a figure-hugging leopard-skin fun-fur dress, black high heels, a gold bow in her hair and an ankle chain. She is carrying a spritzer and a lit cigarette. She looks dressed to kill.*

Viv Go and help Tammy, Manda.

Manda Why?

Viv Coz you'll feel the back o'my hand if you don't.

Manda Who says I'm coming to this bloody party anyway?

Viv Your clothes have got party written all over 'em.

Manda My clothes have got my bloke written all over 'em. (*Points to a different item of clothing as she spells his name.*) S.I.D.D.I.E. Siddie!

Viv *goes and smacks* **Manda** *once over the head.*

Viv Kitchen. Now.

Manda (*tuts*) Didn't hurt.

Viv *smacks her again.* **Manda** *winces, then starts bouffing up her hair.* **Viv** *goes over to the music centre and switches tapes. Dolly Parton's 'Potential New Boyfriend' comes on.* **Manda** *voluntarily gets up and goes out. The doorbell goes.* **Viv** *is too busy boogieing to answer it.*

Kenny, **Viv**'s *brother, comes in, wheeling* **Ivy** *in a wheelchair. He is about thirty, wears a white T-shirt with the sleeves rolled back, displaying chunks of tanned bicep.* **Ivy** *is sixty-five, and wears a mauve terry-towelling tracksuit and slippers. She has gold jewellery draped about her person.*

Viv Oright Kenny?

Kenny Where should I stick her?

Viv In the corner. I'll give you an 'and.

Kenny We'll stick you in that chair Ivy.

Viv Next to the photo of Scottie.

Kenny In case you get bored.

Viv Okay Ivy?

Kenny Let's lift you up.

They wheel her to the corner of the room and get her out of the wheelchair.

Viv Cor, you aint half put on weight Ive.

They put her in the chair.

Kenny Happy now Ivy?

Viv She's all right. Look at her she's in cloud-cuckoo-land.

Kenny (*indicating wheelchair*) Where d'you want this?

Viv Under the stairs.

Kenny *wheels the chair out.* **Manda** *enters with a big cake.* **Viv** *starts boogieing again, in front of* **Ivy**.

Viv D'you like this one mum?

Manda *puts the cake down on the coffee table.*

Viv It's Dolly. You like Dolly don't you? Yes.

Manda The icing's a different colour.

Viv We'll get you up dancing later Ive.

Manda From where you took the lettering off.

Viv (*to* **Manda**) Don't start.

Manda The lettering that said Merry Christmas.

Viv Shut up about Christmas cake, it's still fresh.

Manda You better not give me a Christmas cake for me birthday or I'll feel ashamed.

Viv The only cake you'll be getting'll have a file in it. Coz you'll be inside. For cheek.

Manda Libs!

Viv Have you said hello to your Gran?

Manda Yeah, in the hall.

Viv Yeah well talk to her.

Viv *moves back to the rug and keeps boogieing, now singing as well.* **Manda** *reluctantly goes and squats next to* **Ivy**'s *chair. She points at the photo.*

Manda See that Gran? That's dad. That's Scottie. Your son.

Viv Oh don't start her off. You know what she gets like Mand. Go and get her a drink.

Manda Kenny's getting her one.

Viv You're not on tablets are you mum?

Enter **Sonia**, *hair done, same clothes as before.*

Sonia I heard you were here Ivy.

Viv Yeah, worse luck.

Sonia I heard your wheels on the path. Marvellous things, wheelchairs.

Viv Well don't say it to me, say it her.

Sonia You keeping well Ivy? Good.

Sonia *goes and stands in front of* **Ivy**, *talking loudly and deliberately.*

Sonia Here, that's a nice tracksuit Ivy. I'd like a tracksuit like that.

Manda Marvellous things, tracksuits.

Sonia Is that terry towelling?

Manda No, it's me dad!

Sonia I've gotta pop next door Ive, and get me gladrags on.

Viv (*to* **Manda**) Int she blinding eh? (*To* **Sonia**.) You're a bonus to that rest home Son.

Manda Surprised you aint lost your voice by now.

Viv Don't touch Sonia, Manda, she's got bad back.

Manda Don't worry, I wasn't gonna.

Sonia (*to* **Viv**) Okay? I've gotta feed my Brenda. (*To* **Ivy**.) I'll see you later Ivy, have a nice long chat. Okay?

Viv Huh! You'll be lucky. (*As* **Sonia** *exits*.) See you babe.

Sonia See you later, won't be long.

Viv Ciao for now!

Sonia *exits*.

Viv (*to* **Ivy**, *suddenly shouting*) You remember Sonia, don't you mum? Yes. Ivy? Wake her up Mand. Jesus. (*To* **Ivy**.) This is a party Ivy.

Kenny *enters with a drink for* **Ivy**.

Kenny Got you a drink here Ivy.

Viv What you got?

Kenny Light ale.

Viv Hold it for her Mand.

Manda (*tuts*) God, do I have to do everything round here.

Viv (*to* **Kenny**) You getting off then Kenneth?

Kenny Yeah. You get that money?

Viv In me purse. (*Gets purse off table.*) What time you coming back?

Kenny Soon as I can.

Manda Mum can I go the pub with Kenny?

Viv You're staying here Madam.

Manda Oh it's boring here.

Kenny You don't wanna come with me Mand. I got a few things to sort out. You'd be sat in the bar, bored out your skull.

Manda I'm bored out me skull here. She won't even let me own bloke come to the party.

Viv (*handing* **Kenny** *the money*) Twenty, forty, forty-five, fifty.

Kenny (*gets a cassette tape out of his pocket*) Have it ready to play at eleven. Synchronise watches and all that.

Viv Okay. Mand? Mind that for us will you, and don't tell no one.

Manda What is it?

Viv It's a tape, what's it look like?

Manda I'm not blind.

Viv Well don't ask what it is then. Jesus.

Kenny It's a surprise.

Manda (*sarcastic*) Oh I'm holding me breath.

Viv Don't do that, you might die. And don't smoke in front of your Gran, it'll only set her off.

Kenny (*getting off*) Later then, all right?

Viv Come on Ken, I'll show you out.

Viv *and* **Kenny** *exit*. **Manda** *lights another fag and smiles cunningly at* **Ivy**.

Manda D'you want one Gran? (*Laughs.*) Want some o'your drink? It's got acid in it. (*Laughs.*) Oh wake up Gran!

Viv *comes back in, boogieing onto the rug. The doorbell goes.*

Viv I love this rug. You bought us this rug dint you mum?

Manda She's asleep.

Viv Oh sod her then.

Tammy *enters with* **David**. *He wears a Chelsea top, jeans and trainers. His hair is gelled to perfection.* **Tammy** *has opened his card and shows it to* **Viv**.

Tammy Mum, look what David got me.

Viv (*to* **David**) Oh hello Trouble.

Tammy (*the card*) Look it pops up.

Viv Yeah well I hope that's the only thing that does pop up tonight Dave or there'll be bloody murder. I've told her, no one's going in the bedrooms, you can do your funny business on the stairs. Be warned.

Tammy (*tuts*) God.

Viv Go and get your guest a drink Tam.

Tammy He aint a cripple.

Viv What d'you want Dave?

David Can I have a coke please?

Viv Ooh Mr Teetotal! Coke from the kitchen Tammy please. Hurry up.

Tammy (*tuts*) God. (*Going.*)

Viv He's your guest girl.

Tammy All right all right. (*Exits.*)

Viv Dancing Dave?

David David. No thanks.

Viv (*dancing*) Come on, not often you get an offer from an older woman is it?

David No.

Viv Sit on a high stool so I can speak to you. Cor, you in 'alf small.

David (*climbing onto a bar stool*) Good things come in little packages.

Viv (*laughs*) Don't believe a word of it! (*Laughs.*) Ooh wash my mouth out with soap and water! Take no notice of me Dave. I'm what you call a modern mother.

Manda (*tuts*) And the rest.

David Is Mr Casey coming tonight?

Viv (*laughs*) I hope so Dave!

David David. He's an all right teacher as it happens.

Viv You're telling me!

David He's the best teacher there. Listens to you.

Viv 'Ere, you might be able to answer this. Has he got a girlfriend?

David I don't know. Why, is he bringing someone?

Viv I bloody hope not!

David I know he lives up Charlton. And he comes from Liverpool. And he's vegetarian.

Viv Is he? (*Dances over to food.*) Do vegetarians eat cheese?

David I think so.

Viv Cake?

David I woulda thought so.

Manda Christmas cake an' all?

Viv Shut up!

David I don't see why not. He gave us all a card for Christmas, what he'd designed himself. And a candle, a scented candle. I've still got mine.

Viv Tammy set fire to the bloody mattress with that she did.

Tammy *enters with a glass of coke.*

Viv (*to* **Tammy**) You little cow!

Tammy (*tuts*) Here you are David.

David Cheers Tammy.

Tammy Can I change that tape mum?

Viv What, Dolly Parton?

Tammy Yeah.

Viv You telling me no one wants to listen my Dolly?!

Tammy Manda bought me East 17, let me put it on.

Viv Later Tammy, Jesus you're so impatient! Now David, come and meet Tammy's Gran.

David It's all right.

Viv She won't bite. She's got her teeth out.

Tammy She's had three strokes.

Manda Imagine how you'd feel if you'd had three strokes and stumpy gits wouldn't talk to you.

Viv *slaps* **Ivy** *round the chops lightly three times to wake her.* **David** *gets down off his stool and goes over, sipping his drink.*

Viv Ivy? Ivy? This is Dave, one of Tammy's school friends.

David All right?

Viv (*to* **Ivy**) In'e tiny?

Tammy (*tuts*) Mum.

Viv He's so cute I could eat him. Tell her a bit about yourself Dave (*A la Cilla Black.*) What's your name and where d'you come from? (*Laughs.*)

David D'you mind calling me David, Mrs Williams?

Viv Yeah I do, you snotty brat, now talk to her.

David What's her name?

Tammy Nana Williams.

There is a ring at the doorbell. **Viv** *and* **Tammy** *both make a run for it, leaving* **David** *with* **Ivy** *and a very unimpressed* **Manda.**

Tammy I'll get it!

Viv *I'll* get it!

Manda Talk to her, you stumpy prat.

David All right Mrs Williams?

Manda (*tuts*) You gotta do better than that.

David You all right?

Manda (*tuts*) She's had three strokes you silly prick, would you be all right if you'd had three strokes?!

David I don't know.

Manda (*tuts*) Kids! (*Gets up.*) Talk to her!

Manda *exits.* **David** *is left alone with* **Ivy.**

David You know I said my teacher was from Liverpool? Well it's funny, coz right, I was up Liverpool last week. I was! I was Chelsea's mascot. You know when the teams run onto the pitch? Yeah well I had to run on as well, carrying the ball. I was on 'Match of the Day'. Got it on video if you wanna lend it.

Pause.

Trials next week. Charlton Youth Team. Dad says I'll walk it. And mum says I better not walk, I better get the bus! (*Laughs.*)

Pause.

Can you play any musical instruments? I can. I'm having oboe lessons. Got an exam in a month, Grade Two Practical. It's blinding, the oboe. Well better than football. I gotta play a piece called 'Song Without Words'. This is the fingering.

He mimes playing the tune on the oboe. Then stops.

Can you keep a secret? I aint told me dad I'm having oboe lessons. I was gonna, but . . . I paid for the exam with me paper round. See my dad, he says . . . are you asleep?

Pause.

I hate football. Grown out of it see.

Simone, Kelly, Richard *and* **Tammy** *enter during* **David**'s *last line.* **Kelly** *wears white jeans, a purple NafNaf jacket and trainers. She has a purple bow in her hair and carries a present.* **Simone** *wears a lycra catsuit, high heels, and a leather waistcoat. She carries a massive present.* **Richard** *wears a luminous lime green shell suit, black cap and shades. He carries a pizza box.* **Simone** *has one shoe off and one shoe on. The heel on one of her shoes has come off, and she carries one shoe between her teeth. She takes it out of her mouth as* **David** *finishes his speech.*

Simone (*tuts*) David's pulled.

Kelly He don't waste any time, does he?

David Oh shut up will you? She fought a war for us!

Kelly Yeah and look at the state of her!

Tammy Shut up, that's my gran you're talking about!

David She's had three strokes!

Simone Don't lie!

Tammy She has, so you can shut up an' all. Are they my presents?

Kelly Yeah. Happy Birthday Tammy.

Simone Yeah Tammy. Happy Birthday.

They pass the presents to **Tammy**. **Kelly** *hugs* **Tammy**.

Kelly Oh you're such a good friend Tammy.

Tammy I'll open them on the breakfast bar.

Tammy *exits with the presents*.

Simone You're such a liar Kell.

Kelly So?

Enter **Viv**.

Viv All right kids? (*They all say hello.*) Bloody hell Richard, what have you got on?

Richard Shell suit.

Viv Turn the volume down Rich!

Simone (*to* **Richard**) You got a nob for that?

Viv Is that my pizza love?

Richard Yeah.

Viv (*takes it*) Great. I'll stick on me wotsit. In pride of place. (*Goes to trolley.*) Here, have a sausage roll! (*Laughs.*)

A barrage of sausage rolls comes flying across the room as **Viv** *chucks one to each kid*.

David (*to* **Ivy**) That's Richard, his mum works for Domino Pizzas. That's Kelly.

Kelly My mum's a moany old cow.

David And that's Simone.

Simone All right? (*To* **Kelly**.) I hate old people.

Kelly Stink, dunt they?

Simone I know.

Richard Stink of piss.

Kelly Piss, shit and everything.

Simone Keep away from her.

Kelly Right.

Viv Come through to me kitchen and let's fix you some drinks.

Simone Viv, have you got anything for sticking heels back on shoes?

Viv No.

Simone (*to* **Kelly**) Oh our Sheneel's gonna kill me. She don't even know I've got 'em.

Kelly Don't!

Simone (*to* **Viv**) Superglue'll do.

Viv We got Pritt Stick.

Viv *exits. Followed by* **Richard**, **Simone** *and* **Kelly**. **David** *is left again with* **Ivy**. *He'd like to go through to the kitchen but feels he shouldn't leave* **Ivy** *alone. He stands like a man in a bar, searching for small talk. He finally finds something to say.*

David Was you alive in the war? This was all marshes, wannit? I know coz me dad told me. Did you have a Anderson shelter? My nan did.

Enter **Joe**, *with a bottle of wine. He wears a ravey get-up and a leather jacket.*

Joe Hiya David.

David All right Sir? Put it there mate. (*They shake hands.*)

Joe The front door was open. (**Ivy**.) All right?

David She's had three strokes init.

Joe Oh aye?

David Sad init?

Joe Ah. Is Tammy's mum around?

David Yeah in the kitchen, I'll show you. Here, that's a blinding top you've got on there Sir. Where d'you get that then, Liverpool?

Joe Er . . . no down here.

David Oh what shop was it? Mighta seen it.

Joe Oh it was up in Soho.

David Oh yeah? Which one?

Joe Oh I don't think you'd know it David.

David Might do.

Joe Clone Zone.

David Mmm, nah. Eh! See you've got your Biffa Bacon boots on! Blinding! I've got a pair like that in the house.

Joe Fab!

David Yeah, you come on through to the kitchen Sir, meet Tammy's mum. After you. Age before beauty, as they say. No offence.

Joe Pearls before swine. (*Exits.*)

David See you later Mrs Williams. Nice talking to you. Enjoy yourself, yeah?

David *exits.* **Ivy** *is left alone. Dolly Parton is still playing. She looks lost.*

Scene Eight

Next door

Sonia *is standing on her landing, outside her daughter* **Gemma**'s *bedroom door. She has changed into a canary yellow dress suit top with gold buttons and a pleated floral skirt. She wears black court shoes with gold buckles. As she talks she is slowly opening a can of dog food with a tin opener.*

Sonia I do wish you'd open this door, Gemma. (*Pause.*)
Gemma? (*Pause.*) I know you're in there. Your dad's just
phoned. He's stuck in Birmingham. Ah, I don't wanna go on
me own love. Not really. I wanna go with you. (*Pause.*) All
your friends'll be there. (*Pause.*) What's Tammy going to
think? She won't want to come to your party now. Coz you're
gonno have one. Now I'm working. And you can have all
your friends round. (*Beat.*) Elizabeth, Shirley . . . all the girls
from the Special Class. (*Pause.*) Gemma, is it your spots love?
(*Pause.*) Everyone gets spots at fourteen. (*Pause.*) I had me
flashback before. Wann'alf scary, d'you know what I mean,
that woman. Ooh, makes you think dunnit eh? Mmm.
(*Pause.*) You've got those nice velvetty leggins. Everyone
else'll say. ''Ere, look at Gem, she's got nice velvetty leggins,
see?' (*Pause.*) Are you gonna come Gemma?

*Suddenly, from inside the bedroom, a tuba starts playing loudly. The
tune is 'Au Claire de la Lune'.* **Sonia** *stares at the door and sighs.
She has opened the can.*

Sonia (*shouts*) Well I'm gonna go! I just hope that teacher
doesn't report me for leaving you home alone! I'll be
massacred!

*She starts to walk off, towards her stairs. She waggles the dog food in
front of her.*

Sonia Brenda?! Brenda! Look what mummy's got you!

She exits.

Scene Nine

Viv's *back patio*

*There is a door through to the kitchen, the back door, and a fence next
to* **Sonia**'s *patio. Out the back are* **Simone**, **Kelly** *and* **Richard**,
*having a drinking contest. They count down from ten to zero and then
knock back their drinks.* **Kelly** *and* **Simone** *have large spritzers,*
Richard *has a can of lager.* **Simone** *is now barefoot. Halfway
down their glasses, she and* **Kelly** *burst out laughing and spit their*

drinks out. **Richard**, *laughing, isn't deterred, finishing off the whole can.*

Simone Cor how d'you do it Rich?

Richard Dunno!

Richard *staggers about a bit to entertain the girls. The three of them have a bit of a laugh, a bit too much for what the situation warrants. When* **Manda** *comes to the kitchen doorstep and takes a flamboyant drag on her cigarette, they all watch, impressed.*

Simone All right Manda?

Manda All right, *kids*?

Kelly Does your mum let you smoke in the house?

Manda (*tuts*) Who listens to their mum?

Richard Let's have a bit.

Manda *stares at him. She takes a big drag and then blows the smoke in his direction.*

Manda Suck that in.

Simone We're drinkings spritzers, int we Kell?

Kelly Yeah they're gorgeous int they?

Simone Yeah.

Manda (*tuts*) I used to drink spritzers when I was about three.

Richard What d'you drink now then?

Manda G and T. On the rocks.

Kelly *looks over the fence to next door.*

Kelly Is that Gemma Sweeney up there?

Simone Where?

Kelly In that window.

Manda (*tuts*) Probably. She *is* our next door neighbour.

Simone What a monster.

Kelly Spotty bitch from hell.

Manda Well at least her spots are on her face Kell, and not on her arse. (*Goes indoors.*)

Richard She gets fitter every time I see her.

Simone You wanna get Gemma Sweeney to meet your mum Rich. Use her face for a new design for a pizza.

Kelly (*shouts up to window*) You stay where you are! This aint a dogs' party!

Simone (*holding clenched fist up to window*) Yeah or you'll get that!

Kelly Yeah! Dog!

Simone She's drawn her curtains!!

Richard Only thing she'll ever pull init?

They fall about laughing. **Viv** *and* **Joe** *come to the back door step.* **Tammy** *and* **David** *squeeze past them and out onto the patio.* **Joe** *and* **Viv** *are smoking.*

Viv Here kids, look what the cat dragged in!

Joe Hiya!

Kids All right Sir?

Viv Sir?! He's not your teacher tonight! Call him Joe. (*The kids laugh.*) He's here as a friend of the family's.

Richard All right, *Joe*? (*They laugh.*)

Joe Oh I mighta known you'd be here, Dicky. Okay Dick? (*Laughter.*)

Kelly Sir's got a fag, look!

Simone Oh no! And after all that work we done on it in PSE an' all Sir!

Viv Call him Joe or you'll be out on your arse!

Joe Are yous all enjoying the rave then?

Simone Yeah.

Kelly Richard's pissed, Sir.

Richard I can't help it, I'm a alcoholic.

David You aint old enough to be a alcoholic!

Simone You can't tell us off for swearing, right Sir, coz we're not in school now.

Joe Oh heaven help me. If my mother knew I mixed with the likes of you, she'd have me hung, drawn and quartered.

David I don't swear.

Kelly Boffin!

Simone Viv lets us swear, don't you Viv?

Viv Well I'm not your mother am I?

Tammy She lets me swear all the time.

Viv Only in me own four walls madam. I catch you swearing in school and you'll feel the back o'my hand. Be warned.

David I don't see the point of swearing.

Joe Nice one lad.

Viv Yeah well maybe when you're a bit bigger, eh Dave? Now Joe, tell me, what's your poison?

Joe Ooh a lager wouldn't go amiss Viv.

Viv Nice and frothy hey? I know your sort! (*Exits.*)

Joe Ooh yeah, shove that down me gullet, I'll be laughing!

Simone Sir drinks!

Kelly We've just had a drinking contest Sir. You know, like sports day, only with booze.

David That's stupid.

Richard I won it!

Joe That's coz you've got a big hole Rich.

Simone You can join in the next one if you like Sir.

David Sir's got more sense.

Tammy Call him Joe, that's his name!

Joe I hope none of yous lot's gonno have a hangover on Monday. If there's any absences I'll know why.

Simone Don't be daft, hangovers only last twenty-four hours.

Joe Well pardon me for being alcoholically ignorant.

Richard *attempts to go indoors, squeezing past* **Joe**.

Richard Scuse me, *Joe*! (**Kelly** *and* **Simone** *laugh,* **Richard** *exits.*)

Tammy What's so funny?

David Yeah!

Kelly Nothing. Sorry Sir.

Viv *comes to the door with a can of lager.*

Viv D'you wanna glass for this Joe?

Joe No you're all right.

Viv (*to the kids*) Right I want yous all inside and dancing. Go and keep my mother-in-law company, go on. You're here to party, so be told.

Simone, **Kelly**, **Tammy** *and* **David** *go indoors.*

David See you later Sir.

Viv Joe! (*Smacks* **David** *over the head as he goes in.*)

Joe See you.

Viv *and* **Joe** *are alone together. They stroll onto the patio.*

Joe Lovely night isn't it?

Viv Knockout. 'Ere look, full moon!

Joe Oh yeah!

Viv You know what they say about a full moon dunt ya?

Joe What's that?

Sonia *appears over the fence.*

Sonia My budgie's done toilets all down me curtains. That's three times this month I've had me nets in the Hotpoint.

Viv Oh Sonia no!

Sonia Mm. Here, I can't get me front door to open. Will you go out and give it a push Viv?

Viv Climb over the fence, it's quicker.

Sonia My back.

Viv Don't go away, I'll get the stepladder. (*Exits.*)

Sonia Hello.

Joe Hiya.

Sonia We got a chihuahua cross, three cats, two love-birds and a budgie in there. I think my husband was Noah in a past life. I don't like letting the budgie out, but he says it's only fair. You're Mr Casey, aren't you?

Joe That's right.

Sonia I've seen you before. At Parents' Evening. You had a little card on your desk, said 'Mr Casey'. I'm sorry, I can't remember your first name.

Joe Joe. Joe. As in Bloggs. Or Soap. Or Bugner.

Sonia I'm Sonia Sweeney. My daughter's Gemma Sweeney. She's in Mr Burgess' class, only she don't like him. He's a bit fierce, in'e? Comes over a bit strong sometimes, you know. I'm sure he doesn't mean to, only Gemma's got special needs, you know, and sometimes he forgets. Like say she's not filled in her homework diary, he throws a real tantrum, and see what he doesn't understand is, she can't write. I give her a form, made it up meself on a computer at work, it's like a special sheet. And she's supposed to ask the teachers to fill the homeworks in for her. On the form. Only she's afraid. Coz some of the teachers shout, or haven't got time. I mean I don't blame 'em, they've got enough on their plates with lairy kids and that, you know. So, I write endless letters to him, but he never writes back.

Joe I don't think PE teachers know how do they?

Sonia And see she's got a bad hip. Chronic. So she can't even do forward rolls, so he forgets who she is, coz come PE, she goes and helps Mrs Norman, in the library. She's nice that Mrs Norman, isn't she?

Joe Oh she's marvellous.

Sonia She was ever so nice over the business with the IST. Sorry, Individual Support Teacher. See, they took Gemma's off of her.

Joe Goway!

Sonia Mm. I had to go to an appeal. You know. And they're not the nicest of things, appeals. I come out in a big sweat and kept sliding off me seat. It didn't look good.

Joe Oh they're unspeakable those appeals aren't they?

Viv *guides* **Manda** *on.* **Manda** *is carrying a set of stepladders.* **Manda** *has a fag hanging out of her mouth. They make their way over to the fence.*

Sonia It's Gemma I feel sorry for.

Joe Ah, no luck?

Sonia It's the cuts init?

Joe God, tell me about it! We dunno who's for the chop next.

Viv (*to* **Manda**) Put it on the other side and Joe can lift her over.

Manda You wanna get a gate fitted on this fence Sonia.

Sonia My Brenda might get in and poo on your patio then.

Manda *lifts the ladders and arranges them over the fence.*

Viv Poo?! Nobody says poo any more Sonia.

Sonia Well I do.

Manda Stand back Sonia you're in the way.

Sonia Sorry.

Viv You got big muscles Joe? Up to a spot o'lifting?

Joe Do I look like one o'the Gladiators?

Viv Well I dunno. I'd have to see you in thigh-high lycra before I made me mind up. (*Squeezing his biceps.*) Mind you, you're quite brawny.

Sonia I could always pole vault over. (*She laughs at her own joke.*)

Viv Come on Joe, I'll give you an 'and. (*Winks.*)

Now the stepladders are set up on **Sonia**'*s side of the fence. She climbs up to the top.* **Joe**, **Viv** *and* **Manda** *crowd round ready to lift her down.*

Sonia (*climbing up slowly*) I'm afraid Ernie's stuck in Birmingham.

Manda Oh yes? Working late is he?

Viv Shut up Mand.

Sonia He had a big run on.

Viv You mean he aint gonna come?

Sonia His big end's gone. Who's lifting me?

Viv All hands on deck.

Joe Right then.

Viv And no touching her up Joe, she's a married woman!

Sonia Don't worry Joe, I've always had a strong regard for members of the teaching profession.

Manda If you mean teachers then why don't you just say it? (*Tuts.*)

Sonia *sits at the top of the stepladder with her legs hanging over the fence.*

Sonia Coz some of us have got breeding.

Viv Yeah Mand, that's something you don't know nothing about.

Manda I thank my lucky stars. I wouldn't wanna be like you.

Viv (*to* **Joe**) Are they all as bad as her?

Joe Worse.

Manda Cheeky bitch!

Sonia It's nice up here.

Viv Okay Son?

Sonia Think so.

They each hold onto a part of **Sonia**.

Viv One two three, lift!

They lift her down.

Viv Watch where you're putting them big hands o'yours Joe!

Sonia (*as they lift her*) Gemma's locked herself in her bedroom. (*They put her down.*) Thanks very much.

Viv Take them ladders back in now Mand. D'you know Sonia, Joe?

Manda (*getting the ladders*) What did your last slave die of?

Viv Ugliness.

Joe Yeah, we've met.

Viv Sonia's my next-door-neighbour.

Manda (*exiting with ladders*) Oh you don't say!

Viv (*tuts*) D'you know Sonia's daughter? Gemma? She's got really bad skin. But she's quite pretty underneath it aint she Sonia?

Sonia Well we can't all be perfect can we?

Viv No we can't. Now Sonia, what's your poison? Cinzano and ice?

Sonia Oh fresh orange Viv, it's my back.

Viv You boring old fart! Freeze and a squeeze?

Sonia What?

Viv Ice and Lemon. (*Winks at* **Joe**.)

Sonia Oh why not? Live a little, I say.

Viv You do that Son. (*Exiting.*) Coming right up, as the actress said to the bishop!

Viv *exits, laughing.*

Sonia (*stretching down, as if to pick up an imaginary object*) If I do that, it really hurts.

Joe I bet that's painful.

Sonia I was on a bus yesterday, and I had to get up and lie in the aisle.

Joe Oh you wanna get that seen to.

Sonia And it was the 380, you know those little buses, so there wasn't much room. I don't like those little buses, do you?

Joe Well er, can't say I'm a big fan, no.

Sonia So . . . how d'you find teaching in this neck of the woods? Is it pretty dicey?

Joe Well it's a bit of a challenge like, you know. Dodging the flying bricks, the petrol bombs. I'm getting used to the riot shield but the helmet brings me out in a terrible rash.

Sonia It must help, you coming from Liverpool. Coz that's pretty rough init? And I mean, some of the people round here have just given up. Myself and Vivian excluded. Never miss a Parents' Evening, and we go to all the concerts. My Gemma plays the tuba. She played 'Au Claire de la Lune' at the last concert. Did you hear her?

Joe No. I had a touch o'tonsilitis, but I heard she was very good.

Sonia Well did you go the Christmas Fair? Coz it was my husband what ran the 'Guess the Name o'the Donkey' stall. He got it off a mate of his who has a sanctuary up Erith way.

Joe Oh right I remember. (*Sniggers.*)

Sonia It was a nice donkey, Sophie, they called it. My husband wanted to keep it, but between you and me, my husband aint all there. (*Pause.*) Are you an employee of the Greenwich Council?

Joe For me sins.

Sonia Oh well, you and me both then.

Joe Really?

Sonia I work in a day-care centre up in Woolwich. With old people.

David *comes out and sits on the step with a plate of crisps.*

Joe Oh that's interesting.

Sonia Mm. I'm the secretary. I had untold interviews to get the job. They're an equal opportunities employer, the Greenwich Council, so it wasn't easy . . . me being white and all.

Viv (*off*) Tell him what they asked you!

Sonia They said to me, they said, you know, 'How would you feel, like, if you found you were working in an office with a known gay man.' D'you know what I mean?

Joe Goway!

Sonia I mean I knew it was only put there to fox me, coz I'd been in the office, and it was all women.

Joe Well what did you say?

Sonia Told 'em the truth. Speak as you find, I say.

Viv *comes out with a glass of orange for* **Sonia**.

Viv Okay Dave?

David Yeah, I'm really enjoying myself.

Viv Sonia?

Sonia (*taking glass*) Thanks. Do you believe in reincarnation Mr Casey?

Joe What, Buddhism and all that?

Sonia No, reincarnation. Only I do, right, and let me tell you this, I firmly believe that once upon a time, gay men were women in a past life. D'you know what I mean? And like, now, in their present life, the femininity in them . . . is coming out. To coin a phrase. D'you follow me?

Viv Interesting init?

Joe Yeah. And is that what you said?

Sonia Yeah, well I know a lot about reincarnation. I'm a member of the Erith Nine Lives Association, and we all sit around and connect with our former selves. You call it deja vu. I call it connection. Yeah? I mean if you was to come into my house you'd get quite a shock, coz I firmly believe that once upon a time I lived in a country cottage. And so my house is full of country cottagey type things. It's got a really cottagey feel to it. You know, little cottages made out of stone, a copper kettle over the fireplace, that sort o'thing. And when we go to the country, my husband's a coach driver, so sometimes I sit up front with him. Well sometimes, when we go to the country, I feel really at home. I don't wanna come back. Do I Viv?

Viv Tell him about the woman with the blonde hair Sonia. Listen to this Joe.

Sonia I think I was murdered once. By a woman with a peroxide beehive and a shopping trolley. Well I'm pretty sure of it actually.

Viv She gets flashbacks, don't you Son?

Sonia I do.

Joe God.

Sonia We're in a marketplace. It's a Saturday, mid afternoon. She's holding my hand and I don't want to go. It's busy. There's loads of people about. She talks all northern. 'Come little girl, come.'

Viv Well you know who it is Joe?

Joe No?

Sonia }
Viv } Myra Hindley!!

Sonia You won't tell anyone, will you?

Joe No.

Viv No, don't tell anyone Joe. She might get a reputation for being a loony.

Sonia This is it, init?

Joe But wouldn't you have been alive when Myra Hindley was . . . you know.

Sonia The spirit world moves in mysterious ways I say. I've read 'Devil's Disciples', 'Beyond Belief' and I'm halfway through 'Myra: Inside the Mind of a Murderess' so I'm pretty convinced as it goes.

Viv Know any journalists JoJo?

Joe No I don't.

Viv Oh, shame that. Coz it's a big story init?

Joe Suppose so.

Sonia Is Kenny here yet Viv?

Viv Been and gone, but coming back for more. Just the way I like them.

Sonia Have you met Viv's brother yet?

Joe No.

Sonia Oh he's lovely Kenny, it's a shame.

Joe Oh?

Viv Sonia!

Sonia Sorry.

Joe What?

Sonia Nothing.

Viv David? Go and dance love. Tammy'll be wondering where you've got to.

David I'm all right here.

Viv This is grown-ups talk Dave so shufty please.

David (*gets up*) Sorry. (*Exits.*)

Sonia I'm saying nothing.

Viv See thing is Joe . . . my brother, Kenny . . .

Sonia D'you ever do crosswords Joe?

Joe I have a crack at the *Guardian* now and again.

Sonia Right. Well say we was doing a crossword, yeah, and the word we was looking for was Kenny. The clue would be . . . three letter word rhyming with Fay. Or Fomosexual. Yep?

Viv Comprendez, Joe Boy?

Joe And this is Kenny?

Viv Certainly is.

Joe Oh right.

Viv I love him. Don't get me wrong, but I always feel I gotta warn people before they meet him. Fairer both sides then init?

Sonia Did you get the clue Joe? He's gay.

Viv I mean he aint a pouf or nothing. He's been a boxer, a soldier, he's done modelling . . .

Sonia Catalogue modelling . . .

Viv Yeah. Freemans. He aint . . .

Sonia Effeminatey.

Viv No, he aint what you could call effeminatey. You ask Lulu. She was nuts about him when he did the Freemans catalogue.

Sonia Said he was all man.

Viv All man.

Sonia But some people are prejudiced, int they?

Joe They are.

Viv Just in case . . .

Joe What?

Sonia He tries anything.

Viv I mean he probably won't.

Sonia No he probably won't.

Viv No.

Sonia But you never know, do you?

Viv This is the nature of the beast. Mm?

Sonia Would that offend you?

Joe Oh no. Not at all.

Viv Blinding. Coz I love him Joe, d'you know what I mean?
He's me own flesh and blood, and I'd hate to see him
shunned.

Sonia I told you Viv. I said didn't I?

Viv She did.

Sonia The London Borough of Greenwich is an equal
opportunities employer. Joe must have gay men and lesbian
women coming out of his ears in his line of business.

Viv I can always tell him to steer well clear Joe . . .

Joe Oh there's no need really. Sonia's right, you'd be
surprised at like, the amount of gay people I've actually met.
You know.

Viv Oh blinding. Coz I'd like you to meet him. I'd like you
to meet all the family. And me and him's like that. (*Holds two
fingers up, intertwined.*) Coz he's lovely, inn'e Son?

Sonia Well he's gentle. In a . . . rough . . . sort o'way.

Viv You've summed him up there Sonia.

Sonia (*sniffs*) Well when you've had as many lives as I have, you know your dictionary inside out.

Joe Fab.

Sonia (*sniffs*) I do apologise. (*Looks at her shoe.*) I've stepped in one of my Brenda's little presents.

Viv I wondered what the smell was. Thought it was Joe letting off. I know you vegetarians, it's all beans and roughage init? Very gassy.

Sonia I better wash it off.

Viv Come on Son I'll get you a cloth.

Sonia Oh you're too kind.

Viv No I'll just rip up one of Scottie's old shirts. (*To* **Joe**.) Are you, er, coming in sweetheart?

Joe As the actress said to the bishop. (*Giggles.*)

Viv (*to* **Sonia**) Ooh in 'e saucy eh? I like a man with sauce dun'I Son?

Sonia I wouldn't know.

Viv You see a man to me is like a plate of chips. And a plate of chips aint a plate of chips without a bit o'sauce!

Joe *mounts the step.* **Viv** *smacks him playfully on the bum.*

Joe Ooh! Watch me hoop!

Viv I'm watching I'm watching! (*Laughs.*)

Joe *wiggles his bum and goes in.* **Sonia** *smacks* **Viv** *on the bum as she goes in.*

Sonia So am I.

They go in.

Manda *comes out shortly with a fag and a can of lager. She stares into the audience. Then she reaches her hand inside the kitchen door and* *pulls out a telephone on a long cable – a wall phone. She dials a number, still staring into the audience. She is ringing her boyfriend who lives in the flats at the back of her house.*

Manda (*into phone*) Siddie? Siddie? . . . (*Tuts.*) Go and stand by your window . . . (*She waves.*) Wave back . . . (*Smiles.*) Meet me down the Sewage in ten minutes, I got something for you . . . Well that's for me to know and you to find out init?

Richard and **Kelly** *run out having a peanut fight. They scream as they throw peanuts at each other, darting to and fro on the patio.*

Manda Shut up! Yous two shut up! Can't you see I'm making a call? (*To phone.*) Siddie?

Richard and **Kelly** *calm down and try to fight in silence. They giggle.*

Manda (*into phone, tuts*) What? . . . Who's that at the window with you? Siddie? . . . Is that Pastel Pinkney? . . . oh Siddie . . . oh fuck you then!

She puts the phone back indoors. She sticks two fingers up at the audience.

Ernie *pops his head over the fence.* **Ernie** *is* **Sonia**'s *husband. He is early-forties and wears Farah slacks, with fly down, a sports shirt and Hush Puppies.*

Ernie Manda! Psst! Manda!

Manda (*tuts*) I thought you was in Birmingham.

Ernie Come over here.

Manda Why?

Ernie Come and have a butchers at this!

Manda (*walking over*) Your wife said your big end was giving you jip.

Ernie Hurry up!

He holds a sack over the fence, and opens it so **Manda** *can have a look inside.* **Kelly** *and* **Richard** *share a can of lager.*

Manda Aw Ernie! Let's have it!

Ernie It's a present for the old girl init?

Manda Shall I go and tell her?

Ernie What d'you reckon she's gonna say?

Manda I dunno. I'm not psychic am I?

Ernie Go and get her, but don't let on.

Manda All right, all right, keep your hair on. What's left of it. (*Goes in.*)

Ernie Here, fatty!

Kelly What?

Ernie And you. Hold this while I jumps over.

Richard What?

Ernie Don't drop it, whatever you do.

He hands them the sack. **Kelly** *looks in.*

Kelly Aw, init cute?!

Richard (*into bag*) Boo! (*Laughs.*)

Kelly Don't, you'll wake it up!

Ernie *jumps the fence, and goes flying, falling flat on his face.* **Kelly** *and* **Richard** *have a real laugh about this.*

Ernie Fuckinell! (*Struggles to get up.*) Don't help me will you?

Sonia *comes to the step, wiping one of her shoes with a cloth. She walks a few paces onto the patio. The rest of the cast, bar* **Ivy**, *follow her out gawping.*

Sonia What happened to Birmingham?

Ernie Oh all right love?

Sonia I hope you didn't jump that fence Ernie. You were not, and I stress, were not Olga Korbut in a past life, and never will be!

Kelly (*to everyone else*) Look at this!

Sonia I thought you was . . . Oh don't tell me, Birmingham's gonna be Welwyn Garden City all over again.

Ernie Well it's a surprise, init?

Everyone else crowds around the sack. 'Coos' and 'ahs' from all concerned.

Sonia Your daughter's locked herself in her bedroom. Think she was Rapunzel in another life.

Ernie I got you something there.

Sonia Are you receiving me? Son to Ern. Delta Tango Foxtrot. I said Gemma's locked herself in her room!

Ernie (*to* **Kelly***, taking the sack*) Give us that.

Simone What's its name?

Ernie Cut it out! Have a look in here Sonia love.

Sonia Why do I get the feeling I'm not gonna like this?

Viv Coz you were a chromosome away from being Doris Stokes, Son. Have a look go on.

Sonia Confirm my worst fears.

Ernie Come on babe.

Ernie *holds the sack open.* **Sonia** *peers in. A look of annoyance covers her face.*

Ernie This bird up Birmingham found it at the side of the motorway. Abandoned it was.

Sonia Vivian? Get me that Cinzano.

Manda I'll have it if you don't want it Sonia.

Viv (*exiting*) No you won't Madam.

Ernie It was gonna get put down babe. Look at its face.

Sonia It's rabid.

Ernie Don't say that, it might hear.

Sonia What sort is it?

Ernie Alsatian.

Sonia No Ernie. You know I don't like big dogs.

Ernie It's only a puppy.

Sonia You say that now.

Tammy Can we have it?

Kelly I saw it first!

Manda I fucking did!

Tammy Yeah and it's my birthday!

Ernie This dog's mine! Yous can all stop gawping and piss off inside!

Sonia Ernie!

Ernie Go on!

They all filter back in.

Sonia One of them was a teacher Ern.

Ernie Teachers. Fucking nosiest of the lot.

Sonia Why d'you have to be so moany with kids?

Ernie Oh look, me fly's undone.

Sonia No thank you.

Viv *comes in with a Cinzano.*

Viv Sonia? Get this down you.

Sonia Cheers. I couldn't have an Alsatian Ern. I wouldn't feel in control.

Ernie You would be.

Sonia As soon as you'd go out, it'd turn on me.

Ernie Just shout at it!

Sonia You'll have to get rid of it.

Ernie I saved this mutt from a fate worse than death.

Sonia Nothing wrong with death Ernie. We all come back.

Ernie Oh we'll stick it in the oven and gas it shall we? Come on.

Sonia What would it do Ern? I'll tell you what, it'd chew me furniture and have my little Brenda for afters. She'd be a soft toy within a week.

Ernie I'll take it down the pub then. Someone there's bound to have a bit of feeling in 'em.

Sonia You could try prising your daughter out of her room first.

Ernie Let her stew. I'm going 'The Wildfowler'.

Viv Get us a large bottle o'tonic while you're down there Ern. We're running low.

Ernie If you want.

Sonia I dread every job you do. Dunno what you'll bring back. Snakes and everything I wouldn't wonder.

Ernie I'm an animalist. Can't help that.

Sonia They eat dogs in China.

Enter **Joe** *with an unlit cigarette.*

Joe Got a light Viv?

Viv There you go. (*Passes her fag for him to get a light off it.*) Ern, this is Joe.

Ernie Right?

Viv Tammy's teacher, and a very close personal friend.

Ernie Fuck me, are you a teacher?

Joe Yeah.

Ernie Cor he don't look old enough does he?

Joe I'm twenty-four.

Viv That's a lovely age.

Ernie You don't want a dog do you?

Joe Er . . . no . . . not really.

Ernie Alsatian, fifty quid. But seeing as how you're Tammy's teacher, you can have it for forty.

Sonia Ernie!

Ernie It's a good offer.

Joe No I've only got a small flat.

Viv Live on your own Joe?

Joe No. I share.

Viv What, with a girlfriend or something?

Joe No. Just a friend.

Viv Friendship's a wonderful thing.

Ernie Alsatians make good guard dogs you know.

Sonia That's what he said about my chihuahua. Ern, he doesn't want it.

Ernie Give the man a chance Sonia.

Joe I'm sorry.

Sonia You don't have to apologise to him, he's soft.

Ernie Jees . . . I rescues a little life, and bring it to a good home, where he could have . . . have love, and big long walks . . . instead of getting electrocuted bars shoved through his head . . .

Sonia Got a violin Mr Casey? Play it.

Ernie (*looking in sack*) It's crying Sonia. It's got tears running down its face. I had to Sonia.

Sonia You'll have to excuse my husband Mr Casey, he's had a hard life.

Ernie Not as hard as this poor mutt.

Sonia He was brought up on a barge.

Viv (*to* **Joe**) Tell us a bit about Liverpool. I love the Liverpoolian accent.

Ernie It's shaking Sonia.

Sonia I'll shake you in a minute.

Viv It's probably that Barry Grant off *Brookside*, but I just have to hear a Scouse accent and I go all . . .

Sonia I think he was Tarzan in another life.

Viv Moist. Ah! Weak at the knees.

Ernie If I was Tarzan now, I wouldn't swing through the jungle for you.

Sonia You'd slip off your rope.

Viv D'you watch *Brookside*?

Sonia You'd be wallowing around in swamp.

Joe No, it's not that reflective of how Liverpool is really.

Viv Really? You know, I didn't know that.

Ernie (*to* **Joe**) Hold still, you got a wasp on you.

Joe Have I?

Ernie Don't move.

Sonia Oh flick it off.

Ernie Cut it out Sonia.

Sonia Go on, flick it off before it stings him.

Ernie Are you crazy?

Sonia No!

Ernie How would you like it if a whalloping great big . . .

Viv I'll do it. (*Flicks* **Joe**'s *shoulder*.) Sorry Joe, did I hurt you?

Joe No.

Ernie I don't believe you did that Viv!

Viv (*to* **Joe**) Let me give it a rub.

Joe Er . . .

Viv I didn't mean to hurt you Joe.

Ernie (*making his way out*) I'm surrounded by murderers! (*To* **Sonia**.) I'll be back closing time.

Sonia If you're gonna be like that Ernie, I don't want you coming back.

Ernie Fair enough. (*Exits.*)

Sonia I'm sorry Viv. Really.

Viv (*to* **Joe**, *still rubbing*) You're quite broad shouldered, in a deceptive way.

Joe Am I?

Viv Oh God yeah.

Sonia I think it's on account of him our Gem has special needs.

Viv I got special needs. In the underwear department.

Sonia I think you should have a big black coffee dear.

Viv I wondered what you was gonna say then!

Joe I'll have to go the loo.

Sonia Top of the stairs. It's got 'Yere Tiz' written on the door.

Joe Oh God, call the kitsch police!

Viv What?

Joe Nothing.

Sonia No it's not in the kitchen. Top of the stairs.

Viv Next to my bedroom. No peeking now, d'you hear?

Joe I'll try me best. (*Exits.*)

Viv I can tell him where me own bloody toilet is thank you Sonia!

Sonia You wanna go easy on the drink Viv, d'you hear?

Viv I'm a free agent in'I?

Sonia Think of Scottie, I say.

Viv Oh you're turning into a right little Valerie Pinkney you are! You've got a problem with enjoying yourself you have.

Sonia Scottie died on this patio! I can feel his presence all around me.

Viv Oh Sonia, do you have to?

Sonia He's touching me Viv!

Viv Well don't hold your breath, he was useless at foreplay.

Sonia No Viv, he's communicating with me.

Viv Well if it's a smack in the teeth Sonia, don't say I didn't warn ya!

Sonia You shouldn't say things like that Viv.

Viv Why not? It's the truth init?

Sonia He's listening.

Viv That makes a change.

Sonia He's saying . . .

Viv What?

Sonia He's telling you . . .

Viv No. No Son. I had sixteen years of being told what to do. He's dead Sonia, Scottie's dead. I'm alive. And I wanna enjoy myself. I'm a single woman. Now get in there and get boogieing.

Sonia Yeah well if it's all the same with you Vivian I'm gonna slip next door and see if I can't get my Gemma out of her bedroom. I got an husband tryina convert me home into London Zoo, a daughter in the depths of puberty, and bad back. So actually no Vivian, I don't think I will get boogieing actually.

Viv Oh be like that.

Sonia Yeah I will.

Viv *makes to go indoors, and* **Sonia** *makes to follow. They are about to go in when all the kids come out of the house in a human chain,* *doing the conga.* **Sonia** *and* **Viv** *stand and watch.* **Manda** *and* **Richard** *are at the front, followed by* **Simone**, **Kelly**, **Tammy** *and* **David**. **Sonia** *goes indoors as the conga circles the patio.*

Manda Back in the house!

Richard What?!

Manda Back in the house!

Richard All right!

Manda *swings round, changing the direction of the conga. She heads for the back door and exits. The line follows suit.* **Viv** *brings up the rear, but stops short of exiting and looks up into the sky.*

Viv Yeah Valerie Pinkney! I'm having a good time! I'm loving it! I'll have you Valerie Pinkney! Just you wait and see! I'll fucking have you Valerie Pinkney! Just you see if I don't!

Viv *goes to exit, but it's as though the sky is saying something to her.*

Viv Yeah! Go on! Try it!

Viv *exits.*

Act Two

Scene One

Sonia's *landing*

As before, **Sonia** *stands outside* **Gemma**'s *bedroom door. This time she sings to her.*

Sonia (*sings*) Mister Bear? Are you there?
        Don't you dare to take a bite of me.
        If you do I'll scream and quick
        My ole man'll fetch his stick
        Coz he aint afraid o'bears, not he.
        So if you want a little baby girl
        And you're hungry
        And you can't wait any more,
        I can tell you where there's plenty
        Have a try at number twenty.
        Yes go and bite the little girl next door
        Go and bite the little girl next door.
        (*Soft chuckle.*)
D'you like that Gem? Sang that in nursery I did. (*Pause.*)
You coming the party Gem? You can drink you know. Oh
it's a really lovely party. Real . . . lovely. (*Pause.*) Bathroom's
a bit of a mess Gem. And I did spy with my little eye an
empty bottle of Born Blonde. You . . . experimenting . . .
Gem? I know you got my curling tongs, coz they aint on my
tall boy. Do your hair Gem, doll yourself up. That's the
spirit. We'll all be waiting for you.

She walks off.

Scene Two

Viv's bedroom

As before, double bed, dressing table stool. **Tammy** *and* **David** *sit on the bed.* **Tammy** *has her arm round him awkwardly. He drinks a can of coke. She drinks a glass of what looks like coke.*

Tammy If you had a million pounds, what would you do?

David Give it poor people, how 'bout you?

Tammy I'd give me mum a bit, and me Uncle Kenny a bit. I'd give some to Gemma for facelift, and I'd spend the rest on clothes and world peace.

David Would you?

Tammy Yeah.

David If you had a button, and you had to press that button, and like, a million people would die in Australia or somewhere dead far away . . . would you press it?

Tammy No.

David No. I wouldn't. Richard would.

Tammy Richard's a prat.

David Are you ever gonna smoke?

Tammy Dunno. Might do. In moderation.

David Are you ever gonna drink?

Tammy I'm drinking now!

David Are you?

Tammy Yeah. Only in moderation though.

David What's moderation mean?

Tammy Not much.

David It must mean something.

Tammy No that's what it means, not much.

David Are you gonna have sex before you're sixteen?

Tammy Dunno.

David I'm not.

Tammy No?

David No. Unless I'm in a caring relationship with a bird. And even then, I'll only do it in moderation.

Tammy Oh.

David D'you miss your dad?

Tammy Yeah.

David Did he go all baldy?

Tammy A bit. He was cremated.

David Ah.

Tammy Me mum's got him under the bed, in a pot.

David This bed?!

Tammy She's waiting to take him up Allhallows-on-Sea. That's where they met. They were teenage runaways. But she aint had the time off work yet.

David Right.

Tammy D'you wanna see him?

David Nah. Nah, you're all right. Maybe some other time. Yeah?

Tammy All right.

Kenny *enters.*

Tammy Uncle Kenny!

Kenny All right Tammy? Someone in the bog?

David Sir is.

Tammy Joe is.

Toilet flushes. Off.

Kenny Oh Joe, I've heard a lot about him.

Tammy Joe! Joe!

Joe *pops his head round the door.*

Joe Hiya!

Kenny All right? You Joe then?

Joe Kenny?

Kenny Well if I'm not, me Calvin Kleins are a good fit, d'you know what I mean?!

David (*to* **Tammy**) He's funny in'e?

Tammy (*to* **David**) He's my uncle.

Kenny Down on your own Joe?

Joe (*to* **Kenny**) Fraid so.

Kenny Oh well, we'll have to make sure you don't go lonely. Wait up, I gotta go toilet.

Joe Oh sorry. (*Steps out of* **Kenny**'s *way*.)

Kenny Don't apologise to me, unless you've pissed on the seat. Viv'll get the right hump! (*Laughs as he exits.*)

David You had anything to eat yet Sir? Sorry. I find it hard calling you Joe.

Joe That's okay David.

David There's cheese sandwiches and crisps and cake for vegetarians, so you should be all right.

Joe Sounds good enough to eat.

Tammy Mum's dancing, Joe.

Joe Yeah?

Tammy Have a nice time, won't you Joe!

Joe Okay. I will. (*Exits.*)

David He doesn't fancy your mum does he?

Tammy You saying my mum's ugly or something?

David But he's twenty-four.

Tammy You calling my mum an ole slapper or something?

David He can't go with your mum Tammy.

Tammy Says who?

David He's our teacher!

Tammy But my dad's dead. If they get together . . .

David But Joe lives up Charlton, it's miles away!

Tammy It's only on the fucking 180 bus!

David Don't start swearing Tammy, it aint nice!

Tammy Bloody hell. I'd think you was a boffin if you was brainy!

David I don't like birds who swear!

Tammy I want him to be my new stepdad! I want Joe to be my new dad!

David No!

Tammy Yeah!

David Oh bloody hell Tammy, you gotta put a stop to it before it gets out of hand!

Tammy Oh go and play with your oboe!

Manda *suddenly enters*.

Manda Oi! Who gave you permission to come in here?!

Tammy Oh get lost Manda this is a personal conversation . . .

Manda Out of here now! You know mum don't allow it!

David I'm sorry Manda.

Tammy Don't apologise to her!

Manda Get yourself and your piss ugly boyfriend out of here before I slap the face of you!

Tammy Take that back what you said about my bloke!

David It don't matter Tam!

Tammy (*to* **David**) I'm sticking up for you here!

Manda D'you want me to get mum? Do you?

Tammy We weren't doing nothing!

David I never laid a finger on her!

Manda Oh yeah?

Tammy He hasn't got it in him!

Enter **Kenny**.

Kenny Oi! What's all the bloody noise?

Manda Oh Kenny. Mum said bedrooms was out of bounds. I caught them two at it on me own mother's bed!

Tammy Bollocks!

Kenny Come on yous two, if that's what Viv's said.

David I'm really sorry about this Mr Williams, but it aint the way it seems . . .

Tammy I wouldn't let him near me!

Manda (*to* **David**, *as* **Tammy** *exits*) And don't think you're coming to my party when I'm having one!

David I'd rather stick pins in me eyes! (*Exits.*)

Manda Oi!!

Kenny Manda!

Manda What?!

Kenny Calm down woman.

Manda *gets a fag out and lights up. She is left with* **Kenny**.

Kenny Who rattled your cage, you miserable bitch?

Manda's *not saying*.

Manda (*tuts*) Shut up.

Kenny Who?

Manda (*tuts*) No one. Get outa my face Kenny all right?

Kenny Manda.

Manda Take three guesses. It begins with S and ends in E.

Kenny What did I say?

Manda Oh don't you start.

Kenny What's he done now?

Manda What hasn't he done? I've chucked him anyway.

Kenny Come here you.

They sit on the bed and hug.

Kenny Don't upset yourself.

Manda He's such a bastard.

Kenny He aint worth it. Come on. Plenty more frogs in the pond.

Manda Why's he like that Kenny?

Kenny Law of the jungle babes. That's the way blokes are.

Manda What, like little shits?

Kenny One day, you'll meet a nice bloke. You'll be walking down the street. And he'll catch your eye. And he'll give you the look. And you'll just know he's mad about you. And he'll . . . he'll just be the most gorgeous bloke in the world. A nice bloke . . .

Manda Like you?

Kenny Yeah.

Manda Well he'll be gay then won't he?

Kenny There are some blokes left who aren't. God knows where, but there are.

Manda Kenny?

Kenny Babe?

Manda Is this how you felt after that Reebok-Step-Class Instructor?

Kenny Well . . . that was a little bit different babe . . . he was a waster. Wasters aint worth it. You gotta set your aims high. Little Mister Reebok was goin nowhere.

Manda Yeah. I never liked him.

Kenny I never liked Siddie. Looks like we both need a new bloke.

Manda Yeah. We'll have to find you someone Kenny.

Kenny Find me that teacher then.

Manda You like Joe?!

Kenny I'm aiming high.

Manda He's not one of yours.

Kenny Excuse me but you're speaking to a man with GCSE Queenspotting.

Manda Mum wants to get his knickers off.

Kenny She's not the only one. Anything down there you fancy?

Manda That Richard won't leave me alone. But he's just a kid. I can aim higher than that.

Kenny Ah but once in a while a girl needs spoiling. Come on. Let's get some dutch courage and get ourselves spoilt.

They giggle, get up and leave the room.

Scene Three

Viv's lounge

A loud blast of conga music. Immediately the last scene finishes, a conga procession enters the lounge. **Kenny** *and* **Manda** *gradually join it, with* **Manda** *pushing in and getting behind* **Richard**. *At the front* **Viv** *is pushing* **Ivy** *in her chair. Everyone else is behind. Bringing up the rear is* **Joe**, *closely followed, and snugly held, by* **Kenny**. *Everyone is having a good time.*

Viv Kick your legs Ive, go on!

The conga circles the room. **Viv** *drops out of the line and* **Sonia** *takes over the controls of* **Ivy**'s *chair. She swivels the line round and they start to head for the door.* **Viv** *stands in the middle of the room, conducting them with her outstretched arms. She notices the closeness of*

Kenny *to* **Joe** *at the back, and as the line disappears into the hall she grabs* **Kenny** *and shuts the door.*

Viv What d'you think you're playing at, you ole tart?!

Kenny Same game as you probably!

Viv Yeah well hands off, I seen him first.

Kenny Vivian, the lad's queer.

Viv Oh he is, is he?

Kenny Can't you see it?

Viv No Kenny, and shall I tell you why? Because he's fucking straight! You think you know everything don't you? Well you don't, do you? Every bloke you meet is gay, according to you. Guilty 'til proven innocent, with you.

Kenny And I'm always right, in'I?

Viv Well not this time you aint. Not by a long shot.

Kenny Vivian . . .

Viv No Kenny. Don't wreck my night. He's here in good faith and I don't want him upsetting. Our Tammy idolises that bloke and I don't want him thinking he's stepped into Sodom and Gerfuckinmorrah.

The door opens. **Manda** *stands in the doorway, fingering a drink with a straw.*

Manda Yous two having a row?

Viv Leave it out Manda!

Manda D'you know what I reckon?

Viv Get in the kitchen now!

Manda I reckon he's bilingual.

Viv You! Move it!

Manda (*going*) Touchy touchy! (*Exits.*)

Viv I'll touch you in a minute!

Kenny (*closing the door*) Viv, if you must know . . .

Viv You take the piss once too often you do.

Kenny I've seen him in the pub.

Viv No. You're lying now.

Kenny With a blond lad!

The door opens. **Kelly** *and* **Simone** *come through.* **Richard** *follows shortly, pushing* **Ivy** *in the wheelchair.*

Viv What do you want?

Kelly Get somin to eat.

Simone Blindin' party Viv.

Viv Mrs Williams to you now hurry up!

They hurry up.

Richard Oright Mrs Williams?

Viv Shut up and get a drink. And mind her she's had three strokes!

Kenny Okay Ivy?

Simone, Kelly *and* **Richard** *exit with* **Ivy**, *leaving the door open.*

Viv (*shouting to them as she shuts the door*) Was you born in a stable?! (*To* **Kenny**.) What would a respectable teacher be doing in your fruity pub, hey? You talking through your arse.

Kenny We're not all hairdressers and trolley dollies, dear!

Viv You wanna spoil Tammy's night? Yeah? Well you know what you can do, don't you? (*To* **Kenny**, *as the door opens and* **Joe** *enters.*) You can get out now!

Joe *stands in the doorway and immediately backs away.*

Joe Oh what am I like? I'm the two ends o'Niagara Falls. I've gotta go the loo again. I'm like a tap me, turn it on, turn it off.

Kenny You got a weak bladder, never out that bloody bog!

Viv Shut up! Oright Joe?

Joe Bit pissed really.

Viv Aw, bless!

Joe Toilet. Or as they say on the Continent, dooble-vay-say. Ciao!

Joe *exits.*

Kenny I just don't wanna see you make a fool of yourself.

Viv You're in league with Valerie Pinkney you are. Tryina make me feel guilty, well it won't work.

Kenny Oh you're doing me head in now Viv.

Viv You and me both baby!

Kenny Oh forget I ever said anything.

Sonia *enters as* **Kenny** *attempts to leave. She closes the door behind her, blocking his way, and goes over to the food and starts picking, totally oblivious to* **Kenny** *and* **Viv***'s row.*

Sonia Isn't that teacher a lovely man?

Viv (*to* **Kenny**) Oi! You can't get away with it that easy.

Kenny Spare me the lecture Viv. As per usual, you're lecturing to me about things you know fuck all about.

Sonia We've been having a chat and it looks like, it just . . . looks like . . . he was Bonnie Prince Charlie in a past life.

Viv (*to* **Kenny**) Watch me. I'm gonna ask him. Sort this out once and for all. Watch this.

Viv *flounces out of the room, leaving the door open behind her.* **Kenny** *shouts through.*

Kenny Oh for Gawd's sake! Viv!

Straight into Scene Four.

Scene Four

Viv's bedroom

Viv stands in her room, bouffing her hair up. The toilet flushes off. She goes to the door.

Viv Joe! Get in here!

Joe *entering, sings along to the song playing downstairs. Dancing.*

Viv Sit on the bed Joe.

Joe What?

Viv Just . . . sit on the bed. You all right?

Joe I'm pissed. I've hardly eaten anything.

Viv Can I ask you something? You won't take offence?

Joe Oh Viv I'm off me face.

Viv You see . . .

Joe It's nothing to do with school is it? If I've sent horrible letters home about homework it's only coz o'me Head of Department, she's a real bitch Viv, she doesn't understand me . . .

She joins him on the bed.

Viv Joe . . .

Joe She hates me.

Viv Joe . . .

Joe Mm?

Viv I know I'm being totally out of order here, but Joe, what bus are you on?

Joe Mm?

Viv The queenie bus? Or the straightie bus?

Joe What?

Viv You're not are you? (*Pause.*) Are you queenie? Or not queenie?

Joe Viv . . .

Viv Are you gay or straight?

Joe Oh don't do this to me Viv.

Viv Coz if you're straight, I'll have you, and if you're gay, Kenny'll have you.

Joe Oh ground open and swallow me up.

Viv Are you gay?

Pause.

Joe I'm sorry Viv. Really.

Viv Yeah?

Joe *reluctantly nods his head.*

Viv Jesus. Fucking queers! You're everywhere int you?

Joe Taking over the world Viv.

Viv I coulda sworn you was on my bus.

Joe It's difficult, you know, the kids and all that.

Viv Tell me about it. One whiff o'Kenny being a queer round here and . . . we'd be mincemeat.

Joe I know the feeling love.

Viv Ooh you can call me love any time dear. Here, your secret's safe with me you ole tart. Stay there. (*Gets up.*) Break our Tammy's heart if she knew. I couldn't do that to her.

Viv *exits. As she disappears we hear her calling to* **Kenny**.

Viv (*off*) He's all yours!!

Joe *takes a deep breath, then exhales a big sigh. He rests his head in his hands, still on the bed. Just then the door swings slowly open and* **Kenny** *enters.*

Pause, while **Kenny** *stands staring at* **Joe**.

Kenny Bit of a turn up for the books init.

Joe Christ, you don't waste any time do you?

Kenny Bet you're a big boy int ya?

Joe What?

Kenny (*winks*) Chop me off at the knees and call me tripod.

Joe No. No me dick's tiny. It's like a betting shop biro it's that small.

Kenny *goes over to him and sits on the bed and puts his hand on* **Joe***'s knee. He squeezes it.*

Kenny D'you work out?

Joe No.

Kenny *keeps his hand there, then runs it up and down.* **Joe** *doesn't respond.*

Kenny Just an old fashioned girl eh?

Joe Something like that.

Kenny Bollocks.

Joe I'm a bit pissed.

Pause.

Kenny You courting?

Joe I live with someone.

Kenny Are you faithful?

Joe So far.

Kenny I took one look at you and knew.

Joe Yeah? Well you've had years of practice haven't you?

Kenny Can I see ya?

Joe Where?

Kenny 'The Clutch and Handbag'.

Joe I dunno.

Kenny I can get you in for nothing.

Joe It's . . .

Kenny Embarrassed?

Joe No.

Kenny Good.

Pause.

D'you love him? (*Pause.*) What's he up to tonight then?
(*Beat.*) Out boozin'? (*Pause.*) Pretend I'm a class o'kids, it
might be easier to fucking talk then.

Joe I love him, but . . . he . . . he fucking kills me. (*Beat.*)
D'you know how it feels? To stand in a street in broad
daylight trying to sort your problems out? To stand outside a
pub on a Sunday afternoon and . . . you're talking to him
and you know he's off his face, and this big bastard comes up
– straight as a die, but he knows he can make his money
outa the queens – and he comes up and he says 'Here
Woody' and he hands him a little slip o'paper, the tiniest slip
o'paper with a little blue dot on it, and I feel that much of a
lowy I pay for it and the big bastard goes away. And then
your fella stands there and rips it in two, sticks one bit in his
pocket, and the other in his mouth . . . and keeps on talking
. . . About us, and the way we are, and the way . . . I make
him feel. 'You're hogging me Joe, I need me mates.' And I
just wanna say, 'Can't you wait five minutes? Can't you just
wait 'til I've gone and you're back with your mates? Can't
you take your acid then?' (*Shakes his head.*) I used to like me,
and the way I feel about me. But when you're with someone
else it's like . . . it's . . . well it's like you've got a mirror on
your shoulder, and what you see in them . . . is how you see
yourself. Like it's reflected. And if they're being a twat to you
. . . then . . . you think you're a twat yourself, you don't
question it. You can't. (*Beat.*) Am I talking shite?

Kenny Fucking shut up.

Kenny *lunges at* **Joe** *and snogs the face off him, rubbing his
shoulders as he does. He's really going for the kill. He pulls* **Joe**'s *top
up, pushes him onto the bed. As he does this he takes his own belt off.
On top of* **Joe**, *on the bed he pushes* **Joe**'s *arms above his head and
then ties his hands tightly to the top bed rail with the belt.*

Joe Jesus, what you doing?

Kenny I think it's time you enjoyed yourself!

Joe Untie me you bastard!

Kenny D'you want them kids to hear?

Joe What d'you think you're . . ?!

Kenny Let's get these jeans off.

Joe Oh my God! (*Laughs.*) I'm pissed as a fuckin' Newton and Ridley!

Kenny *has pulled* **Joe**'s *jeans down round his ankles. He has boxer shorts on.* **Kenny** *goes looking under the bed.*

Joe What you doing? Don't hurt me. Don't leave any marks!

Kenny *comes out from under the bed with a vibrator. He stands at the foot of the bed and waggles the vibrator in the air.*

Kenny Let's make babies!

Viv (*off*) Kenny! It's eleven o'clock! He's here!

Kenny Oh shit.

Viv (*off*) Kenny! He's in the bathroom getting changed!

Kenny (*to* **Joe**) Hang on, won't be a tick.

Joe Where you going?

Kenny Shut up!

Joe Lock the door!

Kenny Don't go away! (*Exits.*)

Joe *wriggles his wrists about. He can't release himself.*

Joe Oh mother forgive me! (*Laughs in desperation.*)

Elsewhere on the stage, lights up to reveal **Viv**'s *lounge.* **Simone**, **Kelly**, **Richard**, **Manda**, **Sonia** *and* **Viv** *are singing 'Happy Birthday' to* **Tammy**. *'Til the end of the scene, we can see the bedroom and the lounge at the same time.*

All Happy Birthday to you!
      Happy Birthday to you!

Happy Birthday dear Tammy!
Happy Birthday to you!

Whilst they sing this, **Kenny** *enters.*

Viv (*to* **Kenny**) He's in the bathroom! Get up and see if he's ready!

Kenny *exits. The singing finishes.*

Sonia Lovely.

Viv Not good enough. Do it again. Everybody this time, or you're all out!

They all sing 'Happy Birthday' again.

Viv (*to* **Manda**) Where's that tape? Give me that tape!

Manda *gets the tape from the first act out of her pocket and slips it to* **Viv**. *She sticks it in the music centre. The song finishes. Enter* **Kenny**.

Kenny Okay?

Viv Yep.

Kenny D'you want me to do an intro?

Viv Hurry up.

Kenny Now. Everyone got a drink?

David Where's Sir?

Kenny Bit tied up at the moment. Er, as you all know, this is Tammy's birthday party. And in an hour's time Tammy is going to be fourteen. Now it's been a hard year for Tammy, and Viv and Manda . . . what with Scottie dying and that. So we thought, tonight, to make it an extra special occasion, we'd invite an extra special guest.

Tammy East 17?!

Viv Shut up!

Kenny Now, she's come all the way from Buckingham Palace just to be here. So can we all be upstanding, for the one and only, Her Majesty, Queen Elizabeth the Second.

Viv *switches the tape on. A trumpet fanfare plays.* **Viv** *and* **Sonia** *hold* **Ivy** *up. A* **Drag Queen** *enters dressed as the Queen. He wears a long dress, sash, wig, crown, long white gloves and rings. He goes to the centre of the room and walks round in a circle, waving regally at the assembled company. When the trumpet fanfare ends, the National Anthem comes on and they all sing.* **Sonia** *and* **Viv** *curtsy when he turns to them, and they take* **Ivy** *down with them as they go. The kids are gobsmacked.*

Viv See who it is mum? It's the Queen.

David Tammy! Tammy! Is that a bloke?

Tammy It's the Queen!

David Why?

Tammy It's a laugh, init?

The National Anthem ends. The **Drag Queen** *speaks with a cockney twang.*

Queen Somebody get me a stiff gin.

Kenny Go on Manda.

Manda *tuts and exits.* **Richard** *goes to follow,* **Kenny** *pulls him back.*

Queen Who's the birthday girl?

Viv Tammy.

Tammy *steps forward.*

Queen Happy Birthday dear. You may kiss my ring. (*Holds his hand out to* **Tammy**. **Tammy** *kisses the ring on his finger.*) Have you sung Happy Birthday yet? (*Choruses of 'Yes'.*) Oh well sod that then. Oh hello Viv!

Viv All right Your Majesty?

Queen All these lovely boys and girls. (*To* **Simone**.) You gotta look of my Anne, dear.

Simone (*tuts*) Oh don't!

Queen Here, I had a bugger of a journey to get here.

Manda *comes in with two gins and gives one to the* **Queen**.

Queen Tar babe. Traffic was chock-a-block. We was stuck in this traffic jam, me and my chauffeur, when this bloke in the car next to me starts giving me the eye. I thought, funny. Anyway, he keeps on winking. (**Viv** *laughs*.) I said winking, you dirty bitch. The next thing I know is he's got his dick out. Well I was outa that car like a flash. But d'you know what? I was so excited, I fainted. Ooh what comes next? Oh yeah. So I comes round and I'm lying there on the pavement and there's this big copper standing over me.

Kenny Whoo!

Queen No Kenny, bigger than that. And he goes 'Your Majesty, you must have had a stroke!' I goes, 'I should be so lucky dear.' (*Laughter*.) Now stick the other side o'that tape on Viv. I wanna get warbling. (*As* **Viv** *does this*.) Now can I raise a toast to the birthday girl? What's your name again love?

Tammy Tammy.

Queen To Tammy!

All To Tammy!

David *hasn't been enjoying this. He quietly makes his way out of the room. The tape comes on. It is a backing track for 'I Am What I Am'. The* **Queen** *sings. Everyone left in the room dances. Even* **Sonia** *is boogieing on down.* **Ivy** *motions* **Kenny** *over, and he wheels her out to go to the loo.* **Manda** *goes with them.*

Queen (*croony speaking as music warms up*) It takes a lifetime
        To become the best that we can be
        We have not the time or the right
        To judge each other
        It's one life and there's no return
        And no deposit
        One life
        So make sure you like what's in your closet.

        (*Sings*.) I am what I am
        I don't want praise, I don't want pity
        I bang my own drum
        Some think it's noise

I think it's pretty
And so what if I love each sparkle
And each bangle?
Why not try to see things from a different angle?
Your life is a sham
'Til you can shout out
I am what I am!
I am what I am!

(*Key change.*) I am what I am
And what I am needs no excuses
I deal my own deck
Sometimes the ace, sometimes the deuces
It's my life and I want to have a little pride in
My life
And it's not a place I have to hide in
Life's not worth a damn
'Til you can shout out
I am what I am!
I am what I am!

While all this is going on, **David** *appears in* **Viv**'s *bedroom.*

David Sir?

Joe David?

David Sir?

Joe Untie me, quick.

David Oh Jesus Sir!

Joe Hurry up!

David (*going to the belt*) Was it date rape Sir?

Joe Never mind that, just bloody untie me.

David I'll report her for you Sir.

Joe David . . .

David *unties the belt and* **Joe** *sits up. He hiccups.*

Joe You know you? You're all right you are. And d'you wanna know why?

David Put your clothes on Sir.

Joe Coz you're dead . . . you're dead . . . (*Can't think.*) David. Don't tell anyone.

David I won't.

Joe No you mustn't . . . coz it's all unspeakable.

David Sir you're me best teacher.

Joe Ah I know like but, you know . . .

David D'you wanna talk about it Sir?

Joe David? Phone me a taxi. I need to get a . . . a taxi, yeah?

David Right Sir. There's a cab office round the parade.

Joe We'll go downstairs, and we'll pretend it's for you. We'll make out I'm walking you to the taxi rank. Yeah?

David Nice one Sir.

Kenny *enters with a Tupperware bowl of whipped cream.*

Kenny (*coming in*) Joe? Got some whipped cream here Joe, and guess who's gonna be the . . . (*Sees* **David** *helping* **Joe** *up.*) dish.

David Thanks for a blinding party Mr Williams, but Sir's gonna walk me to a taxi rank init.

Kenny Joe!

David *leads* **Joe** *out.*

Joe (*to* **Kenny**) D'you know him? (*Points to* **David**.) He's bleedin' sound him! And d'you wanna know why?!

David Sir!

Joe (*to* **David** *as he leads him out*) You're dead cosmic you. You know that don't yeh?

They exit. **Kenny** *stands and stares. He dunks his finger in the bowl and takes a mouthful of cream.*

Manda *comes back into the lounge carrying an envelope.*

Manda Another letter mum.

Viv Let's see what the Lady of Letters has got to say for herself this time.

Kenny *comes out of the bedroom and heads downstairs.* **Viv** *rips the letter open and reads it.*

Sonia (*to* **Drag Queen**) Last time I danced like this was at a wedding in Caanan in Galilee. You know, you'd get on with my daughter. She loves experimenting with her appearance. Have you always had a wig?

Viv *switches the tape off.* **Richard** *is pawing at* **Manda**, *who looks at her mum.* **Kenny** *comes in without the bowl.*

Viv Oh shut up Sonia! (*Reads.*)

Simone (*to* **Tammy**) She was murdered once.

Tammy I know.

Simone By a woman with a blonde beehive and a handbag.

Sonia Shopping trolley! (*To* **Drag Queen**.) And d'you know who it was?

Viv I'll have her!

Manda What's it say mum?

Viv I'll fuckin' have her for this!

Sonia (*to* **Drag Queen**) Well it wasn't Valerie Pinkney!

Simone Can we have the music back on?

Viv Where is she?

Richard (*to* **Manda**) Anyone ever tell you you're fit?

Viv The evil cow.

Manda (*pushing* **Richard** *off*) Richard!

Viv Let me at her!

Tammy No mum!

Manda Knock her up mum!

Viv (*forcing back tears*) Says she's written to the council Sonia. Saying I neglect my kids. Do I neglect you Manda?

Manda You're never off me back.

Richard I'm jealous.

Viv The interfering lying little whore. I'll kill her!

Viv *makes for the door.* **Kenny** *grabs her, as do* **Tammy** *and* **Sonia**.

Tammy Mum!

Sonia Vivian think of the kids!

Kenny You stupid cow stay here!

Viv Off of me! I'll have her!

Sonia Calm down Vivian!

Manda *joins in and thumps their arms off her mother.* **Viv** *wrestles free. She runs from the room. Everyone tries to follow but* **Manda** *blocks the door, stopping them.*

End of scene. Straight into next.

Scene Five

Street

In the dark, lit only by streetlamps, **Viv** *appears, staggering into the street with the letter in her hand.*

Viv Written the council? You pissin' no mark! Working in a fuckin' launderette I'll have ya! Where are you? You can hear me, now get out here! Slappery little slap! I'm waiting! Pinkney get your flabby cheeks out here now!

Kenny *comes out of the house, followed by* **Manda**, **Tammy**, **Kelly**, **Richard**, *and then* **Sonia** *and the* **Drag Queen**.

Kenny Vivian!

Viv Keep away from me Kenny I'm warning you.

Kenny Come back in the house now! You'll only get hurt!

Viv She's hurting my girls!

Sonia It'll only end in tears Vivian.

Viv Good. Valerie!! Valerie!!

Manda Knock on her door mum!

Kenny Oi! Manda!

Manda Piss off!

Sonia Language!

Viv I'm waiting Valerie! Give you a taste of your own medicine! You fucking coward! (*To the others.*) She's gone too far this time.

Valerie Pinkney *steps outside, brush in hand. She's wearing a dressing gown, nightie and slippers. She stands with a hand on her hip.*

Val Say that again.

Viv I wouldn't waste my breath.

Val (*sniggers*) Look at you. Miss-Fanny-For-Lodgers, showing your knickers for all the street to see. Aint you got no pride? Wash it down the drain with the memory o'Scottie's name? Eh? Coming in at all hours. Different man every night.

Manda They're all queer!

Val Every time I open me curtains I got a bordello view and the stench o'Merry Widow. Women like you make me sick. Sick!

Viv How dare you spout all this bullshit about me.

Val Well it's a wise bull that knows its own shit.

Viv Come here and say that.

Valerie *walks over.*

Sonia Valerie don't.

Kenny Oi you touch her Pinkney . . .

Val It's a wise bull that knows its own shit.

Viv You little whore!

Viv *lunges at* **Val**. *They roll onto the floor fighting.* **Kenny** *runs over and tries to separate them.* **Manda** *runs over and tries to pull* **Kenny** *off. The* **Drag Queen** *and the* **Kids** *egg them on.*

Sonia Someone call the police!

David *leads* **Joe** *out of the house.*

Joe (*to* **Sonia**) What's going on girl? Oh it's all unspeakable.

Sonia Oh Mr Casey, phone the police! Phone the police!

Joe Aray girl I'm off me face. I'm bladdered.

David Taxi rank's this way Sir.

David *leads* **Joe** *off.*

Sonia *screams up to her house.*

Sonia Gemma! Gemma! Phone the police!

Tammy Don't Sonia!

Richard *decides to join in the fight, trying to save* **Manda**'s *skin.*

Sonia Gemma! Gemma!

A figure appears out of **Sonia**'s *front door.*

Sonia Gemma, how d'you get that door to open? Gemma?

Gemma *is dressed up in sixties clothes. Her blonde hair is up in a beehive and she pulls a shopping trolley. She speaks with a northern accent.*

Gemma Come little girl. Come with me!

Sonia *screams and collapses into the arms of the* **Drag Queen**. *A police siren wails in the distance, getting nearer all the time.*

The **Drag Queen** *lies* **Sonia** *on the floor and slaps her round the face trying to resuscitate her.*

Kelly Oright Gemma? You look good like that. Can hardly see your spots.

Viv *and* **Val** *still fighting.* **Kenny** *still trying to stop them.* **Simone** *lights a fag up and watches.* **Manda** *holds* **Richard** *off.* **Tammy** *starts to cry and screams down the street.* **Gemma** *takes* **Kelly**'s *fag off her and has a long drag, watching.*

Tammy Joe! Joe! Come back! Come and help me mum! Joe! Joe!

The police car gets nearer. Blackout.

In the blackout 'To Sir With Love' plays, by Lulu, linking to the next scene.

Scene Six

Joe's *flat*

Lights up on **Joe** *sitting cock-eyed in the easy chair. He holds his stomach, groaning.*

Woody *comes in dressed for bed in boxies and a ravey long-sleeved sweatshirt, his hair skew-whiff. He holds an open bottle of Evian and a paracetamol tablet. He stands there.*

It's dark. A shaft of light creeps in from the kitchen.

Woody (*tenderly*) You soft get.

Joe I'll never live it down.

Woody What?

Joe Puking up in front of the kids like that.

Woody Well you will go gallivanting off to the backwaters of the Big Smoke. Come on. Take this. (*He squats down next to* *him.*) It'll knock your hangover on the head in the morning. (*Tries to give him the paracetamol.*)

Joe (*struggles with him*) I don't want that!

Woody It's a paracetamol!

Joe It's an E!

Woody It's a paracetamol!

Joe You're trying to kill me!

Pause. **Woody** *sighs.*

Woody God, you've got E on the brain.

Joe Is it any wonder living with you? Y'vile mong.

Woody Joey.

Joe What?

Woody You can always tell us to go you know.

Joe I know.

Woody It's your flat.

Joe I know. (*Beat.*) No it isn't. It's our flat.

Woody If I'm doing your head in.

Joe Shut up will yer?

Woody You told us to before.

Joe Where did you go?

Woody Stormed off down the street. Went and sat in the launderette, watching other people's crusty undies going round. Got back just in time for the feature length edition of *Taggart*. So I numbed me brain on half o'pound o'telly. Was the party shite?

Joe Yeah.

Woody Acting straight. Avoiding all references to Doris Day.

Joe I know, it really takes it out of yer.

Pause.

So you never went the Fridge?

Woody No.

Joe And you never done E?

Woody No.

Joe I wish you'd done E.

Woody (*tenderly*) You dickhead.

Joe I know. That's why you love me.

Woody I know yeah.

Woody *gets on the chair with him and puts his arm round him. He chuckles quietly and then kisses* **Joe** *softly on the head.*

Scene Seven

School playground

The next Monday back at school. A tall wire mesh fence separates the playground from the playing fields. **David** *sits huddled in a corner to the left, the other side of the fence, hugging a football.*

Kelly, **Simone** *and* **Richard** *are walking away from him, this side of the fence, sharing a cigarette inconspicuously. When taking a drag they turn their back to the school (audience).*

When they've just about reached the right end of the fence, **Joe Casey** *enters with his school bag. He stops to talk to* **David**. *The others hastily stub out their fag and walk briskly to the front of the stage and off.*

Joe Morning, David.

David Sir.

From the way **David** *speaks it is obvious he is crying.*

Joe David? What's the matter?

David Nothing. Leave me alone.

David *jumps up and runs right, quickly, along the side of the fence.*

Joe David!

David *stops and, holding onto the fence, stares through at* **Joe**. *Then he runs again, round the fence and in the direction of the school.* **Joe** *raises his voice.*

Joe David Dobson stop right there!!

Joe*'s tone is severe.* **David** *freezes.* **Joe** *walks towards him.*

Joe What's been said David?

David I can't say, it's not nice.

Joe (*more insistent*) David?

David I wish I'd never gone to that fucking party!

Joe There's no need to swear David.

David Oh . . . (*Wants to swear but can't bring himself to.*)

Joe Oh fucking swear then.

David It's Kelly, and Simone. They reckon they're gonna spread it round the whole class that I wanted to have sex with Tammy. And I never, I swear. All we talked about was . . . in moderation.

Joe *starts to chuckle.*

David And Richard reckons he's gonna tell everyone you dance like a queer.

Joe (*chuckles*) Is that all?

David Oh that's easy for you to say.

Joe True. (*Puts his arm round* **David**.) This sex. It's a scarey business isn't it?

David You're telling me.

Joe I'll have words with them.

David Don't tell 'em I said nothing.

Joe Don't worry. I owe you one.

David Cheers Sir. I can call you Sir now, what a relief. Sir?

Joe What?

David What happened the other night. What Tammy's uncle done to you. It aint right, is it?

Joe Well. Takes all sorts to make a world.

David Right.

Joe Have a hanky. (*Gets a tissue out of his bag for him.*)

David Tar.

Joe Now come on, or we'll both be late.

Joe *and* **David** *walk towards the school.*

David Tammy aint gonna be in today Sir.

Joe Surprise surprise.

David I knocked for her and her mum said they've all got twenty-four-hour flu. Yeah well, we all know what that means, don't we eh?

They keep walking.

Did you puke in the taxi Sir?

Joe No.

David Oh that's good.

Joe Aye.

David Coz it's a fiver extra if you do Sir.

They exit. Seven warning pips herald the start of a new school day.

Boom Bang-A-Bang

Boom Bang-A-Bang was first performed at the Bush Theatre, London, on 19 July 1995, with the following cast:

Lee	Chris Hargreaves
Wendy	Jane Hazlegrove
Steph	Gary Love
Roy	Francis Lee
Tania	Elaine Lordan
Nick	Karl Draper
Norman	Rob Jarvis

Directed by Kathy Burke
Designed by Robin Don
Lighting by Paul Russell
Sound by Paul Bull
Costumes by Becky Hewitt

Characters

Lee, *about thirty, soft Liverpudlian accent.*
Wendy, *his younger sister, late twenties.*
Steph, *early thirties, camp male Londoner.*
Roy, *about twenty, from Rochdale.*
Tania, *late twenties, loud north Londoner.*
Nick, *her boyfriend, possibly a bit younger, slight Northern accent. An actor often typecast as a wife batterer.*
Norman, *about thirty, ugly Liverpudlian, lives upstairs from Lee.*

Setting

The play is set in the lounge of Lee's Kentish Town flat on the night of the 1995 Eurovision Song Contest.

There's a three-piece suite, a glass-topped coffee-table, a chest of drawers housing a modern stereo at the back of the room, an old television at the front of the room. On one wall a mirror, on another a blown-up photograph in a clipframe of a man who bears a striking resemblance to Johnny Logan. There's a radiator at the back as well which has hanging on it a mini clothes-horse with a few T-shirts drying on it. Another small table houses a few bottles of mineral water, brandy, wines and fruit juice. Two doors, one to the kitchen, one to the hall etc. Another door, glass, next to the window, which leads out on to the balcony. We must be able to see out of this. On the wall next to the hall door there is an entryphone and buzzer, which lets people into the flat. His proper phone sits on the floor next to one of the armchairs.

Act One

As the lights come up we see **Lee** *in casual clothes and slippers, placing some bowls of nuts on the coffee-table. The stereo is on and he is playing his Eurovision Song Contest medley tape. 'Boom Bang-A-Bang' by Lulu is playing. He inspects the room, then goes off to the kitchen. He returns with a few ashtrays and places them at strategic points around the room. There is a knock on the door. He looks suspiciously at the door then goes and opens it to* **Norman**, *the bloke who lives above him.* **Norman**'s *no oil painting, and speaks quite slowly in a Liverpool accent stronger than* **Lee**'s. *He is carrying an armchair a lot less stylish than* **Lee**'s *taste.*

Norman   Any room at the inn, girl? Hiya.

Lee   Oh hiya, Norman.

Norman   Another chair and you're almost there!

Lee   Oh thanks, Norman.

Lee *helps* **Norman** *carry the armchair in and they arrange it at an appropriate part of the room.*

Norman   Well, another chair and you are there really. Hey, you've got it looking nice in here, haven't you eh? Eh?

Lee   Thanks.

Norman   It's a transformation. It's a make-over. It's a before and after. It is! I mean, between you me and the shag (*Indicates carpet.*) the people who were here before you. They didn't know the first thing about decor. I think to them, decor was a foreign word.

Lee   Ah, thanks a lot for this, Norman. I really appreciate it.

Norman   Well, you see, Lee. I know what it's like when you're doing the entertaining. If you've got nowhere to sit everyone you're fucked. Ah, I hope yous have a fabulous time anyway.

Lee   Thanks. You going out tonight?

Norman   No. I think I'll just sit in and mong around the flat. Have something to eat and . . . (*Sniffs.*) . . . ooh, something smells nice.

Lee   Garlic bread. Listen, Norman –

Norman   Ooh, it's nice that, isn't it? Hey, you don't know how many minutes it takes to do a pot noodle, do yeh?

Lee   Won't it say on the side?

Norman   Spose. (*He's seen the photo on the wall.*) Ah, was that him?

Lee   Yes.

Norman   Mm. He doesn't half remind me of someone.

Lee   I mean, all the people coming tonight were quite close to him. I mean I'd love to invite you down, but –

Norman   Now who does he remind me of?

Lee   I mean it's a sort of tradition we've always had. Getting together to watch the Eurovision. I know it sounds silly.

Norman   I'm a great stickler for tradition meself. Is that a new telly?

Lee   No.

Norman   Mm. I've just bought a new one. Eighteen-inch screen, dolby sound system and a thingy –

Lee   Remote?

Norman   Control. Oh, it's marvellous you know. Set me back a bob or two, mind. Speakers everywhere.

Lee   This is ancient. Sentimental value really.

Norman   Oh God, tell me about it, you wanna see the state o'my stereo. But it was me Aunty Edie's, you know. Knocked her head on a downspout and never woke up. Death, it's dead . . . final. Isn't it?

Pause.

Oh well. Back upstairs. To me place on the shelf. Enjoy your meal. And your party.

Lee   It's not really a party.

Norman (*sees the clothes-horse*)   Oh God, look at that, isn't it gorgeous?

Lee   Oh, I've been meaning to put that away.

Norman   Oh, where'd you get this? (*Runs his hands over it.*)

Lee   Er, it was a present.

Norman   Goway! Oh, it's really nice, isn't it? You got a washing-machine?

Lee   Yeah.

Norman   Tumble-drier?

Lee   Yeah, but I'm just airing these.

Norman   Dunno where I'd be without mine.

Lee   The launderette probably.

Norman (*without laughing*)   D'you know what? That's funny that is. And d'you wanna know why? Coz it's the Liverpool sense of humour. And down here us Scousers should stick together coz I'll tell you this for nothing, Lee. There are some really boring people in London. And that's no word of a lie. B. O. R. I. N. G. Boring. I can't get over it, you know.

Lee   I should be getting on really.

Norman   Well, if there's anything you need just give us a shout.

Lee   Okay then.

Norman (*sniffs again*)   It's good for you garlic, you know.

Lee   I know.

Norman   Might put some in my pot noodle coz I think I'm coming down with something terrible.

Lee   See you.

Norman   Trar, kidder.

Norman exits. **Lee** *brushes some dust off* **Norman***'s chair. His sister* **Wendy** *enters from the kitchen. She is smoking a joint.*

Lee   Norman. Upstairs.

Wendy   I've badly mistimed this garlic bread.

The door buzzer goes. **Lee** *gets up and goes to the wallphone.*

Wendy   It's nearly ready.

Lee   We can always bung it in the microwave later. (*To phone.*) Hello? Oh hi, Steph, push the door. We're on the first floor. (*Replaces the receiver.*) Steph.

Wendy (*not impressed*)   Steph.

Wendy *swiftly exits to the kitchen.* **Steph** *appears from the hall. He speaks fast and officiously, and is wearing an overcoat and carrying a bottle of wine and a bumbag. He has brought a huge picture in a frame wrapped in pink crêpe paper as a house-warming present. He plonks the bottle of wine down on* **Lee***'s drinks table and looks around the room.*

Lee   My new abode.

Steph   I thought it'd be bigger than this.

Lee   Well –

Steph   Had a picture of it in my head.

Lee   Size isn't everything.

Steph   No, it's what you do with it. And if you don't mind me saying you seem to have done with it reasonably well. Oh, a balcony. How sixties. (*Looks out of window.*) That Hampstead Heath?

Lee   Yeah.

Steph   Handy. For those late-night walks.

Lee   I find all that a bit of a bore really.

Steph   When you're bored with the Heath m'darling, you're bored with life.

Lee   Oh, I'm not bored with that just yet.

Steph   Pleased to hear it. *Pour vous, s'il vous plaît.*

He hands **Lee** *the house-warming picture.*

Lee   Oh, Steph, there was no need . . .

Steph   Nonsense, it's house-warming, init?

Lee (*joking, shaking it*)   Is it a jigsaw?

Steph   No, it's a picture. Get it opened.

Lee *rests the picture on his settee and rips open the crêpe paper. It is a Tom of Finland print showing a man with a huge penis.* **Lee** *thinks it is vile but daren't say.* **Steph** *is beaming.*

Lee   Oh, Steph . . .

Steph   I thought of you as I seen it you know. I said to the man in Clone Zone, I said, 'You know this is *so* Lee.'

Lee   Oh, it's . . . yeah . . .

Steph   It's gorgeous, isn't it?

Lee   It's a bit big, isn't it?

Steph   Well, you've the length of wall fortunately. Look good over the telly actually. Do I get a kiss?

Lee   Cheers, Steph. (*Kisses him.*)

Steph (*suggestively*)   You gonna take my coat?

Lee   Where to? (*Laughs.*)

Steph (*taking coat off*)   It's nice to see you smile again, Lee. You suit it. Mourning didn't suit you. I hate to see a man frown. (*Passing coat to* **Lee**, *he grasps hold of* **Lee**'s *hand and speaks in a faster, hushed conspiratorial tone.*) Top Man in Oxford Street. Get your arse down there. Communal changing rooms. I was in for hours. Had to buy this to keep the store detectives happy. Not a big fan of store detectives. Are you?

Lee   Can't say I am.

Steph   No, me neither. (*The wine.*) New Zealand. Thought you might like a drop of Maori in you.

Lee   Oh tar. I'll just . . . stick this in the bedroom. Might get in the way a bit.

Steph *winks.* **Lee** *exits to the hall with* **Steph***'s coat and the picture.* **Steph** *sits and gets cigarettes out of his bumbag. He has to root around to find them, and in so doing gets out a pair of handcuffs and some nipple clamps, which he returns to the bumbag as he lights up.*

Steph   Is this your Eurovision medley tape?

Lee (*off*)   Yes.

Steph   Thought so. (*Looking around room.*) Actually you know, this is spesh. *Bijou,* but *très* spesh.

Lee (*off*)   I can run you a copy off if you want.

Steph   That's kind of you. (*Pause. He's having a good nose around.*) How's that vile bitch from hell Wendy? Is she out of that wheelchair yet?

Wendy (*off*)   Yes, I am, thanks for asking!

Wendy *enters from the kitchen, lurking in the doorway with a roll-up.*

Steph (*thinking very quickly*)   Just my joke! Knew you were here. Hi, Wend. Smelt your perfume.

Wendy   Hello, Steph.

Steph (*kissing her*)   Terrible accident, Wend. So I heard. Lee showed me the clipping from the *Bromley Gazette.* You could've died, couldn't you, Wend?

Wendy   Well . . .

Steph   All that crazy paving stacked up one minute. Next thing you're under it. Suppose it was like dominoes, wasn't it? One goes, they all go. Not nice.

Wendy   No.

Steph   No. And my heart bleeds for you, Wendy. Every time you look out your window you gotta look at that damn patio. Did you manage to scrape all the blood off the crazy paving?

Wendy   Yeah. I get the pins taken out on Thursday.

Steph   Great. Great. No, that is great actually, Wend. You're up and about at last and that's great. Wasn't aware that you were a fan of the Eurovision actually.

Lee *enters.*

Lee   Wendy didn't have anything to do, so . . .

Steph   I thought of you the other day actually. I saw a woman in a wheelchair in Marks and I thought 'I wonder how Wendy is?'

Wendy   That was kind of you. I'm just going to check the garlic bread.

Wendy *exits.*

Steph (*quieter, more urgently so* **Wendy** *doesn't hear*)   You might have told me.

Lee   I was about to.

Steph   I wanna get on with your family, even if they are vile.

Lee   Oh, thanks.

Steph   Well, how you and her could have sprung from the same womb I'll never know.

Lee (*tuts*)   Steph.

A look of horror covers **Steph**'s *face.*

Steph   Oh, Lee, I'm sorry. I forgot you were one of Barnardo's finest.

Lee   Forget it, it's okay.

Steph   All the same I don't see the point in having a Eurovision Song Contest party and inviting people who don't know their Clodagh Rogers from their Jahn Teigen. It's ridiculous.

Lee   She'll enter into the spirit of things, don't you worry.

Steph   This night is the highlight of my year if you must know. (*Jovially.*) You'll be telling me you've invited Nick and Tania next. (*Pause. He gets more serious.*) You haven't.

Lee   Well, loads of people dropped out.

Steph   Nick and . . . ? I don't believe it!

Lee   Oh, they're lovely.

Steph   Oh, really!

Lee   Nick has been a tower of strength to me lately.

Steph   I bet he has.

Lee   Steph!

Steph   Well, it's a bit rich if you ask me.

Lee   Well, I didn't.

Pause.

Steph   I'da come round at the drop of a hat if I wasn't working.

Lee   I know.

Steph   I read this article the other day in this magazine. 'Straight Men Who Suck Dick.' It sounded like a character description of Nick.

Lee   God, Steph, I don't understand you at times.

Steph   Yeah, well, what's new? Pour me a wine.

Lee   Red or white?

Steph   Surprise me.

Lee *goes about trying, with some difficulty, to open the wine* **Steph** *brought.*

Steph   Has he ever watched a Eurovision Song Contest?

Lee   Probably.

Steph   But you don't know for sure.

Lee   No.

Steph   The key to a perfect Euro evening, Lee, m'darling, is relaxation. I can't stress that strongly enough. And if there are non Eurovision fans present we'll feel oppressed.

Lee   I won't.

Steph   I will. They'll talk through the songs.

Lee Well, that's part of the fun.

Steph Part of the fun, Lee, my darling, is being amongst friends. Fellow enthusiasts. (**Wendy** *has come in with her joint which has gone out.*) Did you know Nick was coming?

Wendy Yes. Got a light? This has gone out.

Steph (*passing his lighter*) I'm just ... I'm just a bit on edge if you must know. Ignore me.

Wendy Something wrong?

Steph You wouldn't understand.

Wendy Try me.

Steph For the first time in Eurovision history we have a rap group representing us. Okay, so it's a novelty. Last time we won we did so on the novelty of the Bucks Fizz skirt rip. But what I'm beginning to get a tad anxious about is ... what if nobody likes it? What if we get *nul points*? We won't be able to take part in next year's contest if we come in the final four. And that would be a catastrophe ... See? I told you you wouldn't understand.

Lee (*having no success with opening the wine. Offers it to* **Wendy**) Can you have a go at this? (**Wendy** *tries to open the bottle.* **Lee** *looks at his watch.*) Twenty past seven. Excited?

Steph I suppose so. So who else is coming?

Lee Er, well ...

Wendy Nick and Tania.

Lee Roy ...

Steph Roy? Very good. At least if we lose we've got something nice to look at.

Lee And that's it I think.

Pause. **Steph** *looks confused.*

Steph But what about all the others?

Lee Well, Billy's having people round to his.

Steph Billy's not coming here?

Wendy (*shakes head*)   Throwing his own do.

Steph   Well, what about Alan and Kevin? They'll be coming here surely.

Lee   Going to Billy's apparently.

Steph   But. I don't under . . . last year there were twenty or thirty of us.

Wendy   Steph.

Steph   What?

Lee   It's all right, Wend.

Steph   What?

Lee   I think people would rather go to Billy's this year.

Steph   Well, I think I would too from the sound of things.

Lee   I don't think people wanna come her coz of Michael.

Pause.

Steph   Well, it didn't stop me.

Lee   I know. And I'm glad. I mean that, Steph. I'm glad you've come here. We could've all gone to Billy's but, I just wanted to be in me own place.

Wendy   Far from the madding crowd.

Lee   Maybe next year I'll fancy going somewhere else.

Wendy (*giving up on bottle*)   The cork's buggered. You'll have to use a knife.

Lee *goes into the kitchen.*

Steph   I saw Billy in Sainsbury's last night. I thought his trolley looked a bit full. Thought he'd started seeing somebody. Should've known. Didn't breathe a word of it to me. Ignorant bastard, I've never liked him.

Wendy   Well, obviously the feeling's mutual.

Steph   Well, if he's not gonna come here just coz Michael's popped his clogs I don't think I want him liking me. Bellringers, never trust 'em.

Wendy   I think some people just don't know what to say.

Steph   Well, they should make something up. Poor Michael.

Wendy   Poor Lee.

Steph   Had a terrible row with Michael last year. I said Frances Rufelle was far superior to that Irish pair that won. He was having none of it.

Wendy   Didn't see you at the funeral.

Steph   I was in Tenerife. I was all set to cancel but Lee insisted I go.

Wendy   Not much of a tan to show for it.

Steph   I was in bed a lot.

Wendy   Diarrhoea?

Steph   Dream on, Wendy.

Lee enters with three glasses of wine. He hands them out.

Lee   We have a result. *Douze points*! Cheers.

Wendy   Cheers.

Steph   Cheers, Lee. I hope Nick and Tania aren't going to be late. There's nothing worse than having the first song obliterated by straight people taking their coats off. No offence, Wend.

Wendy   I'll check my bread.

She exits.

Lee   She can't help being straight.

Steph   If you ask me she's borderline Lebanese.

Lee   What's got into you?

Steph   She's the first straight woman I've met that can play pool.

Lee   Oh, fucking hell, Steph. How d'you explain that fella she was seeing?

Steph   Smokescreen. I could spot it a mile off.

Lee (*laughs*)   You're good value, I'll give you that!

Steph   Well, if she starts wearing sandals and humming Patsy Cline don't say I didn't warn you. So, it's still all on with Nick and Tania, is it?

Lee   Yeah.

Steph   Well, I wish they'd make their minds up and save us all the heartache.

Lee   They have made their minds up.

Steph   Yeah, but how long's it gonna last this time? I wouldn't be surprised if they've split up by the time Croatia are on.

Lee   They'll be fine. We'll all be fine.

Steph   Yeah, well, I think you're forgetting Abergavenny. It was like sharing a caravan with Barry McGuigan and . . . some other bloody boxer. Fight fight fight, and they call that love. Yeah, well, if that's love, you can take it, put it in a bin-bag and drop it in a very huge skip.

Lee   You don't mean that.

Steph   If I want personal fulfilment I just hang around the Coleherne at closing time. You can get whatever you want at those traffic lights, it's better than IKEA.

Lee   I couldn't.

Steph   Bollocks, you like hot sex like the rest of us m'darling. Hot sex is a prerequisite to happiness. I'm very safe, don't get me wrong, but there's never a dull moment in my life believe you me.

Lee   And where does love fit into the picture?

Steph   I'm not knocking love, I'm just saying that till you find it you should get some hot sex. It's the nature of the beast m'darling. The human machine has three carnal drives: to eat, to shit, and to mate: I love restaurants, I love a good crap and I like hot sex. I'm completely normal.

Lee   At least you're honest about it.

Steph   You'll find no skeletons in my closet. Scuse language. Mind you, I'm getting on a bit now. I quite fancy a shot at monogamy.

Lee   D'you think you're capable of it?

Steph   Course I bloody am. (*Winces.*) My right nipple.

Lee   What?

Steph   Red raw.

Pause.

Chewed to buggery last night. Nice bit of trade from the footwear industry. I sat him down, his name was Dave. Was it Dave? No, it was Darren. I sat him down and I said, 'Darren, I'm into non-penetrative safe sex.' It's so refreshing to have trade who understand four syllable words.

Lee   I couldn't imagine going to bed with anyone just yet. Me head's chocka.

Steph   Oh, they'll come crawling out of the woodwork for you. You must have a nice little nest egg if you don't mind me saying.

Lee   Michael left me a bit.

Steph   I know the sort of money architects earn. All I'm saying is be careful. There's some who'll be after you for it . . . whereas if it was me . . .

Lee   You'd be after me for me devastating looks and personality?

Steph   Why not?

Lee   I know you too well.

Steph   Oh, everyone thinks they know me. When really. No one knows no one. Anybody. Whatever.

Pause.

His name wasn't Darren last night it was Delyth. Welsh piece.
(*Beat.*) How's Norman No-Mates upstairs?

Lee   Fine.

Steph   Still pestering you?

Lee   A bit.

Steph   Well, be grateful you've got a queen on top of you. I've
got heterosexuals either side and if it's not R.E.M. it's Lou
Bloody Reed morning noon and night.

Lee   That's his chair.

Steph   And what does *he* look like?

Lee   A cross between Marty Feldman and Mr Bean.

Steph   I might have to pop up there later. The ugly ones are
often so much better in bed. More desperate. More . . .

The door buzzer goes.

Lee   That's probably Roy. (**Lee** *goes to wallphone.*) Hello? Come
on up Roy. The door's on the latch.

Wendy (*off*)   Is that Roy?! (*Enters.*)

Steph   Gonna make him straight, are you, Wend? Gonna show
him the pins in your knee?

The door opens. **Roy** *enters. He's a lot younger than everyone else and has a
Rochdale accent. He wears a ravey get-up, tight T-shirt with his belly-
button showing, jeans and a coat that looks like a sheepskin rug, he carries a
bunch of flowers and a bag of booze, he enters the room and starts dancing,
singing 'Love City Groove' by Love City Groove.*

Roy (*sings*)   In the morning, when the sun shines.
Down on your body,
And now we're really making love now baby.

(*Speaks.*) We're not gonna win, are we? We're gonna be a
laughing stock, aren't we? I'm convinced. Hiya.

Steph   Hi, Roy.

Wendy   Roy.

Roy Give us a hug you. (*Hugs* **Lee**.) I bought you these. (*Gives him the flowers.*)

Lee Ah, they're lovely. What a sweetie. Oh, aren't they nice?

Steph Got anything for me, Roy? Like a peck on the cheek?

Roy I've got a coleslaw. How's your leg, Wendy?

Wendy Fine. They're coming out on Thursday.

Roy Marvellous. (*He gets champagne and orange juice out of his bag.*) Champagne and orange juice, thought we could all have a Bucks Fizz.

Wendy Oh, brilliant. Let me . . . (*She takes them off him. To* **Lee**.) Shall I put those in water? (*She takes the flowers.*)

Lee Tar, Wend.

Wendy Right, I'll rustle something up in the kitchen.

Steph She knows her place.

Wendy (*exiting*) Put a personality on the top of your next shopping list, Steph.

Roy *laughs uproariously.* **Wendy** *has gone into the kitchen.*

Roy How are you feeling, Steph?

Steph Well, hardly 'Rock Bottom' now you've arrived.

Lee Sit down.

Roy I can't I'm too excited. (*Starts to dance on the spot.*) I was gonna take an E before I came but I thought no, I'm gonno enjoy this straight. I'm thinking of going to Trade after this, anyone coming?

Steph Now there's a thought.

Roy Lee?

Lee I don't think so.

Roy Ah, will you be too depressed if we don't win?

Lee It's not that. I'm off clubs at the moment.

Roy Well, fair enough.

Steph I might be up for that Roy.

Roy Bona. Bonerata! What time is it?

Lee Twenty-five past.

Roy Whoo!! Not long now. Ay, int your sister lovely?

Lee Yeah.

Roy Int she lovely, Steph?

Steph Unique.

Roy I know. I was down the Black Cap the other week and Lee dragged her along and we gabbed all night. Oh, I think she's fab.

Steph You've started going to the Black Cap?

Lee Yeah.

Steph Didn't realise that was your scene.

Roy It's been refurbished.

Steph Oh, you must let me know the next time you go, I worship the Black Cap.

Roy Eh, we'll all go one night and have a laugh.

Steph Yeah, that would be phenomenal actually.

Roy Ah, yeah!

Steph (*to* **Lee**) You're off clubbing but you'll go to the Black Cap. Forgive me for appearing ignorant, but isn't there a little inconsistency in your rationale there?

Lee We just went for a few drinks.

Steph I seem to recall leaving a few messages on your answerphone drinkswise but you never got back.

Lee This was a spur of the moment thing.

Steph Oh, well, you know who your friends are.

Lee Since Michael died I've preferred an early night, that's all. This particular night I didn't.

Steph   Roy, will you sit down please? You're making me nauseous.

Roy   Don't you think I'm a good dancer? I won a tennis racquet once in the youth club disco dance championships.

Steph   A tennis racquet, Roy? That's handy.

Roy   Me bastard brother broke it the next day. Smashed it over his girlfriend's head. She had to go to hospital and everything.

Steph   Heterosexual men. Never trust 'em.

Lee   Was she all right?

Roy   Yeah you could hardly notice the stitching on the wedding photos.

Wendy *enters with a tray. A jug and glasses of Bucks Fizz stand on the tray.*

Wendy   Bucks Fizz anybody?

Roy   Ah fab! Eh, Steph. Are you in two minds about this or are you 'Making your Mind Up'?! (*Laughs.*)

They all help themselves to a glass of Bucks Fizz.

Steph   'One Step Further' and I might be pissed!

Roy   I'd 'Beg Steal or Borrow' for a drink right now!

Lee (*raising glass*)   'Better the Devil You Know Than the Devil You Don't.'

Steph   Just quoting UK Eurovision song titles, Wendy. Hope you don't feel left out.

Wendy   I don't, Steph. And please don't 'Save Your Kisses for Me' tonight.

Pause.

Steph   I hear you've sampled the delights of the Black Cap, Wendy. Did all the queens shout 'Fish!' when you went in?

Wendy   No, and I didn't shout 'Cheese' at them.

Roy (*to* **Wendy**)   Ah, haven't you got a fab sense of humour? Ah, and you're dead pretty you know, dunno why you haven't got a boyfriend.

Steph   Coz she's a dyke.

Roy   Ah, leave her alone.

Wendy   What if I was?

Steph   Well, you're butch enough.

Roy   Copped off lately, Steph?

Lee   Last night.

Steph (*to* **Lee**)   Bless you, my darling.

Roy   Ah was he gorgeous? What was he like? How old was he?

Steph   Twenty-five? Circa twenty-five anyway.

Wendy   Name?

Steph   Danny.

Roy   Nice?

Steph   Mm, brought up in Bristol actually.

Wendy   Will you see him again?

Steph   No.

Roy   Would you like to?

Steph   No. And I didn't take a polaroid of him either before you ask.

Wendy   You wanna be careful, Steph.

Steph   I'm into non-penetrative safe sex, Wendy, actually.

Wendy   Well, I'd hate to open the paper one morning and see you've been butchered by an axe-wielding maniac.

Roy   I know.

Steph   Bless you, Wendy, what a special thought.

Wendy   You should always let someone know where you're going.

Steph Would you like to give me a guided tour of your new flatette, Lee, my lovely?

Lee Gladly.

Steph Come on, tresh. (*Stands, to* **Wendy**.) Lee's just gonna give me a guided tour of his flat, Wendy. So if I don't come back either Lee's killed me or he's at least a witness. Okay?

Wendy I'll look forward to it.

Steph And hands off my bubbly.

Lee This is the kitchen.

Lee *and* **Steph** *exit to kitchen.*

Roy Ah, Wend, don't you look gorgeous tonight?

Wendy I haven't made any extra special effort.

Roy Ah, you look really special.

Wendy Well, this lipstick's new.

Roy I always wanted a big sister. Someone you could watch getting ready to go out. Painting their nails for 'em, plugging in their Carmen rollers. We used to watch *Tenko*, d'you remember *Tenko*? All them fabulous women.

Wendy In the concentration camp?

Roy Yeah, and me mam used to say, 'If you could choose one of the women from *Tenko* to be your big sister, who'd you choose?'

Wendy Which one did you pick?

Roy The Australian one.

Wendy I remember. Vaguely.

Roy Big piece, blond hair. You never see her now, do you?

Wendy No.

Roy No. Shame really coz she was dead nice. I think the Japs got her.

Lee *and* **Steph** *enter from the kitchen and go towards the hall door.*

Steph Well, I've always been a big fan of pine. Okay, Roy?

Roy   Yeah.

Steph   Great guns.

Steph *and* **Lee** *exit to hall.*

Roy   He was in Tenerife when Michael died, want he?

Wendy   Yes.

Roy   It's not right that.

Wendy   I didn't miss him.

Roy   Who else is coming?

Wendy   Nick and Tania.

Roy   Ah, fab, I've not met them, have I?

Wendy   Well, they were at the funeral.

Roy   I spent all day with Michael's sister. I think she fancied me. Kept asking did I do sports.

Wendy   Funny place to pull, a funeral.

Roy   Still . . . Nick and Tania eh? I can't wait to meet that Nick. He looks gorgeous in that Tango advert. I've never met a real actor before. Oh, tell a lie. I met Gail Tilsley once when I were home coz she opened a new MFI round the corner to me mam's. She's good that Gail Tilsley, isn't she?

Wendy   Yes.

Roy   She's got a lovely head of hair on her. I think if I were going to do it with a woman it'd have to be her.

Lee *enters.*

Lee   Steph's abluting.

Roy   Ah, you all right, Lee?

Lee   Yeah, I'm fine.

Roy   Ah, great. What time are Nick and Tania getting here?

Lee   Soon.

Roy   Ah, fab. We're gonno have a great time, aren't we?

Lee   I hope so.

Roy   Ah, we will though. I love the Eurovision me. Well, that's how we got to be mates, int it? Coz I walked in the pub that night and saw you with your Michael and I thought he was Johnny Logan. Ah, he was the two ends of Johnny Logan, wasn't he?

Lee   He did look like him.

Roy   Ah, they coulda swapped heads, couldn't they, Wend?

Wendy   Yeah.

Roy   And I made an absolute pratteth of meself, dint I?

Lee   No!

Roy   Oh, I did though. Asking for his autograph.

Lee   It was funny.

Roy   On a beermat. God, I shoulda known when I heard him speak, he weren't Irish.

Lee   No.

Roy   Johnny Logan. Still, we couldn't stop gabbing could we?

Lee   No.

Roy   Gabbed all night.

Lee   Yeah.

Roy   He were special your Michael. He was.

Lee   He was to me.

Roy   Ah, he was lovely. He looks dead handsome on that photo.

Lee   (*looks at photo on wall*)   Like a model.

Roy   Though that was before he lost that weight. I mean, he missed his opportunity there. Modelling and that. I mean, you never know, do you? I mean, look at Kate Moss. She had to start somewhere, and now she's practically running the country.

Wendy   (*to* **Lee**)   Are you okay?

Lee   Yeah.

Pause.

Roy   Have I put me foot in it?

Lee   Not at all.

Roy   Tell me if I have.

Lee   You haven't.

Roy   It's a lovely picture. I used to be jealous.

Lee   Did you?

Roy   Yeah.

Lee   That's nice.

Roy   Yeah.

Steph *enters from toilet.*

Steph   I'm still alive, Wendy. You can stop worrying now.

He sits down and lights up a cigarette.

They don't make brown toilet paper, do they.

Nobody seems very interested.

Think about it. You wouldn't know when to stop.

Wendy   Oh, Steph, do you have to?

Wendy *hurries out to kitchen.*

Steph   Is it premenstrual?

Wendy (*off*)   No, it's bloody well not!!

Steph   Have you seen the time? Come on, Nick and Tania.

Lee   They'll get here.

Steph   Probably having a row in the middle of Camden High Street, as per.

Lee   No.

Steph   You drinking my wine, Lee?

Lee   What? Er, no, this is some that was left over from the other night.

Steph Lee?

Lee Mm?

Steph Tell Aunty Steph all the gory details please. Who were you drinking wine with?

Lee Nick.

Roy Nick and Tania?

Lee No, just Nick. I went to see him in a playreading in Richmond, then we came back here for wine and Pringles.

Steph And where was Tania? Had they had another row?

Lee No. She was visiting her mother.

Steph She didn't go to see his playreading?

Lee It was on for three nights, she went on the last night.

Steph So it was just you and Nick here on your own?

Lee Yes, Miss Marple.

Steph And . . . was the wine racy?

Lee Oh, shut up, Steph.

Steph Well, I do think it's a very odd friendship you have with that boy. You live in each other's pockets. Nick this, Nick that, Nick Nick Nick Nick Nick, I'm sick of the sound of him.

Lee What's odd about our friendship?

Steph Nothing, he's obviously an S.B.S.C.

Roy S.B.S.C.?

Steph Straight but sucks cock.

Lee There's nothing odd about a gay man and a straight man being mates.

Steph I think it's unnatural.

Roy I think it sounds dead nice.

Steph And nothing's happened between you two?

Lee Steph.

Steph   Well, I think there's something you're not telling us. It'll all end in tears.

Roy   D'you think all the groups'll be getting nervous now?

Lee   I really don't know, Roy.

Lee *exits to the kitchen.*

Steph   Methinks I hit a raw nerve.

Roy   If Nick was gay, why would he have a girlfriend?

Steph   Well, I slept with a woman once.

Roy   What was it like?

Steph   Nothing to write home about.

Roy   I wouldn't know what to do.

Steph   Close your eyes and think of Jason Orange.

Roy   I often wonder whether I've cut meself off. Whether I've put all me eggs in the one basket. Maybe I'm missing something.

Steph   Do something about it then.

Roy   There was this girl at Michael's funeral. It was his sister, Louise. She were dead pretty.

Steph   So?

Roy   We went round the back of the church hall and had a snog.

Steph   Did you like it?

Roy   It was all right.

Steph   Did you do anything else?

Roy   Two Es.

Steph   You really paid your respects, didn't you?

Roy   At least I was there.

Steph   You don't know how much I regret that. I love Lee. I hated every second of his mourning.

Roy   So why did you go to Tenerife then?

Steph He insisted.

The door buzzer goes.

Roy Have you seen Nick in that advert?

Steph · It's on often enough.

Lee *enters and goes to the wallphone.*

Roy Don't you think he's gorgeous?

Lee (*to phone*) Hello? Okay, push the door.

Steph He's okay in a rough tradey sort of way.

Roy Is it Nick and Tania?

Lee Yeah.

Roy Ah, fab.

Steph (*to* **Roy**, *about* **Lee**) Look at him, he's all a quiver.

Lee Shut up, Steph.

Steph You are, you're trembling!

Lee Will you just give it a rest, Steph? Please. Just. Give it a rest.

Steph Okay okay.

Lee Thank you.

Steph Your secret's safe with me, Tania!!

Tania *enters with a petrol can with the lid missing.*

Tania Oright? I couldn't bring Nick so I brung this. (*Laughs, holding the can up.*) He's parking the car. Has it started yet?

Lee No, it doesn't start till eight.

Tania I told him. He reckoned it was seven, stupid wanker. Oright, Steph?

Steph Yeah, great guns.

Lee This is Roy.

Tania Oright?

Roy   Hiya.

Lee   This is Tania.

Roy   Hiya, Tania.

Tania   (*gives* **Lee** *wine*)   And can you stick this somewhere, I don't want it stinking out my motor. (*Hands him can of pretrol as well.*) He's had it in there since he broke down the other night. You know he broke down, duntcha?

Lee   When?

Tania   When he came round here. Breakdowns, nothing new with him. Shouldna been driving anyway, state he was in. Can you stick it somewhere?

Lee *is putting the petrol can out on the balcony.*

Lee   Yeah, how's your mum? (*He spills some petrol on the balcony.*)

Tania   I don't wanna talk about it. Sorry, there's no lid on it.

Lee   I love the smell of petrol. (*Shutting balcony door.*) D'you wanna Buck's Fizz?

Tania   No, get us a lager.

Lee   Okay. (*Smells hands as he gets her a can of lager and starts pouring it into a glass.*)

Steph   I hear Nick's had some work.

Tania   Nick? Yeah, he done an episode o' *The Bill.*

Steph   Oh? I heard he'd been in a playreading.

Tania   Oh yeah, above a pub.

Steph   Any good?

Tania   No, it was crap. It was all about this fella called Jung, yeah? I felt totally ignorant watching it. He introduced me to the writer in the pub afterwards. I said, 'Listen, mate, don't give up the day job.'

Roy   Do you work?

Tania   Yeah. Cor, this is a nice suite, init? Where'd you get this?

Lee (*passing her a can and glass*) Habitat.

Tania Don't like that chair. (*She means* **Norman**'*s.*) Cheers,
Lee, so we all watching this song contest shit, are we? Christ.

Steph No one made you come.

Tania Didn't they?

Roy Aren't your shoes fab?

Tania Yeah.

Wendy *enters.*

Wendy Hiya, Tania, you all right.

Tania Right, Wend? Eh, big day Thursday.

Roy Oh, yeah, she's having her pins out.

Tania I bet you can't wait, it's been months anit?

Wendy Yeah, six.

Tania National Health Service, they want shooting.

Wendy Where's Nick?

Roy Parking the car.

Tania He'll be fucking hours. Good.

Steph You two not getting on, Tania?

Tania He's all right. In small doses.

Steph Like thrush.

Tania Yeah, 'cept if I chuck a tub o'live yoghurt on him he
don't go away. (*Offers cigarettes.*) Anyone?

Roy *takes one, and* **Wendy** *takes another and sits to build a spliff.*

Roy Tar.

Wendy How's work?

Tania Ah, God.

Roy (*to* **Lee**) Where's she work?

Lee Hospital.

Wendy   Tania's a psychiatric nurse.

Steph   Auxiliary, if you please.

Tania   We got this new bird started Tuesday. She fucking stinks. I went in that ward and I nearly keeled over with the smell. It was disgusting. I had to sort her out. I said, 'Listen love, I dunno whether you've heard of deodorant but you wanna fucking start using it.'

Lee   There's nothing worse, is there?

Wendy   And has she?

Tania   Says she don't believe in it, see. Says she wants to be how nature intended. I said 'Oh yeah? What's that? A smelly cunt?' I'll fucking deck her on Monday if she ant bucked her ideas up.

Roy   Is she a nurse? Or a patient?

Tania   Director of Finance. It's not on is it, Lee?

Lee   No, it's not.

The door buzzer goes.

Tania   Ignore it.

Lee *presses the button by the phone.*

Tania   Ask him about his audition today. He made a right prat of himself.

Roy   I've seen him in the Tango ads.

Tania   We had a gorgeous holiday out of the money from that. Fuerteventura. What were them pictures like I shown you, Wend?

Wendy   Oh, it looked idyllic.

Tania   It is a class restort. (*To* **Roy**.) What's your name?

Roy   Roy.

Tania   Roy, you have never seen water like it in all your life.

Roy   Blue?

Tania   Clear as crystal.

Nick *enters.*

Tania   That was quick, get back out again we're not ready for you yet.

Nick   Good evening. (*Kisses* **Lee**.)

Everyone greets **Nick**.

Lee   Now you know everyone except Roy.

Nick (*shaking his hand*)   Hello, Roy.

Roy   Ooh, big hands! Hiya.

Tania   I was just telling Roy about Fuerteventura.

Nick   What a location, man.

Wendy   Bucks Fizz, Nick? Or d'you want a can?

Roy   What of? Tango?

Nick   Er, Bucks Fizz, please. May as well slip into the character of the avid Song Contest fan.

Tania   Nick?

Nick   Mm?

Tania   It starts at eight.

Nick   Right.

Tania   He thought it started at seven.

Roy (*to* **Nick**)   If I move up, you can sit down.

Nick   Thanks, Roy. So! What's new in Kentish Town?

Nick *joins* **Lee** *and* **Roy** *on the couch,* **Steph** *is in one armchair,* **Tania** *the other.* **Wendy** *will have* **Norman**'s *chair. She pours* **Nick** *a glass of Bucks Fizz.*

Steph   Hear you were in a fiasco of a playreading the other night, Nick. Tania says it was deplorable.

Nick   Oh now, Tania, it wasn't that bad.

Roy   What were it called? I might've heard of it.

Nick 'Psychodrama' by Chuck Finnegan. (*To* **Tania**.) You met him, didn't you, Babes?

Tania Chuck Finnegan? More like Chuck Up.

Nick It was quite meaty. The thing with playreadings is that you actually don't get much rehearsal time – a day if you're lucky – and then you're sort of semi-performing it.

Tania Nick, nobody's interested.

Roy I am.

Pause.

Roy I were in 'Dracula Spectacular' at senior school. I played Helga the tavern wench.

Pause.

Steph And you've done *The Bill* again?

Nick Yes.

Lee Fourth time.

Tania Tell them what you were playing.

Nick Barry Miles.

Tania Wife batterer.

Steph Again?

Tania Typecast, mate.

Nick No, this wife batterer was different. He'd been abused as a child.

Lee I don't remember that bit.

Nick Oh, it wasn't in the script. It was sort of unspoken. I got the penultimate line. 'There's no justice in this world.' And sort of sneered angrily at camera while that really great Asian WPC put the handcuffs on. She's delightful.

Wendy Is she? Yes, she looks nice.

Nick Well, they're all pretty cool. Great team. Great spirit. And bloody good.

Steph   Fascinating.

Lee   And you had an audition today?

Wendy   Oh, really? For what?

Nick   Danish sandwich spread.

Tania   Tell 'em what you had to be.

Nick   A wholemeal loaf. Medium sliced.

Tania   Ah, what a cunt! Who'd be an actor? Not me.

Lee   D'you think you'll get it?

Nick   Well, the director said he really liked my characterisation, so . . . fingers crossed.

Tania   Put the telly on, I'm bored.

Lee   It's not time yet.

Steph   I hope you're not gonna talk all the way through, Tania.

Tania   Nah, I'm looking forward to this. I love nothing better than sitting in a chair for three hours listening to crap music with words I don't understand and seeing the British fail miserably at everthing they do. Wend, you coming the pub?

Steph   That's not a bad idea actually.

Tania   You can't get rid of me that easily.

Nick   That's true.

Tania   (*to* **Nick**)   Oi! Three thirty this morning, mate, you weren't complaining then. (*Winks at* **Roy**.)

Wendy   Roy's a big fan of yours, Nick.

Roy   Have you ever met Gail Tilsley? I have.

Nick   No. I did audition for the *Street* though, years back.

Roy   Really?

Lee   Yeah, to play thingy.

Nick   Medical student.

Lee   They said he was too old.

Tania Well, they got tact, ant they.

Nick You'll have to excuse Tania, her mother's not very well at the moment.

Pause.

Roy Ah, what's wrong with her?

Wendy Emphysema.

Nick Tania's been under a lot of strain.

Tania Shut up, Nick, nobody's interested.

Roy I am.

Pause.

Roy Is it fatal?

Pause.

Lee I've made scoring cards.

Lee goes to the chest of drawers and gets out some pieces of paper and some biros and starts giving them out.

Lee And we'll all need a pen.

Roy D'you like the Eurovision, Nick?

Nick My hobby's, like, experience. I think the only way you progress as a human being is by opening yourself up to new experiences.

Steph Really?

Roy It's been going forty years!

Nick I'm really looking forward to this.

Roy You're a lot taller. In the flesh.

Nick You'll have to adjust your horizontal control.

Steph Yeah, fiddle with your nob, sweetheart.

Tania I'm starving. Any grub going?

Wendy Five minutes.

Roy   I always fancied being an actor. Did you have to go to drama college and learn how to do accents?

Nick   You don't have to. There's plenty of guys around who are untrained and some of them, not all of them mind, are shit hot.

Lee   You did though, didn't you.

Roy   Do us a brummy accent, go on. I think it's dead difficult that one. I come out in Liverpool.

Nick (*Birmingham accent*)   Y'oright, our kid? Hey, you looking forward to the Eurovision Song Contest, our kid?

Roy   Ah, int that brilliant. It is, you know, it's brilliant that!

Tania   Comes in handy, dunnit, Nick? For when you're down the pub with the luvvies and you can pretend you're a snobby git.

Wendy (*reading score card*)   I didn't know Israel was in Europe.

Steph   Course it bloody is. They won two years running.

Roy   Seventy-eight and seventy-nine.

Lee   'A-ba-ni-bi' and 'Hallelujah'.

Steph   Though between you and me I think their best entry was 'Halila', which is Israeli for 'Tonight'. It was performed by a group called Habibi, the lead singer of which was heavily pregnant.

Lee   Eight months pregnant.

Steph   Was it eight? I thought it was nine. Coz Terry Wogan said Habibi might be Havinababy. Yeah, I thought that was pretty droll actually.

Roy (*to* **Nick**)   What drama college did you go to? Corona Kids?

Steph   The RADA, wasn't it, Nick?

Nick   RADA, yeah.

Steph   The RADA, Roy. Pretty impressive, yep?

Roy   I've heard of that. Isn't that where Julie Walters goes in *Prick Up Your Ears*?

Nick   No, Gary Oldman. My hero.

Roy   He got murdered, didn't he? By that one out of *Letter to Brezhnev*. And that one from *The Bill* finds them and then her out of *Howards End* buries the pair of them. I loved that movie, it were dead real.

Tania   My pen don't work.

Lee   Oh. (*Gets her another.*)

Nick   I'm parked on a yellow line. I'll be all right, won't I?

Lee   Yeah.

Steph   You should've tubed it like me.

Lee   Nick gets panic attacks on tubes.

Steph   Since when?

Lee   Since he got stuck on the Central Line for forty minutes in a tunnel. The lights went out and everything.

Steph   Heaven.

Tania   He's seeing an analyst.

Roy   Ah, fab.

Lee   He'll be all right, won't you, doll?

Nick   Katriona's very pleased with my progress.

Roy   Is she?

Steph   Katriona?

Tania   His analyst.

Roy   Ah, fab.

Nick   She's dutch.

Wendy   Dutch?

Nick   Yeah.

Steph   You'll have to ask her if she knows Teach-In.

Lee   Teach-In were a Eurovision group.

Steph   A Dutch Eurovision group.

Roy From Holland. They won as well.

Steph Quite spectacularly actually, and with a fantastic song.

Lee ⎫ Ding A Dong
Steph ⎬ Ding A Dong
Roy ⎭ Ding Dang Dong

Steph (*to* **Roy**, *snapping*)   It was Ding A Dong!

Roy It was Ding Dang Dong.

Steph Lee?

Lee It was Ding A Dong. I had the single.

Steph B-side was 'Let Me In'.

(*Sings.*)   Let me in.
Don't say goodbye
Let me in
Oh me oh my.

Tania *yawns very loudly.*

Nick (*scolding*)   Tania?

Tania Nicholas?

Wendy Is the treatment counselling based?

Nick For the time being. It's just such a relief to talk to someone who understands at last.

Tania I understand.

Nick A professional. My locum was useless.

Lee Put him on Prozac.

Nick Told me to grow up. I was disgusted.

Roy Have you still got 'em?

Nick The panic attacks?

Roy No, the Prozac.

Nick Chucked 'em.

Roy Ah, I coulda sold them in the clubs.

Wendy (*reading scoring card*)   Lot of songs, aren't there?

Steph   There's only twenty-three.

Lee   It'll be over in the blink of an eye, Wend.

Tania   Good.

Nick   She's not really an analyst, she's an occupational therapist.

Steph   Well, let's face it, most actors go mad at some stage in their careers, Nick. Look at whatsisface . . .

Roy   Yeah.

Tania   Who?

Nick   I wouldn't say I was going mad exactly . . .

Steph   That one out of *Coronation Street*.

Roy   Gail Tilsley?

Steph   No.

Roy   I was gonna say! When I met her she didn't seem the slightest bit potty. She was ever so nice. She signed me a card. 'To Roy. Best Wishes, Helen Worth.' That's her name. She's very pretty in the flesh. I felt sorry for her. She was opening this new MFI and it was only me and me mam turned up to see her. They let her go early. Hey, just think, Nick, you coulda been in that and then I'd be sitting on the same couch as a *Street* star!

Tania   Shame he failed the audition really.

Lee   It's not really failure though, is it.

Roy   No.

Nick   No.

Wendy   More . . .

Steph   Losing.

Roy   Yeah.

Steph   Yeah.

Pause.

Nick (*to* **Tania**)   Babes? (**Tania** *looks over.*) Isn't that a cool picture of Michael?

Tania   Ah, Lee, you must be so happy you took that photo.

Lee   Wendy took it actually. Had her David Bailey hat on there.

Steph (*laughs uproariously*)   Hahaha! It's terrible!

Wendy⎫ Oh, shut up.
Nick ⎭ Have some fucking manners, Steph.

Tania   Yeah, Steph, be fair, that's a good picture.

Lee   It really captures something about him. I just look at it and . . . oh you know.

Tania   Yeah, Lee, I know exactly what you mean. To Michael. Miss you, you cunt. (*Raises glass.*)

All   To Michael!

Roy   Ah.

Tania (*going in her bag*)   Here, Lee, look what I found this morning. I was cleaning out the kitchen and this was down the back of the fridge. (*Gets postcard out of her bag.*) It's the postcard he sent me from Paris, right after he'd met you. (*Passes it round to him.*) Had a right little cry when I seen that.

Nick   Isn't that beautiful?

Lee   Yeah.

Tania   You can have that.

Nick   He was one happy man.

Tania   He was.

Nick (*puts his arm around* **Lee**)   You brought a lot of happiness into that guy's life. Don't be too hard on yourself.

Pause.

Nick   How was Tenerife, Steph?

Steph   Bloody hot if you must know.

Roy Mandy Smith's been to Tenerife.

Tania Has she?

Roy Yeah.

Pause.

I'm reading her autobiography at the minute. No, she likes
Spain. She likes the balmy heat and the mañana mood. Says
everyone's dead *laissez-faire*, you know.

Tania Did you get laid?

Steph *Naturellement.*

Wendy Well, let's face it, when did Steph never get laid?

Steph Thursday night, Wend, why?

Wendy You're slipping.

Steph Well, warn me if I'm reaching your level.

Lee Should I go and have a look at the food?

Wendy No, I'll do it. (*Exits.*)

Tania I'm starving.

Roy Are you on a diet?

Tania Cheeky bastard, no!

Roy Oh, sorry.

Nick She's constantly on a diet.

Tania Nobody's interested, Nick.

Nick You've just bought that video!

Roy Ah, which one?

Tania Nick!

Nick 'Linda Robson's Light As A Feather.'

Roy Oh, I've got that, it's brilliant, isn't it?

Nick I was quite impressed actually, it's like, she's bringing
nutrition to the people.

Steph   Really?

Nick   Yeah.

Steph   Great.

Nick   No, seriously.

Tania   He's being serious.

Roy   Eh, Nick, just think, one day you might be doing your own diet video.

Tania   Called 'Nick East's ballooned since RADA'. He has, you know, he's put on so much weight.

Roy   Is that your surname? East?

Nick   My real name's Ross, so I had to change it for Equity's purposes.

Roy   Where d'you get East from? Your mam's side?

Nick   No, my first job was *Eastenders*. I took it from that.

Steph   Good job it wasn't *Country Practice*.

Roy   Who were you in *Eastenders*?

Nick   Robbie McFee.

Roy   Who was he?

Nick   I was drunk and abusive in the Queen Vic.

Steph   Fifteen minutes to go.

Roy (*to* **Nick**)   Are you fat?

Nick   I've been thinner. I lost two stone for a part last year.

Roy   Which part?

Nick   It was set in a hospice.

Roy   Oh, was that that thing about the fella who was dying and his dream was to buy his wife an engagement ring so he went on the rob and ended up in jail? She was in it, her off *Desmond's*, ah, it was great that!

Nick   No, this was called 'Heartbreak Holiday'. It was a . . .
fringe production.

Lee (*proudly*)   The *Jewish Chronicle* said he was really good at
misery.

Roy   Why are they called hospices?

Steph   Can we get into Eurovision mood please? If it's not too
much to ask? I mean, that is the reason why we are all here.
Thank you.

Roy   Me Uncle Albert were put in a hospice. I remember me
mam saying, 'Your Uncle Albert's gone in a hospice.' I thought it
were just a trendy way o' saying hospital.

Pause.

So when me mam went into hospital for her women's operation I
told me teacher me mum'd gone in a hospice. She let me draw all
afternoon. Everyone else was doing maths.

Pause.

There was bloody murder when she came to sports day.

Lee *has rushed out to the bedroom.*

Roy   I wonder if it's Greek, meaning 'A place you go to die'.

Steph   That's not hospice, that's Bury St Edmunds.

Nick   I'm . . . (*Gets up to follow* **Lee**.)

Tania (*to* **Nick**)   Leave him, Blobs.

Nick   I better . . .

Tania (*to* **Nick**)   He might wanna be on his own.

Nick   I'll check.

Nick *exits.*

Tania   Can't be easy, can it? If this time o'year holds big
memories and that.

Steph   I believe Nick's been a tower of strength.

Tania   Yeah, well, he's a man's man.

Steph   Oh, yeah?

Tania (*tuts*)   Him and Lee have always been close.

Steph   Inseparable.

Tania   Mike was my mate right from school. Nick and Lee were our partners. They formed a special bond.

Roy   Like footballers' wives.

Tania   Nick aint queer, Steph.

Steph   I never said he was.

Tania (*getting up*)   Not tonight, no. (*She goes towards the kitchen.*) Need hand, Wend?

Wendy (*off*)   Please!

Tania *exits to kitchen, leaving door open.* **Steph** *and* **Roy** *are left on their own.*

Steph   And then there were two.

Roy   Two what?

Steph   Eurovision fans.

Roy   Did I . . . ?

Pause.

I did, didn't I. Oh, God, I'm always saying the wrong thing. All the time. I get nervous see. (*Starts to cry.*)

Steph *gets out of his seat and goes and sits next to* **Roy**.

Steph   Oh now, Roy, m'darling. Roy Roy Roy Roy Roy. What are we gonna do with you?

Roy   Nothing.

Steph   Now, Roy, come on. Unburden those humungous woes please. (*Puts his arm round him.*)

Roy   Get off.

Steph   I know how it feels you know, to feel you can't do a thing right. Every time I try and get close to Lee, Nick gets in the way.

Roy *gets up.*

Steph Where you going?

Roy Nowhere.

Roy *goes and stands on the balcony.*

Steph Well, let . . .

Roy You stay right there I'm all right.

Roy *has his back to us, leaning over the railings looking out, possibly crying.* **Steph** *is left alone on the sofa. There is a knock at the door,* **Steph** *goes and answers it. It's* **Norman**.

Norman Hiya, I'm Norman.

Steph Hi there.

Norman I'm from upstairs. Well. I'm from Liverpool really, but I live upstairs. I was just wondering if the chair was all right.

Steph It's great actually, now thank you so much for making tonight a possibility bumwise.

Norman God, where is everyone? Have they all done a runner?

Steph Just . . . powdering their various noses. And . . . any other body part you care to mention. Only joking, yep?

Norman Oh well, just thought I'd check.

Steph Well, it's nice to know that manners are alive and well and living in Kentish Town actually, Norman.

Norman Sad time o'the year the Eurovision, isn't it?

Steph Well . . .

Norman Don't worry he told me everything. And I mean everything. Thought I'd pop down now coz I know it's starting soon.

Nick *enters from the bedroom. He collects his and* **Lee**'s *glasses.*

Steph What?

Norman The contest. (*To* **Nick**.) Hiya.

Nick   Hi. Just taking these through to the bedroom.

Steph   Everything hunky-dory with Lee in there, Nick?

Nick   Nearly. You don't know where he keeps his hankies, do you?

Steph   No.

Nick   It's all right, I'll get some toilet paper.

Nick *exits to bedroom.*

Norman   God, Richard Gere or what?

Steph   Actually...

Norman   Been round an awful lot lately that one, you know. Still, if they've made it to the bedroom tonight of all nights, all I can say is about time too. I know they haven't been at it yet coz me floorboards are like that. (*Shows just how thin they are with his finger and thumb.*) Toilet paper eh? I prefer a hot towel meself. Best be getting back. Ah, it was nice to meet yer anyway.

Steph   I'm Steph incidentally.

Norman (*shaking his hand*)   That's an unusual surname. Only kidding yer.

Steph   I hope we meet again, Norman.

Norman   Oh, you can come up any time, you know. I'm the youngest of twelve, I'm used to having people round me.

Steph   I might just have to do that. Run along now.

Norman   Trar.

Steph   Ciao for now.

Norman *goes.* **Steph** *goes to the kitchen door.*

Steph   Okay in there, girls, are we?

Wendy (*off*)   Fine!

The kitchen door slams shut in **Steph**'s *face. He goes towards the balcony.*

Steph   Roy.

Pause.

You've done nothing wrong, you know. If Lee can't bear to hear the word hospice then that's his lookout.

Pause.

I'm all on my ownsome lonesome in here actually, Roy.

Pause.

Roy, this is Steph. Your old buddy.

Roy   Buddy off.

Roy *closes the balcony door and goes back and leans on the railings.* **Steph** *sits down and has a swig of his drink. He pours himself another Bucks Fizz. He reads his scoring card. He looks at his watch. He gets up and goes to the television set. He switches it on. Nothing. He bangs on it. Nothing. He hits it again. Nothing. He checks it is plugged in. It is. He switches it off then on again. Nothing. This time he slaps it in annoyance. A small explosion is heard inside the TV. He looks horrified. Another small explosion. Terror. He looks around. He switches the telly on and off. Nothing. It's dead. He retreats to his chair and sits uneasily looking round at the various doors. He looks at his watch. He gets the phone off the floor and dials a number.*

Steph (*on phone*)   Hello, Billy. Steph. Hi. What you up to then? Well, I was just sitting in at home and, you know, having bumped into you at Sainsbury's last night I thought, 'I know what. I'll give Billy a ring.' Not going to Lee's tonight? No, me neither. It's a bit awkward, isn't it? Yep. Yep. I mean, between you and me, he tends to get just a little too over emotional for my liking, so. No. No. No, I didn't go whole hog for the brain tumour story either. I mean it's obvious, isn't it? And I mean, we both saw the state he got into on World Aids Day. I mean it's not everyone who sticks a red ribbon on their hatchback. Mm. So. What you up to tonight? Right. Is that voices I can hear in the background? Oh. Must be my party line. Oh, is it? Oh, right, well, I better get the telly on, hadn't I? Oh, there's my doorbell, must go. I've got a couple of friends round from the London Nude Swimmers so. Okay, Billy. You too. Fingers crossed for Love City Groove eh? Yeah. Ciao for now. Bye. Bye.

He puts the phone down. He goes in his bumbag for a business card. He gets it out, he picks the phone up again and dials the number from the card.

Hi, Victor? Steph. Hi. Remember when we played that trick on your ex? That's right, that's the one. Well, I need you to do it for me now. Yeah. To Billy's house. Well, I can't coz I'm round at Lee's. You got Billy's address? Great. Remember, different cab company each time. Get your Yellow Pages out. Okay, Victor. Let your fingers do the walking. Love you for it. Yeah. Bye.

He puts the phone down. He doesn't know what to do. He switches the TV off then runs off to the hall and shuts the door. At the same time the kitchen door opens and **Wendy** *enters with a plate of garlic bread, she comes in and puts it on the coffee-table.* **Tania** *follows with a selection of dips.* **Wendy** *stands looking at her. It's important that they are positioned so neither of them can see* **Roy** *on the balcony.*

Tania   Where is everyone? (*Beat.*) What?

Wendy   I dare you.

Tania   What?

Wendy   Here.

Tania   Are you bleeding mad?

Wendy   I think I must be.

Tania   You are, you're a bleeding nutter.

Tania *moves towards* **Wendy**. *They giggle then kiss.* **Tania** *backs off.*

Tania   Wend.

Wendy   I know.

Tania   Shut up.

Wendy   (*nodding towards kitchen*)   Crudités.

They go off to the kitchen. **Roy** *comes back in to get a cigarette. He takes one of* **Steph**'s, *lights it, and returns to the balcony, shutting the door behind him. He leans against the railing, looking down, his back to the lounge.* **Tania** *and* **Wendy** *enter again with trays of sliced vegetables.*

Wendy   They must all be in with Lee. Probably having an orgy.

She opens the door to the hall.

Why don't we?

Tania   No.

Wendy   No?

Tania   No.

Wendy (*advancing towards her*)   No?

Tania (*whispered but insistent*)   NO!

Wendy   You know what they say about women who say no.

Tania   No?

Wendy   No. Neither do I.

They kiss again. **Roy** *wipes his eyes and turns round to come back in. He sees* **Wendy** *and* **Tania** *kissing. He is gobsmacked. His jaw drops and the cigarette falls to the ground. Immediately it ignites the spilt petrol and a modest fire begins to burn on the balcony.* **Wendy** *and* **Tania** *are oblivious to this.* **Tania** *stops the snog.*

Tania   No.

Wendy   Okay.

Tania   No. Kitchen.

They hurry off to the kitchen and close the door. The fire is getting bigger. **Roy** *can't get back into the flat because the fire is blocking his way. He screams.* **Nick** *enters with his drink from the bedroom.*

Roy (*from balcony*)   Shit! Shit! Shit! Shit! (*Sees* **Nick**.) Tango! Tango!!

Nick   Shit!

Nick *gets some damp tops from the clothes-horse. He opens the balcony door and slaps the fire out with the tops, then jumps up and down on it. Soon the fire is out.* **Nick** *stands in the lounge with the tops and* **Roy** *stays on the balcony.*

Roy   I'm sorry. I forgot your name.

Nick   Are you okay?

Roy   Yeah.

Nick   What the fucking hell happened, man?

Roy   I dropped a ciggie.

Nick   In that? Jesus Christ, come in.

Roy   Can't.

Nick   What?

Roy   I can't.

Nick   Eh?

Roy   I've wet meself.

Nick   I'll get a cloth from the kitchen.

Roy   No! No!

Nick   Well . . . I'll get some trousers from Lee.

Roy   Please.

Nick   What?

Roy   Don't tell anyone I went on the balcony. It's Lee, see. He told me not to. He didn't want anyone on here. You mustn't tell anyone I was here not even your wife.

Nick   Partner.

Roy   Tania, don't tell her, promise?

Nick   Well . . .

Roy   It'd mean a lot to me. I loved the Tango advert. And . . . I haven't told you this before but you were belting in that *Bill* episode.

Nick   Which one?

Roy   All of 'em. I saw 'em all. Please. I'm a kleptomaniac.

Nick   Sorry?

Roy   I'm addicted to setting fire to things. You understand. You're having treatment. Please. Our secret.

Nick   Okay.

Roy   I really appreciate this.

Nick   Come in.

Roy   Tar.

Roy *comes in off the balcony. He has a wet patch down one of the legs of his jeans, emanating from his crotch.*

Nick   I didn't realise you erm, had followed my career so closely. I mean, the core of my work's been theatre but. Well. What can I say?

Roy   Mm.

Nick – I appreciate you holding back. I get it a lot. You know.

Roy   Adoration?

Nick   Well.

Roy   I'm not surprised.

Nick   Makes a refreshing change when someone . . . Hey, thanks.

He hugs **Roy**.

Roy   Close the door.

Nick   What? Oh right.

Nick *shuts the balcony door.*

Roy   He won't notice for ages, he never goes out there. (*Looks at his trousers.*) Oh, God, does it show?

Nick   Well. It's nothing to be embarrassed about, you're amongst friends. Where's Steph?

Roy   Dunno. I'll soak them. In the bathroom. You look hungry. Have something to eat. Don't, whatever you do, go in the kitchen.

Nick   Why not?

Roy   Coz Wendy's . . . talking to Tania about the pins in her knee. I think it's like counselling.

Nick   Tania? Counselling?

Roy   Have you noticed they've been spending time together lately?

Nick No, her mum's been ill. Emphysema.

Roy Oh. Well, that's what's happening now. And treatment's like, confidential. Isn't it?

Nick Strictly.

Roy Start the food off, go on.

Nick Right. You okay?

Roy Yeah. Are you gay?

Nick No.

Roy No, I didn't think you were. I can spot it a mile off.

Nick *sits to eat.*

Roy So you're not shagging Lee or owt?

Nick Roy, mate, listen.

Roy I don't mind. I won't tell anyone.

Nick Roy!! For fuck's sake! I'm straight. I wish I wasn't half the time, you guys can get it when you want.

Roy And you're not in an open relationship?

Nick Roy. You're a nice lad. Handsome. But threesomes aint in our line, mate.

Roy I'll put these in to soak in the bathroom.

Lee *enters.*

Roy (*to* **Lee**) What do you want?!

Lee Food!

Roy Sorry. I've spilt Bucks Fizz down me jeans, I'm gonna soak 'em in the bathroom.

Lee (*sees stain*) Oh no! (*Realises.*) Steph's in there.

Roy Where?

Lee In the bathroom.

Roy Right.

Lee   Look if you stick them in the washer on an economy wash they can be dry by the end of the contest. I've got a drier.

Lee *heads to the kitchen.*

Roy   No!!

Lee (*stops*)   You what?

Roy   They're handwash only.

Lee   They're 501s, aren't they?

Roy   No! Oh . . .

Roy *bursts out crying.*

Lee   Oh, Roy, love eh? Eh? (*Goes to him.*) It's only a bit of Bucks Fizz. (*Wipes his hand on* **Roy's** *wet patch and then licks his finger.*) Mm? (*He hugs* **Roy.**)

Roy   It's not that.

Lee   Well, what is it?

Roy   Erm . . .

Tania *and* **Wendy** *enter from the kitchen.*

Nick   Everything okay, ladies?

Wendy   Fine.

Tania (*to* **Nick**)   Why aren't you eating?

Nick   I am.

Wendy   Oh, Roy, puppy, what's up?

Roy   Nothing.

Tania   Eeh! What've you spilt down your strides, Roy?

Roy   Nothing.

Wendy   Roy, what is it?

Roy   Bucks Fizz.

Wendy   No. What's the matter?

Lee   Eh?

Nick   I think I know.

Tania   Yeah, well, you think you know everything, duntcha?

Roy   Tania!!

Tania   What?!

Roy   Don't have a go at him!

Tania   Do what? And just who d'you think you're talking to eh?

Nick   Tania!

Tania   I am not having him talk to me like that!

Lee   He's upset.

Nick   Actually, if you must know.

Tania   What?

Lee
Wendy } What?

Nick (*beat*)   His . . . his dog died this afternoon.

Steph *enters from the bathroom.*

Steph   Ooh, had a right lamppost to get rid of there. Beautiful. Just about time, isn't it? Stick the telly on, Nick.

Pause.

Nick   Isn't that right, Roy?

Roy   Mm.

Lee   I didn't know you had a dog, Roy.

Roy   I only got her this morning.

Wendy   Oh, Roy, how did she die?

Nick   Run down. On her first walk.

Lee   Come and sit down, Roy.

Wendy   Yeah, oh, baby. Get him a brandy, Lee.

Roy   Oh, yeah, I need a drink.

Lee *goes into the kitchen.* **Roy** *ends up wedged between* **Tania** *and* **Wendy** *on the couch.*

Steph   Nick? Stick telly on. I'm hopeless with them old contraptions.

Tania   This boy's just lost his dog.

Steph   Have you got a dog, Roy?

Tania   Not any more, obviously.

Wendy   What was her name?

Roy   Dyke . . . andra.

Steph   I love it!

Roy   Dykandra.

Lee *enters with a bottle of brandy and a glass. He starts pouring one for* **Roy** *on the coffee-table.*

Nick   Dykandra.

Tania   What sort was she?

Roy   Lesbian.

Lee   What?

Nick   It was a very special dog. Female. And attracted only to other bitches.

Steph   Well, she'd be better off dead.

Roy   We're going to miss the opening.

Wendy   Oh, Nick, you're nearest.

Lee   I'll do it, it's a bit temperamental.

Wendy (*to* **Roy**)   Oh, you poor baby.

Roy *sips the brandy as* **Lee** *switches the television on. He messes around with the switches on it till his next line.*

Roy   I'm all right. I think it's the excitement of tonight. And . . . I'll be all right when the contest's on.

Wendy   Can you eat something?

Steph   I'm ravenous actually.

Tania (*to* **Roy**)   Try and eat something, mate. Wend's gone to a lot of trouble with that.

Lee   I don't believe it.

Nick   What?

Lee   I was right.

Tania   What?

Lee   He *is* here.

Steph   Who?

Lee   Michael.

Wendy   Lee?

Nick   Lee. Is it plugged in?

Lee   He doesn't want me to see it. He doesn't want me to enjoy it without him.

Steph   You're not trying to tell me the telly's broken down, are you?

Roy   What?

Nick   Lee, we've talked about this.

Lee   Haven't we just.

Nick   You said.

Lee   Yeah.

Nick   What did you say?

Tania   Nick?

Nick   You said . . . you were going to move forwards.

Lee (*joining in*)   Move forwards. (*Clears his throat.*) Move forwards and see it through. I'm going to watch it. I'm going to fucking well watch it! But how can I when the telly's buggered?

Roy   It's not, is it?

Tania   I'll phone Billy. We can all go over to his.

Steph   Now *that* is the most ridiculous thing I've ever heard in my life!

Roy   Why is it?

Steph (*to* **Lee**)   After the way he's treated you? Snubbed you? On your special night?

Wendy   Steph's got a point.

Steph   You and Michael threw the best Eurovision parties around. But now Michael's gone Billy can't even bring himself to come. Don't do it, Lee.

Roy   We were all invited.

Steph (*not impressed*)   Were we?!

Wendy   Steph's right.

Steph   Well, there's a first.

Lee   How am I going to watch it?!

Wendy   Isn't it on Radio Two?

Lee
Roy   } IT'S NOT THE SAME!!!
Steph

Tania   She's only trying to help.

Wendy   Well, there's only one thing for it.

A knock at the door suddenly. **Steph** *gets it. All eyes on the door. It's* **Norman**.

Norman (*peering in*)   Have I called at a bad time?

They all look at each other.

Blackout.

In the blackout the Eurovision theme music begins to play.

Act Two

Bucks Fizz plays 'Making Your Mind Up'.
Lights up on **Wendy** *and* **Tania** *putting the food from the coffee-table onto trays to be carried upstairs.*

Wendy   We could say we're going to the pub.

Tania   Ssh. (*Nods in the direction of the main door.*) Nick.

Wendy (*loudly, deliberately*)   I don't know whether I fancy this Eurovision lark. Don't want to come to the pub, do you, Tania?

Pause.

Tania (*quietly*)   He's going through a hard time. I know I take the piss but . . .

Pause. **Tania** *continues to fill her tray.* **Wendy** *watches her, hurt. Just then* **Norman** *enters from the hall.*

Norman   Oh, aren't yous marvellous?

He picks up his armchair.

I think we'll be wanting this, don't you?

Tania   Yeah.

Tania *exits hurriedly with her tray.*

Norman   You know where it is, don't yer?

Wendy   Yeah. Thanks.

Wendy *hurries out.* **Norman** *puts the armchair down, looks at photo of* Michael.

Norman   Ah, God love him.

Goes to **Tania**'s *handbag, looks in and sniffs it. He puts it on his shoulder and goes to the mirror.*

Well, tonight, Matthew, I'm going to be . . . Kiki Dee.

Waves to mirror. Puts bag down. Taps coffee-table.

(*To chair.*) That's glass.

Sits on sofa.

(*To one chair.*) I know. (*To other chair.*) I know. I said to the fella I want from there to there covered in pine. Well, I can afford it, you know. (*Up, to the kitchen doors.*) This is the saloon bar effect.

A toilet flushes off and **Nick** *enters.* **Norman** *sees him.*

Norman   He's got some lovely bits, hasn't he?

Nick   What? Yeah. Got it really homely.

Norman   Sort of place you could envisage yourself living in, is it?

Nick   Well. It's central.

Norman   I'm not being lesbophobic or nothing, but them two are really pretty.

Nick   Sorry?

Norman   Them lesbians.

Nick   Actually they're both straight.

Norman   Oh, well, I was right then, wasn't I?

Roy *enters from hall. He wears a towel round his waist instead of jeans.*

Nick   Oright, Roy?

Norman (*laughs*)   God! Fancy me thinking they were lesbians! God, I can't get over that, can you? Aray I'll see you upstairs then, yeah?

Norman *picks up his armchair and exits.* **Roy** *stands looking sheepish.*

Nick   Roy?

Roy   Erm.

Nick   What's up?

Roy   Nothing.

Nick   I hope you're not embarrassed that I know.

Roy   Know what?

Nick   What happened.

Roy When?

Nick Look if it's any consolation, I shat myself on stage once.

Roy What?

Nick Admittedly I had gastroenteritis but, hey, the show must go on. It was a three-hander Julius Caesar. We were all in togas, so I got stage management – they're these guys who, kind of, well, they . . . do stuff, set the props, prompt your lines. Not that they had to prompt me – I was off the book at the read through . . . unlike Derek. Anyway, yeah, I got them to make me a nappy out of towels and masking tape. Nobody knew. But I did. And, Christ, did I feel humiliated.

Roy stands up and heads for the hall. **Tania** *enters.*

Nick Where you going?

Roy Toilet. I need an E.

Nick An E?

Roy I brought two for later. I'm gonna take one now.

Nick Right.

Roy I've got to.

He exits. **Nick** *sits down on the settee and rests his head in his hands, thinking.*

Tania You coming up or what?

Nick Yeah, I'll be up in a sec.

Tania I mean, you know, you drag me over for some piece of shit and then . . .

Nick I did *not* drag you over. Christ! I couldn't believe you said you'd come.

Tania I'm not totally heartless, you know. Mike was my mate!

Nick It's the first time in fucking ages you haven't had to go running off to bloody Islington every five minutes.

Tania My mum aint well!

Nick Yeah, well, I wish she'd save us all the hassle and die now.

Pause.

Tania   Well, I'm sorry to disappoint you, Nicholarse, but she happens to be making a recovery.

Nick   Oh, maybe I'll get to see you once in a blue moon.

Tania   I can't help it if me mum's ill.

Nick   Convenient, isn't it?

Tania   What?

Nick   That she gets ill all of a sudden.

Tania   She's been up and down for years, you know that.

Nick   Oh, do I?

Tania   You think I'm making it up?

Pause.

You are gonna regret you even thought that, you cunt. I want an apology. And I aint moving one cell till I get one.

Roy *enters from the bathroom, relaxed.*

Roy   Where are they up to?

Tania   Sorry but I can't see through ceilings.

Roy   God, imagine what it'd be like to see through ceilings.

Nick   Roy . . . er . . .

Tania (*to* **Nick**)   I'm waiting.

Roy   I best get up.

Roy *exits.*

Tania   You know what you do? You make me wanna heave. If I was anorexic I wouldn't waste me time with laxatives or sticking knitting needles down me throat, I'd just take one look at you.

Nick   I'm sorry.

Tania   You wanna be glad you've got me. I'm a fucking result.

Tania *pours herself a drink and lights herself a cigarette.*

Nick It's all this freedom. Not working. My mind works overtime.

Tania You haven't got a mind. Look at you. You're a waste of space. I'd be better off having an affair. Don't look at me like that, all doey-eyed, you said it.

Nick I didn't.

Tania What do I do then? If I aint visiting my mum?

Nick (*shrugs*) Got a fancy man?

Tania A fancy man. I've already got a fancy man. Very fancy. Fancies himself as a fucking star. And I have to put up with his fancy ways, dunn'I? No. I don't. And won't. Grow up, Nick.

Nick I wouldn't blame you. I'm not much cop to live with at the moment.

Tania You never were, darling.

Nick Your mum can't stand the sight of me, I can't stand the thought of her. Ideal excuse. See? Got it all worked out. (*It's obvious he doesn't believe this.*)

Tania D'you know what you are? You're one sad bastard. You don't even believe that.

Nick I think I might be depressed.

Tania Oi! There's somebody else in the room! Jesus. Even when you're accusing me of sleeping around, it's gotta get back to you!

Nick It's this freedom thing.

Tania Is someone paying you to say that word?

Nick I have all this time to myself to think the stupidest things. To hatch the stupidest schemes.

Tania Well, here's a little scheme for you to hatch. You'll like this one. You get on the blower, you hire a removal van and you get out sharpish. Like that one, do ya? Thought you would. You're spoilt. God help the poor mug who gets you next.

Nick Fine I'll move out.

Tania (*rubs hands together*)   Excellent. A result.

Nick   I can't remember the last time you said you loved me.

Tania   Me neither, shame that.

She goes to the door.

(*Sarcastic.*) I love you. How's that?

Nick   You'd make a crap actor.

Tania   You *are* a crap actor.

Tania *exits to go upstairs.* **Nick** *is left on his own. He begins to recite a speech from the last play he was in.*

Nick   Why is my life such a mess? In tatters? Shattered like a piece of broken glass you take your fist to. Clenched first, broken wrist, Rizla papers torn to shreds. Shredded beds of nothingness. I am a mess. Guess. Bless this House. I no longer live here. The psychic spines of broken glass that pierce this very skin, but where do I begin to even lick the wounds you cause me?

Lee *enters behind him.*

Nick (*continues*)   I loved you once. I loved you all. But fall is the season of distrust. I must. I must. I must. Depart. (*Sees* **Lee**.) 'Psychodrama' by Chuck Finnegan.

Lee   Don't let me stop you.

Nick   I think it's all over with me and Tania. I'm being as horrible as is humanly possible.

Lee   I think Jeffrey Dahmer pipped you to the post on that one. (*Tuts.*) Surely it's not irretrievable.

Nick   Christ, Lee, why aren't I gay?

Lee (*shrugs*)   Too close an association with your father in your pre-school years?

Nick   We'd make a great team.

Lee   Yeah, but the sex'd be pretty lousy.

Nick   I'm a quick learner.

Lee   But would your heart be in it?

Nick   Me arse would! (*More serious.*) I envy you bastards.

Lee   I think it's a case of the grass is always greener, dear.

Nick   Shit. I'm sorry. See? I can say sorry to you at the drop of a hat and mean it, but Tania?

Lee   D'you love her?

Nick   I'm used to her.

Lee   Isn't that the same thing?

Nick   No.

Lee   No.

Nick   I dunno.

Lee   Where would you go?

Nick   I don't know.

Pause.

Lee   You could always come here you know.

Pause.

Go up and talk to her.

Nick   And tell her what?

Lee   I don't know.

Nick   I can't talk to her like I can talk to you.

Lee   Get up there and salvage it, Nick.

Nick   Right.

Lee   If you want to.

Nick   Yeah. I do.

Lee   Well, hurry up.

Nick   You're a fucking good mate, Lee.

Lee   Everything's easier with mates.

Nick   You are.

Lee   Go on, you're beginning to sound like someone from *The Wonder Years*.

Nick   That's an excellent show.

Nick *exits.* **Lee** *moves to the stereo and puts on a CD of Annie Lennox singing 'Why'. He looks at the CD cover. He fights tears. He takes the photo of Michael off the wall and holds it to him. He sits on the sofa and hugs the photo to him. On the line 'This boat is sinking',* **Steph** *enters, he sees* **Lee** *sitting on the sofa fighting tears.* **Steph** *tries to stop* **Norman** *entering but he does.* **Steph** *pushes* **Norman** *out of the room then re-enters.* **Steph** *turns the sound down.* **Lee** *looks round.*

Steph   Annie Lennox? Sacrilege tonight, dear.

Lee *turns the sound down a bit.*

Lee   Sometimes we had taste. It wasn't all tack. I used to play this whenever . . . I always opened my big mouth, then he'd open his, then silence. It was easier to say sorry by playing this, than actually working up the courage to . . . And now it's . . . He'd be standing there, where you are. I'd put this on. And there'd be no need to talk.

He gets up, snaps the stereo off, then sits down again.

I don't know whether to phone Billy. We had a row in Sainsbury's last night. Frozen foods. When I saw him reach in that freezer and bring out a party-bag of mini sausage rolls I just saw red.

'He had a brain tumour you stupid soft prick!' I yelled. 'He had a fucking brain tumour!'

Maybe it would have been easier if he had had AIDS. We certainly wouldn't have hidden it. Well, you don't, do you? But oh no that's not good enough for the likes of Billy. It couldn't possibly have been a brain tumour. 'He lost three stone!' he yelled at me. God, he was on a fucking diet, wasn't he? He was on a diet because I didn't fancy him with a beer gut and a bit of a double chin! If he'd had AIDS I'd've been prepared for it . . . this . . . and been able to say . . . I should phone Billy. I hit him round the head with a frozen chicken.

Pause.

I said some terrible things. Personal. He must think I hate him. My parting retort was, 'I'll get my own back on you!'

Pause.

We're okay with AIDS. We expect AIDS. We don't expect a brain tumour. I thought he'd gone off me coz it was always 'Not now Lee I've got a headache.' I should phone Billy.

Steph   Don't phone Billy. He's not worth it. I wouldn't piss on him if he begged me. I'd piss on you. If you asked nicely.

Lee   You mad bastard.

Steph   Well . . . in the immortal words of Teach-In, seventy-five,

> 'When you're feeling all right,
> Everything is uptight,
> Try to sing a song that goes
> Ding, Ding a Dong.

> And the world is sunny,
> Everyone is funny,
> When they sing a song
> That goes Ding Dang Dong.'

Lee   Sometimes the Dutch put it so much better than we ever could.

Steph   I feel a bit silly now.

Lee   What?

Steph   No, it's nothing.

Lee   What?

Steph   Well . . .

Lee   Steph?

Steph   Can I borrow your bedroom for five minutes? No longer, I promise.

Pause.

It's Norman. He's er . . .

Lee You what?

Steph Well, Nick and Tania are in his bedroom and Love City Groove are on shortly. I won't be long, I promise. We'll clean up after ourselves.

Pause.

I never once doubted the brain tumour story.

Lee It wasn't a story.

Steph Exactly.

Lee (*nods*) Yeah. Go'ed.

Steph *is delighted.*

Steph You know, I think he's rather sexy, in a Chaucerian sort o'way. (*Calls.*) Norman?!

Norman *enters sheepishly.*

Steph Now the very marvellous Lee has kindly given his permission for us two to use his boudoir. Say thank you, you ungrateful little slut!

Norman Thanks, Lee. It's dead kind o' you, y'know. No, it is.

Steph (*conspiratorially to* **Lee**) Don't have a spare table-tennis bat knocking about, do you?

Lee No. There's a fish server in the kitchen.

Steph Stainless steel? (**Lee** *nods.*) Cheers m'darling. (*Making his way to kitchen, hollers at* **Norman**.) And you can get in the bedroom!

Steph *exits to the kitchen.* **Lee** *picks up the phone. He rings a number, waits, then puts the phone down.* **Steph** *returns with a stainless-steel fish server.*

Lee Engaged.

Steph *goes in his bumbag and gets the handcuffs out.*

Steph Have you got a radio through there?

Lee   Yeah.

Steph   What's its Radio Two reception like?

Lee   Fine.

Steph   Good.

Steph *exits with the fish server and handcuffs. Presently* **Roy** *ambles in.*

Roy   Are my pupils dilated?

Lee (*looks at his eyes*)   No.

Roy   I'll kill that dealer.

He gets a wrap of coke out of his pocket and a credit card out of his wallet and starts chopping up some coke on the glass coffee-table.

Didn't feel I could do it in front of Wendy. She'd probably think I had a drug problem.

Lee   Is Wend on her own?

Roy   Yeah. D'you want some?

Lee *shakes his head.*

Roy   D'you think I've got a drug problem?

Lee   Do you?

Roy   Not sure. I hope not. (*Slicing it into a line now.*) I . . . only . . . do it . . . of an evening. I mean, it's not like I . . . wake up of a morning and . . . neck three Es. It's just . . . I've gotta stop it. It's no wonder . . . I'm always so skint. (*He gets a twenty-pound note out of his wallet and rolls it up.*) Sure you don't want any?

Lee   Sod it, why not.

Roy   You take first half. You'll feel better for that.

Lee (*sticking the note up his nose*)   I don't think you've got a problem. (*Snorts half the line.*)

Roy   No, neither do I. (*Snorts the other half.*)

Lee   I better get up and check on Wendy. And the contest.

Roy   You do that.

Lee I will. (*At the door now.*) I was sorry to hear about your dog.

Roy So was I.

Lee *exits.* **Roy** *slices up a second line then snorts it. As he is cleaning up after himself.* **Steph** *comes in with the fish server and heads for the kitchen.*

Steph Don't want a go, do you?

Roy No, tar.

Steph Fair enough.

Steph *exits to kitchen. He returns carrying a spiky wooden spaghetti server.*

Roy Steph, you know Wendy?

Steph Unfortunately.

Roy Has she ever had a fella?

Steph A guy from Stevenage, didn't last. Knocked her about a bit, sensible man.

Roy Don't be horrible, you.

Steph Why do you ask, m'darling?

Roy D'you ever get the feeling she's dykey?

Steph Well, put it this way, if she hasn't got k.d. lang in her CD collection I'd be pretty fucking surprised.

Roy No, but do you?

Steph I don't think so. Why?

Roy Oh, nothing really.

Steph Right.

Roy It's just that I saw her snog the golly off Tania before and I just put two and . . . (*Stops himself.*)

Pause.

I didn't really, that were a joke.

Steph Was it?

Roy I think I'm coming up on me E.

Steph   Roy?

Roy *starts stretching his arms in the air like he is waking up. The Ecstasy he took earlier is beginning to take effect. He rolls his head round.*

Roy   In here. Bold as daylight. Don't tell no one.

Steph   You really saw . . . no! No!!

Steph *sits down, mulling this over.* **Roy** *doesn't really take much care with what he says now as he is enjoying his ecstatic state.*

Roy   You mustn't tell anybody. Least of all Lee. I mean. Ah, wow, I feel great. Do you feel great? Oh, I feel fab! Oh, I wanno stretch out and, oh, this is really nice. Ah, Steph, will you rub me head?

Steph *gets up, stands behind* **Roy** *and rubs his head for him.*

Roy   Oh, that's so good. That is just, ah, wow.

Steph   Wendy and . . . It's all beginning to make sense now.

Roy   I know it's fab, isn't it?

Steph   I don't believe . . .

Roy   You haven't taken an E, have you?

Steph   What would Michael say?

Roy   I don't think he ever did it, did he?

Steph   What?

Roy   E!

Steph   They've been . . . all o'them . . . bloody hell, Roy. D'you realise what this means?

The phone rings. **Steph** *exits for the bedroom in a daze.* **Roy** *slowly goes to the phone, his eyes rolling and answers it lying on the floor. Rolling around.*

Roy   Hello? Hello? No, it's Roy. Do I sound like Lee? I didn't think I did. Do I sound like I'm on helium? Good, it's embarrassing when I get like that. Don't shout. Who is it? Billy, hiya! Oh, Billy, don't shout, there's no need to shout. Okay I'll get him. Billy, I don't know whether I've told you this before but I love you. I think you're fab. Ah don't shout.

Roy *gets up and goes to the door. He softly calls out.*

Roy　Lee! Lee, it's Billy!

Steph *comes out from the bedroom and into the lounge with the pasta server.*

Steph　Did you just say Billy?

Roy　Yeah. He's shouting. Why's he shouting?

Steph (*shouts*)　Lee!! Lee!!

Roy　Will you rub me head again?

Steph　Couch.

Roy *sits on the couch,* **Steph** *rubs his head.* **Roy** *is in ecstasy.* **Lee** *enters.*

Lee　What?

Steph　Billy on the phone. Seems to be getting a tad terse.

Lee　Billy?

He goes to the phone. He sits to speak.

Hiya, Billy. Bill, do you have to . . . (*Shouts.*) Bill, I'm not deaf!! (*More calm.*) You cheeky get, as if I'd do a thing like that. Billy! Billy! Now hang on a minute! (*Pause.* **Lee** *puts the phone down.*) The cheeky bastard. He's had taxis coming every five minutes and he's tryina make out I ordered them! I'll fucking . . . says he's gonna get his own back.

Steph　Maybe you did do it, Lee.

Lee　What?

Steph　Maybe you did.

Lee　Steph . . . you've been here all night, you'd've seen.

Steph　Well, I seem to recall you saying earlier you'd seen Billy in Sainsbury's and said you'd get your own back.

Lee　I wouldn't do a thing like that.

Steph   Wouldn't you? You're probably right. What would I know?

Lee   You should know that's not my style. Where's Norman?

Steph   Fuck him, where's Nick?

Lee   Nick's talking to Tania. Isn't he?

Steph   What are they talking about?

Lee   What's the matter, Steph?

Steph   We're your mates. Don't you think if you've got something to tell us, we've got a right to know? Out of common courtesy. Manners.

Lee   Y'what? Like what?

Steph   Lee, we know what's going on.

Lee   What's going on?

Roy   Yeah, what's going on?

Steph   I'm going home.

Steph *heads for the door.*

Lee   What? Steph, what's the matter?

Steph   I'm not jealous.

Lee *stops him from leaving the room, grabbing his arm.*

Lee   Steph?

Steph   Do I have to spell it out to you?

Lee   Well, I wouldn't mind. Have I done something to upset you?

Steph   No.

Lee   What then?

Steph   I worry about your head, Lee. You're so caught up in 'doing the right thing'. The man of principle. When all along you're just a bloody great hypocrite.

Lee   How come?

Roy Rub me head.

Lee I dunno what the fuck you're talking about, Steph!

Steph You and Nick, dear.

Lee What about me and Nick?

Steph I really thought you were my friend.

Lee Yer are. What about me and Nick?

Steph Oh, how much more bullshit have we got to take? Your secret's out, m'darling. Roy saw Tania and Wendy snogging, okay?

Lee What?

Steph I suppose Mike did have AIDS after all, but you had to hoodwink us into believing it was something else, just because you and your twisted little mind can't own up to being just a little bit human. I know you laugh at me behind my back but at least I'm honest about what I do. At least I can sleep at night.

Lee *punches* **Steph** *in the face, knocking him onto the couch.*

Roy Ah, don't hit him.

Lee (*to* **Roy**) What d'you have to go and say a stupid thing like that for?

Roy Stop shouting at me.

Lee I'll shout at who I fucking well like, now why?

Roy Eh?

Steph My nose is bleeding.

Lee (*to* **Roy**) Why?

Roy I don't know what you're talking about.

Lee You *have* got a drug problem.

Lee *pours himself a drink.*

Roy I've put me foot in it again, haven't I?

Lee (*to* **Roy**) Have you got a cigarette?

Roy   I don't know. Probably.

Lee   Then give me one.

Roy   You don't smoke.

Lee   Why, Roy?

Steph   Oh, Lee, stop it, you know why. Because it's true.

Lee (*lighting one of* **Roy***'s cigarettes*)   When? When did you see them kissing?

Roy   I don't know. Oh, yes I do. Before. Before I set fire to the balcony. There's not much damage.

Lee (*to* **Steph**)   See? He's barmy.

Steph   You just can't bear the fact that you've been caught out.

Steph *exits to kitchen.*

Roy   I'm sorry, Lee.

Lee   Oh, you will be.

Roy   It's just that I saw them kissing and me fag dropped out me mouth and went in the petrol and . . . oh, I feel fab.

As **Roy** *goes into an ecstatic trance,* **Lee** *goes and opens the balcony door. He inspects the burnt damage.* **Steph** *returns, nursing his nose with a wet tea towel and sits on the sofa.*

Steph   We don't care, you know. We don't care that you're getting your end away with him. And as for Tania and Wendy, well, yes, it does turn my stomach, but you know, I'm broad-minded. And even if Michael did have AIDS, so what? It's nothing to be ashamed of you know. You wanna be like me, practise non-penetrative safe sex. Simple solution. Q.E.D.

Lee *goes and punches* **Steph** *again.*

Lee   Get Wendy down here now.

Steph   Why should I?!

Lee   Just get her down here.

Steph   No, I will . . .

Lee *goes to punch him again.* **Steph** *rolls out of his way.*

Steph   I'm going.

Steph *exits.*

Lee (*to* **Roy**)   You did, didn't you?

Roy   I know. Eh? What did you just say?

Lee   You saw them. Oh, Roy. Was all that stuff about the dog crap?

Roy   You don't see white dog crap any more, do you?

Lee *sits down.*

Roy   D'you feel fab?

Pause.

I feel great.

Lee   Look, Roy.

Roy   What?

Lee   Do one, will you.

Roy   What?

Lee (*shakes his head, confused*)   Do one.

Roy   Another one? I've only got the one left but I'm saving it for later.

Lee   Go upstairs or something. Please.

Roy   Oh. Oh, okay. Okay.

Wendy *has just entered.* **Roy** *passes her to exit.*

Wendy   Okay, Roy?

Roy   I feel great.

Roy *exits.* **Wendy** *sees that* **Lee** *is smoking.*

Wendy   Put that out.

Pause.

Come on. Four months is a record for you.

Pause.

Lee. You throw a party to watch your favourite programme and then you spend all your time down here smoking. I wanted to go to the pub earlier, but I'm quite getting into it now. Some of those songs are really crass. Love City Groove are in with a pretty big chance I woulda thought.

Lee   I couldn't give a shit about Love City Groove to be honest with you.

Wendy   Now, come on, you don't mean that.

Lee   I'm afraid, Wendy, that I do.

Wendy   There's no need to get like that about it. Okay, so it's not as catchy as the usual entries but I don't believe for one minute it's put you off the Eurovision.

Lee   Nothing's put me off the Eurovision. Why, Wendy? Why?

Wendy   Why what? Put that out. You spent a fortune on hypnosis.

Pause.

Lee   I mean, it's not like I don't know how it feels.

Wendy   What?

Pause.

Lee   Look. Nick's my best mate. I love that lad. He's been like a brother to me since . . . I know things are dodgy between him and Tania. But. Why get yourself involved? Just. Wendy.

Pause.

Wendy   He's a bastard to her.

Lee   Kill it. Right?

Wendy   You don't know half the things . . .

Lee   I said kill it!

Pause.

Wendy   And what did you say to me at the age of sixteen when I couldn't understand why there was a fella in your bed? Eh?

What did you say then? Come on, lad. You've said it often enough to me mum and dad. Say it. Go on. Remind me what you said then, I've forgotten.

Pause.

'You can't choose who you fall in love with. If we could, the world'd be an easier place.'

Lee   I can't believe it.

Wendy   She's leaving him, Lee.

Lee   Why didn't you tell me?

Wendy   I've handed my notice in and I've got a job with a temping agency in Crouch End. Begin first of the month. Anyway, now you know. She's everything to me.

Lee   If you throw another cliché at me I'm gonna be sick.

Wendy   I'll be taking possession of a flat in Crouch End at the end of the month. Tania will be joining me just as soon as she sells up. So. I'll be able to pop round to see you as often as I like.

Lee   I'd like you to go now, Wendy.

Wendy   You've pigeon-holed yourself you know. I'm glad I never. At least I can go through life not regretting anything. You wanna really look at yourself.

Lee   Just go.

Pause.

Wendy   You're homophobic.

Lee   Oh no I'm not. You can call me what you like but don't you ever call me that. You should've told me. If that lad's feelings are . . . I'll fucking . . .

Wendy   What? Hit me? He hits her, you know. Your whiter than white best friend hits my lover. You're all the same.

She gets up.

Lee   No wonder you were so keen to come tonight.

Wendy You didn't think I'd come to see you, did yeh? Oh, what for? To thank you for pushing me round in a wheelchair?

Lee He'll be better off without her.

Wendy I believe this is mine.

She starts folding away the clothes-horse hanging from the radiator. She is beginning to get a bit manic. **Nick** *enters.*

Nick Oright, Wend?

Wendy Where's Tania?

Nick Gone for a walk. Clear her head, usual story.

Wendy Split up, have you?

Nick What? (*Laughs.*) No. No. I salvaged it. Again. Christ knows how long for. Christ knows why. Routine, I guess. Can't help but love me, warts and all, silly moo.

Wendy Pretty big warts!

By now **Wendy** *is hysterical.*

Lee Wend.

Wendy Oh, I'm Wend now, am I? Five minutes ago I was Wendy, now I'm Wend. There's progress.

Nick What's up?

Wendy You hit her.

Nick What?

Wendy Oh, so you're gonna deny it then?

Nick (*laughs*) Where'd you get that idea from?

Wendy From my girlfriend.

Pause.

Tania.

Nick (*laughs*) Am I the only person at this party who hasn't taken drugs?

Wendy (*to* **Lee**)   Denial. He's in denial. Look at him, he's got it written all over his abusive face.

Nick   Grow up, Wendy, a joke's a joke.

Wendy   Oh, you gonna hit me now, are yeh?

Nick   Lee?

Wendy   Fraid I might report you to the police? Like she did? (*To* **Lee**.) Bet you didn't know he had a record as long as his arm.

Nick   What the fuck are you on about woman?

Wendy   I'm a lesbian! All right?!

Pause. Then **Norman** *shouts through from the bedroom.*

Norman (*off*)   I told yer she was! Didn't I say?!

Wendy   Oh, now he can just shut up.

Wendy *exits towards the bedroom. A lot of slapping and moaning is heard off.*

Nick   What's going on mate?

Lee   Oh, Nick. Nick. Come here. (*Draws* **Nick** *to him and hugs him.*)

Nick   Steph's got a broken nose, Roy's off his box . . .

Wendy *re-enters.*

Lee   Wend, what were you . . .

Wendy   Oh, shut up, he enjoyed it! Hey, what does a lesbian take on her first date? The removal van. Well, it's no joke. Now you were under the impression Nick that Tania was visiting her mother in Islington, well she was, but what you and her mother don't happen to know is that actually . . . I'm sorry . . . (*Almost crying.*) it'll all be fine and . . . just . . . just . . .

Nick *looks to* **Lee**, **Lee** *shrugs.* **Wendy** *bursts out crying.*

Lee   Oh, bloody hell, my heart's going. Feel that.

Nick   What? (*Feels* **Lee's** *heart.*) Shit. Breathe. Breaths, big breaths.

Wendy (*to* **Nick**)   React! You bastard!

Lee   I had a line of coke from Roy and . . .

Nick   Come on, mate, just . . . breathe . . .

Just then **Tania** *enters carrying a tower of pizza boxes.*

Tania   I couldn't get out the bloody door. Which soft git ordered twenty quattro formaggio pizzas? Coz there's a geezer on the doorstep waiting to be paid.

Pause. **Tania** *puts the boxes down. She realises* **Lee** *is having some sort of anxiety attack and that* **Wendy** *is distraught.*

Nick? Did he order twenty pizzas from Pepino's Pizzas? That man's doing his nut.

Nick   I don't know.

Tania   Oh, for fuck's sake. (*Puts pizzas down.*)

The phone rings. **Nick** *picks it up.*

Nick   Hello? No, he's er . . . he's busy at the moment. What? Billy?

He puts the phone down.

Billy.

Tania   Well, what did he want?

Nick   He just said . . . 'Enjoy your meal.'

Lee   Tell the pizza man there's been a mistake go on.

Nick   Right.

Lee   Hurry.

Nick *exits.*

Tania   Wend?

Wendy   Crouch End.

Tania   Shut your big fat mouth, will ya?

Lee   I need a glass of water, Tania.

Tania (*pouring one*)   You've gone and blabbed. You stupid cow.

Lee   Steph told me.

Wendy   Steph?

Lee   Roy told Steph.

Wendy   Roy?

Lee   He saw the two of you kissing or something.

Wendy   Us two?

Tania   Keep going, Wend, you're working your way through every git at this party. You've only got Nick and Lee to go.

Lee   Steph of course, surprise surprise, assumed me and Nick were having a bit of a thing as well.

Tania   Yeah, well, Steph's the biggest arsehole going.

Lee   Not from where I'm sitting he isn't.

Tania (*to* **Wendy**)   You stupid cow.

Wendy   You've got to ring your mother.

Tania   Shut up.

Wendy   You told me to remind you.

Pause.

Tania   Cheers, Wend. Appreciate it.

Wendy   Crouch End. The swinging bed.

Lee   It's not her fault. She'da been quite content to keep it under wraps if you hadn't been seen.

Tania   Look, I haven't agreed to marry the bastard or nothing.

Wendy   He knows. I told him. Me and you.

Tania   Probably turned him on.

Wendy   He won't want you now.

Lee   I think I'm going to be sick.

Lee *runs off to the kitchen.* **Wendy** *tries to hug* **Tania**. **Tania** *shrugs her off.*

Wendy   You're a man. You do the sort of things men do. Fuck women up.

Enter **Nick**.

Nick   He's a pretty big guy. Pretty insistent. He's got a baseball bat down there. Wants a hundred and twenty quid.

Pause.

What should I do?

Pause.

Nick   Right, well, you can go and deal with him. (**Tania** *makes no attempt to move.*) Where's Lee?

Tania   Puking in the kitchen.

Pause.

Nick   She wasn't joking was she? (*Pause.*) Roy. Roy tried to tell me.

Nick *starts to kick the settee.*

Tania   Oi, watch it! Nick! Nick! Don't be a prize cunt!

Wendy   Don't say that word, Tania. You know it goes right through me.

Nick *looks at them. He starts to retch. He runs off to the kitchen.*

Tania   Christ, I said I'd ring me mum.

A fight breaks out in the kitchen, off. **Tania** *goes on the phone and dials a number.*

Wendy   What would she say if she knew what we'd been up to in the spare bedroom while she lay poorly?

Tania   Probably have a heart attack and die.

Wendy   Is my face a mess?

Tania   Shocking.

Wendy   I'd never hit you.

Tania   (*on phone*)   Hello? Hiya, Paul, what you doing there? No, I've been out all night. Lee's.

Lee *enters from the kitchen with sick down his front.* **Nick** *is behind him. They are holding onto each other in mid fight.* **Wendy** *tries to split them up.*

Wendy   What the fuck are you doing?

Lee   Tell him. Tell him I never knew.

Nick   Tania.

Wendy   He was in the dark, Nick, I swear.

Nick   I want to hear it from her.

Wendy   Get off him, you battering bastard.

Tania (*on phone*)   Okay. I'll be over as soon as I can. (*Puts the phone down.*)

Lee   Me face, don't mark me face!

Wendy   Nick! Jesus! Me knee! (*Falling.*)

Nick   Tell him. And her. I never hit you.

Tania   Never.

Wendy   But the bruises!

Tania   I'm a psychiatric nurse for fuck's sake. I get manhandled!

Nick   She says you told her.

Tania   Well, that's bollocks then, isn't it!

Pause. **Lee** *lets go of* **Nick**.

Nick   Tell me. Tell me he didn't know.

Tania   Course he didn't. D'you think he'da kept silent with you?

Nick *lets go of* **Lee**.

Lee (*to* **Wendy**)   Nick wouldn't hurt a fly.

Wendy   I just saw the bruising and . . . Tania? What's the matter with your mum?

Tania Oh, something and nothing. Had heart attack and died. Actually I better be going. Nick, you better run me to the hospital.

Wendy I've got my car.

Lee You've been drinking . . .

Tania I don't care who takes me just hurry up. (*Getting stuff together.*)

Nick No. I'll . . .

Wendy I can . . .

Lee Nick?

Wendy I've only had a glass of Bucks Fizz. Which hospital is it?

Tania They've taken her to the Royal Free.

Nick I'm covered in sick.

Tania Oh, come on, Wend, look sharpish.

Tania *and* **Wendy** *exit.* **Nick** *and* **Lee** *sit down side by side on the sofa.*

Nick I'm sorry, Lee. Are you all right?

Lee Yeah, I'm fine.

Nick No, come here. (*Looks at* **Lee**'s *face.*) Let's have a . . .

Lee (*shaking him off*) I'm fine.

Pause.

You moving in then?

Nick I don't want to put you out.

Lee If you were putting me out I wouldn't have offered!

Nick Sorry. Yeah, why not.

Lee Oh, Nick, I . . . I'm so sorry.

Nick Bet I can say sorry more times than you.

Lee Christ, Nick, don't you feel like hitting someone?

The ridiculousness of this strikes them both at the same time. They start giggling. The doorbell rings, three times.

Nick   Pizzas.

Lee   I'll talk to him. If words fail I'll call the police.

Nick   I can always do that. I've done four episodes of *The Bill*.

Lee *exits.* **Nick** *takes his shirt off. He rolls it into a ball and sticks it on the sofa beside him.* **Steph** *enters.*

Steph   They've been on.

Nick   Who?

Steph   Love City Groove. *Royaume Uni.*

Nick   Any good?

Steph   What do you really care?

Nick   Fuck all, I guess.

Steph   I don't like you.

Nick   It's no big deal. I'm used to rejection.

Steph   I don't like what you've done to our friendship. I don't like any of you any more. And if anyone's taking minutes let it just be said that I don't wholeheartedly approve. Anyway, Roy's just necked his second E and we are leaving. There's a bar in King's Cross which is showing the contest on a wide screen. Roy can dance his little tits off, I can watch the scoring. Leave you two to it. (**Nick** *raises a thumbs up and smiles.*) You probably think I'm stupid. Well, let's get one thing clear. I knew all along. You see, I can sniff trade at twenty paces. Just one thing, Nick. D'you feel guilty?

Pause.

Does he make you feel guilty?

He chucks **Nick** *the photo of Michael.* **Nick** *looks at it.*

Nick   He puts a smile on my face. Happy memories.

Steph   You can tell that boyfriend of yours I never wanna clap eyes on him again till the day I die.

Nick I'm sure he'll crack open the Dom Perignon.

Roy *enters.*

Roy Oh, here you all are!

Steph Get your slacks on, we're going.

Roy (*to the topless* **Nick**) Ah, haven't you got nice tits?

Steph Hypocritical tits, that's what he's got.

Roy Can I feel your chest?

Nick For you, dear boy, anything.

Roy *sits next to* **Nick** *and runs his hands over his chest.*

Roy Ooh, it feels lovely. You're dead straight-looking.

Steph If you chopped him in half he'd have QUEEN written through him like rock.

Roy Ah, you're lovely, you.

Nick Well, I think you're lovely too.

Roy D'you wanna come out and play?

Nick No.

Roy Ah. (*To* **Steph**.) Int he lovely?

Steph How can a slut be lovely?

Roy (*to* **Nick**) I love you.

Steph No you don't. (*To* **Nick**.) He's on drugs, ignore him. (*To* **Roy**.) I'm getting your slacks.

Steph *exits to kitchen.*

Roy I think he's jealous. He doesn't really mean it. I think he wishes he were you.

Enter **Lee**.

Lee I think we better call the police.

Nick Okey-dokey.

Roy We've got to go. Steph said. Sorry.

Nick *removes* **Roy's** *hands and finds the phone.*

Roy (*to* **Lee**)   I always fancy your fellas.

Lee   Roy, I'll speak to you about this tomorrow. When you're a bit more *compos mentis.*

Roy   Fab.

Steph *enters with* **Roy's** *jeans. He throws them at him.*

Steph   Get them slacks on I want out.

Lee   Actually I don't think it's a very good idea to go down there just yet.

Steph   Hurry up, Roy. (**Roy** *puts the jeans on.*)

Lee   There's a brick shithouse of a queer-basher on the doorstep wanting the money for twenty pizzas.

Steph   You'll try every trick in the book to get me to stay; won't you. Well tough, we're going and that's that. Roy?

Roy   I've got both legs in t'same hole.

Steph   No, dear, they're in different holes.

Roy   Are they? They feel dead close.

Steph (*to* **Lee**)   I blame you for this boy's dependence on drugs. Roy!!

Lee   Roy, don't go down there.

Nick (*on phone*)   Police please.

Steph (*to* **Nick**)   Where d'you think you are? Sun Hill?

Steph *exits.* **Lee** *grabs hold of* **Roy.**

Lee   Roy. You don't wanna get hurt, do you?

Roy   No.

Lee   No. Well just stay here a second.

Roy   Why?

Lee   Just sit down.

Roy   I wanna dance.

Lee   Well . . . dance then.

Roy   Tar.

Nick (*on phone*)   Yes, we're having a spot of bother with a pizza delivery man.

Roy *starts to dance.* **Lee** *looks to* **Nick**. *Suddenly a scream of agony from* **Steph** *downstairs.*

Blackout.

'Rock Bottom' by Lynsey de Paul and Mike Moran plays.

Act Three

Steph *is nursing a black eye on the couch with a bag of frozen peas.* **Roy** *sits nodding his head.* **Nick** *and* **Lee** *are drinking.* **Nick** *has put a top on from the clothes-horse.*

Steph Not a big fan of the police. Borderline brusque if you ask me. If you ever do *The Bill* again, Nick, tell 'em it aint true to life.

Roy You oright, Nick?

Nick Yeah.

Roy Great.

The doorbell goes. **Lee** *gets it. He hears who it is on the entryphone then presses the buzzer. Soon* **Wendy** *enters, out of breath.*

Nick How is she?

Wendy Remarkably composed. She's in the car. Actually, she's asking for you. Wants both of us to go back with her.

Nick Where?

Wendy Your place.

Nick Both of us?

Wendy She knows it's cheeky but. You'd be on the couch.

Nick Where would you be?

Wendy Not sure yet.

Nick If you were in bed with her . . .

Wendy Aha?

Nick Could I watch? (*Pause, then tuts to* **Lee**.) Tell her I don't mean that.

Lee He didn't mean that.

Wendy I could kill a drink.

Lee You're driving.

Wendy I'll stop off at an off-licence. (*To* **Nick**.) Coming?

Nick (*to* **Lee**) I will go.

A derisory grunt from **Steph**.

Wendy Me and Tania . . . well, you know that much. But these two aren't. (**Nick** *and* **Lee**.) Okay?

Steph Losing you as a friend's no sad loss.

Wendy Well, let's face it, Steph, there was never anything to lose.

Roy Can you give us a lift to King's Cross?

Wendy Sure.

Lee Steph?

Steph *shakes his head*.

Wendy Bye then.

Lee Take a bottle of wine.

Wendy Right. Can I take two?

Lee Take the lot if you want.

Roy What's meat got? It's got the lot!

Wendy *goes to kitchen*.

Lee (*to* **Nick**) You gonna be all right?

Nick I'll bring a car-load of stuff over tomorrow.

Lee Phone me if you need to talk.

Nick I'll hang onto this feeling. I might get to play a jilted lover one day. Hey, it's research.

Wendy *returns with two bottles of wine*.

Wendy Roy?

Roy Yeah.

Wendy Nick?

Nick Down in a sec.

Wendy (*to* **Lee**)   Bye.

Lee   Let me know the details of the funeral.

Wendy   Will do. Farewell, Steph.

Steph   I hope you crash and the pins in your knee get smashed.

Wendy *goes.* **Roy** *goes to follow.*

Roy   See you.

Lee   Ring you tomorrow, yeah?

Roy *goes.* **Nick** *goes over to* **Lee** *and hugs him. He starts to cry.*

Lee   Hey. Hey. Be strong.

Nick   I don't want to go. Make me stay.

Lee   Come on.

Nick   I'll see you tomorrow then, yeah?

Lee   Yeah, darling.

Nick *nods. He takes a deep breath then goes.* **Steph** *is left alone with* **Lee**. **Lee** *pours two brandies.*

Steph   Well, let's hope Billy gets his comeuppance. I should sue that pizza pillock.

Lee   Cheers. (*Hands him a brandy.*)

They clink glasses. **Lee** *puts his Eurovision medley tape back on. It takes a while for the next tune to start.*

Steph   Think I'll stop in and watch it on me own next year.

Lee   Yeah.

The song comes on. It's 'Love Enough for Two' by Prima Donna.

Steph   1980?

Lee   Yeah.

Steph   Sally Ann Triplett went on to be a member of Bardo in eighty-two. Still didn't win. You've got to admit. It has gone off. There's no novelty value any more. No dance routines. No skirt-ripping. Dunno when I last heard a boom bang-a-bang or ding

ding-a-dong. It's asking for trouble taking Euro into the twenty-first century. I want it to be like it used to be.

Lee   I used to wonder if being gay was genetical. Something I'd got from my real parents. Or was it the way you were brought up, something I'd got from my adoptive parents. I finally decided it was just something I got from myself. It was just me. Something special. (*Beat.*) It still hasn't sunk in.

Steph   Norman's still through there with Radio Two on. Fabulous bedstead incidentally. Very handy for the old handcuffs. Did you see that policeman's handcuffs? A marvellous feat of metalwork.

Lee   Why don't you go in and finish Norman off?

Steph   How can a master be bruised?

Pause.

Steph   Where's the best place to get a cab round here?

Lee   Kentish Town Road.

Steph   Right.

He looks in the mirror. He inspects his eye.

If this comes up I'm not gonna get trade for months, am I?

Lee   About time you had a rest.

Steph   I hate Billy.

Lee   I'll see him in court.

Steph   Oh, before I go. Meant to show you this earlier. (*Gets photo out of his bumbag.*) Recognise her?

Lee (*studying photo*)   She was in the New Seekers. Who's the little boy? It's not you!

Steph   Bumped into her in a hotel in Scotland. Holiday. Eve Graham. She was ever so nice. Little poodle. I said, 'Shame you didn't win.' I must have been all of about eight. She said, 'It was rigged.' 'Beg, Steal or Borrow'. 1972.

Lee   She's beautiful looking.

Steph She had it all, didn't she? It's all ballads and techno now.

Steph *puts the photo away.*

Lee See you then.

Steph (*knocks back his drink*)   Verged a tad on the prattish side, haven't I, m'darling?

Lee What's new?

Steph So long then.

Lee Bye, Steph.

Steph Billy'd be sick if he knew you'd seen that. (*Taps bumbag.*)

Steph *goes.* **Lee** *starts tidying up the debris. He switches the tape off and rewinds it. Suddenly* **Norman** *shouts through from the bedroom.*

Norman (*off*)   Norway! Norway have won! The bastards! I don't fucking believe it!

The tape comes on. It is 'Ding-A-Dong' by Teach-In.

Some soft get on a violona! There's no words! It's not even a song it's just a tune! (*Beat.*) My wrists are killing!

Lee *goes to his chest of drawers. He gets a huge whip out. He runs his hands over it.*

Norman (*off*)   Norway! Norway have won! It's not even a fucking song!!

Lee (*to himself, extremely angry*)   Oh, have they now?!

He brandishes the whip then whips the back of the settee. He looks to the hall door that leads to the bedroom. He looks at the whip. He heads off for the bedroom and shuts the door behind him. The lights fade and the music gets louder.

Rupert Street
Lonely Hearts Club

Rupert Street Lonely Hearts Club was first produced by English Touring Theatre and Contact Theatre Company. It opened at the Contact Theatre, Manchester, on 27 September 1995 prior to a run at the Donmar Warehouse, London, with the following cast:

Shaun	Scot Williams
Marti	Tom Higgins
George	Lorraine Brunning
Clarine	Elizabeth Berrington
Dean	James Bowers

Directed by John Burgess
Designed by Jackie Brooks
Lighting by Gerry Jenkinson

With thanks to Angela Clarke, Karl Draper, Suzanne Hitchmough, Morgan Jones and Andy Serkis for the first draft reading at the Royal National Theatre Studio.

The play subsequently transferred to the Criterion Theatre with one cast change;

George   Wendy Nottingham

Characters

Shaun, *twenty-three, a pretty, straight lad from Liverpool.*
Marti, *thirty-three, his louder, camper, elder brother.*
George, *lives downstairs to Shaun. She is in her late twenties and from Kent.*
Clarine, *twenty-eight, quite portly. She has a repertoire of different personalities, and although she is from Kidderminster, she speaks usually in either a London or a Rochdale accent. Lives upstairs to Shaun.*
Dean, *twenty-six, a friend of Marti's. Broad London accent.*

Setting

The play is set in Shaun's bedsit, east London, in the spring of 1995.

There are two doors, one the main door leading to the landing, the other leads to the kitchen. There is a big sash window stage left with a rafia blind over it. There is a three-quarter bed stage right, and centre stage a settee with stretch covering and matching chairs. A coffee-table sits between the three. There is a gas fire, plants, a phone, standard lamps and a chest of drawers. On the wall are various posters, and a mirror. The feel is youthful, slightly bohemian and occasionally ethnic. Front of stage there is a telly and video and a music centre.

Note
An oblique/stroke within a speech serves as the cue for the next speaker to overlap with the first.

Act One

Scene One

*In the dark before the lights come up, the opening of Jam and Spoon's 'Right In The Night' plays loudly. As the music fades, the lights come up gradually on **Marti** and **Shaun**, pissed in the middle of the afternoon. **Shaun** is in the right armchair, **Marti** on the couch. There are bottles of wine on the coffee-table, finished and unfinished, a bottle of Jack Daniels and they each have a glass. **Marti** and **Shaun** are reciting the cheque scene from* Mildred Pierce, *with **Shaun** playing Mildred (Joan Crawford) and **Marti** playing Veda (Anne Blyth). They start speaking before or as soon as the lights start to come up, and the music fades underneath their voices. **Marti** is wearing PVC trousers, and a big baggy mohair jumper. Importantly, his hair is shaved to a number two all over. (M) indicates an impersonation of Mildred, (V) an impersonation of Veda. Sitting in the left armchair, nursing a big bottle of water is **George**, who is not drunk, but a bit bewildered by their venomous display.*

Shaun (*M*) I've never denied you anything. Anything that money could buy I've given you. But that wasn't enough, was it? All right, Veda, from now on things are going to be different.

Marti (*V*) I'll say they're going to be different. Why d'you think I went to all this trouble? Are you sure you want to know?

Shaun (*M*) Yes.

Marti (*V*) Then I'll tell you. With this money I can get away from you.

Shaun (*M*) Veda!

Marti (*V*) From you and your . . .

Shaun (*prompting him*) . . . chickens . . .

Marti (*V*) Chickens and your pies and your kitchens! And everything that smells of grease. You think just because you made a little money . . .

Shaun You've skipped a bit!

Marti   Shut up. (*V*) . . . you can get a new hairdo and some expensive clothes and turn yourself into a lady.

George   This is amazing.

Marti (*V*)   But you can't, because you'll never be anything but a common frump whose father lived above a grocery store and whose mother took in washing.

Shaun (*M*)   Veda! Give me that cheque!

Marti (*himself*)   I haven't finished yet!

Shaun (*M*)   I said give it to me!

Marti (*himself*)   I haven't . . .

Shaun (*M*)   Get out, Veda.

Marti (*himself*)   I haven't slapped you.

Shaun (*M*)   Get out before I throw you out. Get out before I kill you.

Small Pause.

George   Wow, that's like, pretty emotive stuff.

Marti   It's also completely wrong. It's (*M*) 'Get out, Veda. Get your things out of this house right now before I throw them into the street and you with them. Get out before I kill you.' (*Himself.*) actually.

Shaun   Fuck off, Marti.

Marti (*imitates him*)   Fuck off, Marti.

Marti *and* **Shaun** *giggle. The last bicker reminds* **Shaun** *of something and he launches straight into a scene from* Whatever Happened to Baby Jane? *He's playing Blanche (Joan Crawford).* **Marti** *then plays Jane (Bette Davis).*

Shaun (*B*)   Oh Jane I'm sorry. I didn't mean to ring for my breakfast. I was just wondering who all those people were at the back door.

Marti (*J*)   It wasn't anything.

George   Oh, I've seen this one.

Marti (*J*)   Just that nosy Mrs Bates going on about your picture last night.

Shaun (*B*)   Oh, really? Did she like it?

Marti (*J*)   Oh, really? Did she like it? She liked it.

The lads laugh.

George   I have. I've seen that with Malcolm.

Shaun (*à la Bette Davis*)   Enjoying yourself?!

Marti   Malcolm?

George   Isn't that the thing about the two feuding sisters, one of whom's a wheelchair/user?

Marti   Wheelchair-bound./yeah.

George   Malcolm loved that/flick.

Marti   Joan Crawford's confined to a wheelchair/in it.

George   Oh, now come on, Marti, wheelchairs are liberating, not confining.

Shaun   Sort yer nouns out,/Mart.

George   What was that movie called? Malcolm adored/it.

Marti   Who the fuck's Malcolm?

Shaun (*to* **George**)   *Whatever Happened to Baby Jane?*

Marti   She's here and she's thirsty. (*Helps himself to another drink.*)

George   Malcolm's my ex.

Shaun   He dumped her.

Marti (*raising his glass*)   To Malcolm. A man with taste. Oh, but it's so passé that movie now. Everyone's got their hands on it. But only us two know the cheque scene from *Mildred Pierce*. I weaned him on it, didn't I?

George (*getting up*)   You'll have to forgive me. I'm having terrible cystitis.

Shaun (*screams*)   Get out! Get out before I throw you out! Get out before I kill you!!

George   Right.

George *exits awkwardly.*

Marti   God, how big's her bladder?

Shaun   You heard what she said.

Marti   Christ, I've never known anyone go the loo as much as her.

Shaun   You don't know the first thing about the female anatomy, do you.

Marti   I know this much. Your little friend's near bored the slingbacks off me.

Shaun   Her heart's in the right place.

Marti   Her mouth isn't, she talks shite.

Shaun   She's Juliet's friend really.

Marti   Oh, so you can't stick her.

Shaun   She lives downstairs. She's all right.

Marti   Your girlfriend's got dodgy taste in mates, that's all I can say. Who else does she knock about with? Eva Braun?

Shaun   It was you that asked her in! She only came round to pick up a knitting pattern.

Marti   What's she trying to knit herself? A sense of humour?

Shaun   She's nice enough.

Marti   She's a cunt.

Shaun   Didn't you know that word's offensive in polite company?

Marti   Polite company? Where d'you think you are? The Ritz? God, that girlfriend of yours has really got to you, hasn't she.

Shaun   She's got a name.

Marti I remember a time when every single one of your sentences was prefixed by the word fucking. Now look at you. Cast adrift in a sea of political correctness. This is offensive. That's offensive. I tell you what *is* offensive. Your hair's offensive.

Shaun There's nothing wrong with my hair.

Marti What d'you wash it with? Lard?

Shaun Ah, you're just on one now.

Marti And with every right. God knows what your customers must think. You're hardly a walking advertisement for hairdressing. Must be like getting your eyes tested by a blind man. Or is that offensive? Ah, who gives a fuck.

Shaun You, for some reason.

Marti I forked out five hundred quid for that van. If you're gonna go all camp on me and run a mobile hairdressers then I'm entitled to give a fuck. Get it washed! (*Slaps him over the head.*) If you mess this business up while Juliet's away.

Shaun I love getting pissed with you. You just stand there ragging me ...

Marti You deserve it.

Shaun ... and telling me things I already know like I haven't washed my hair.

Marti I have a degree in ragging. A double degree with campery. Don't knock it, it's a lethal combination.

Shaun There's no such thing as a double degree. It's joint honours.

Marti Oh, you think you know it all coz you've got your City and Guilds in hairdressing and you've done a bit of a business course at night school. (*Joan Crawford.*) Well, you don't, and you never will!

Shaun You can't stay here all day, you know.

Pause.

Shaun I'm cutting someone's hair at six.

Marti   God, you really live life in the fast lane, don't you.

Shaun   Oh, I'm sorry, I don't sell stretch covers./I can't be . . .

Marti   There's nothing wrong with selling stretch covers.

Shaun   There is if you're a twat.

Marti   Fine. If you don't like my stretch covers then you don't have to have them disgracing your sumptuous first-floor apartment.

Marti *starts clawing at the cover on the couch to get it off.*

Shaun   Oh, you always have to get the last word.

Marti   No no, it's quite all right.

Shaun   Marti!

Marti   I can take a hint.

Shaun   Oh, come on, Marti . . . Marti! Marti!!

Shaun *scrambles over and wrestles with* **Marti** *over the stretch cover.* **Shaun** *trying to get the cover back on,* **Marti** *trying to get it off.*

Marti   No. If you don't want it . . .

Shaun   I do.

Marti   You've just . . .

Shaun   Put it . . .

Marti   Eh?

Shaun   Just leave it on!

Marti   All right, all right!

Shaun   Sit down.

Marti   Okay. Jesus. What's got into you?

Shaun   Nothing.

Marti   Eh?

Shaun   Sit down, Marti.

Pause. **Marti** *sits down.* **Shaun** *stays standing behind the couch, holding onto it for support.*

Marti   What's up? Cat got your tongue?

Small pause.

Marti   Well, here's a clue then. 'I'm sorry I insulted your job.'

Shaun   I'm sorry I . . .

Shaun *goes and sits on the bed, head in his hands fighting tears.*

Marti   Oh, Christ. Young love! (*Tuts.*) If you're looking for sympathy you'll find it in the dictionary between shit and syphilis. (*Tuts.*) D'you think she's crying in Barbados?

Shaun   Of course she's crying. She's burying her grandad.

Marti   She hardly knew him.

Shaun   He's still her grandad.

Marti   She was brought up over here.

Shaun   You're so racist.

Marti   Am I fuck racist. I know Juliet, she'll be a tower of strength to people she hasn't even met. She'll be a shoulder to cry on. She certainly won't be sitting in a messy flat feeling sorry for herself.

Shaun   I told her I wouldn't look at another woman while she was away.

Marti   So?

Shaun   The first woman I meet and I'm talking to her.

Marti   George? But she's a mate of Juliet's.

Shaun   When I went the chippy.

Marti   Oh, so you can't talk to someone in the chippy now? How else are you supposed to order? Sign language?

Shaun   No. When I come back, coming up the stairs. This new bird's moved in upstairs. We chatted like. She's coming later. I'm gonna do her hair.

Marti   Oh, aye? On the make, is she?

Shaun   I hope not. She's a dog.

Marti   Well, what you worried about then? God, you get yourself into some states. You never used to be like this.

Shaun   I can't help it, Mart.

Marti   It's all right, lad.

Shaun   Have you ever felt like this?

Marti   Ooh, well . . .

Shaun   No funny voices.

Marti   Course I have, doll. Who hasn't? But . . . this is your first time. Oh, I know you've notched 'em all up on your bedpost, but even I can see it's different with Juliet.

Shaun   It is, man, it is.

Marti   It's just . . .

Shaun   What?

Marti   You've got to be in control of your feelings. Don't relinquish it to some other twat. Oh, I'm a bitter old queen, I know, but I've had a lot o' knocks, haven't I? Been let down more times than a lilo. When you get to my age you don't expect anything. Then what you do get is a bonus.

Shaun   I told her I wouldn't have chips.

Marti   Your cooker's on the blink. We've all got to eat.

Shaun   I tried sticking me fingers down me throat after I'd had them, like she used to, but it only brought up bile. (*He holds up a stained pillow.*)

Marti   Oh, you soft get. Come here. (*Goes and sits on the bed with him and hugs him.*) I should be slapping you really. You're just pissed.

Shaun   I'm not.

Marti   Sometimes being a bit down, Shaun, it's just God's way of showing yeh you're human.

Shaun   Who you being now? Mrs Overall?

Marti   I'm being serious. D'you feel really low?

Shaun (*shrugs*)   I just miss her.

Marti   I mean, you don't feel like doing anything daft, do yeh?

Shaun   Like what?

Marti   I dunno.

Shaun   Like killing meself?

Marti   No, I didn't mean/that.

Shaun   Yes you/did.

Marti   Well, it's best to check. I mean, it's happened before in the family.

Shaun   Thanks a lot, Mart.

Marti   I didn't think you did, you know.

Shaun   No?

Marti   It's actually er . . . it's actually a counselling technique. The Samaritans are trained to say that in every call.

Shaun   Are they?

Marti   Yeah. Not that . . . I've ever rung them or anything. Seen it on . . . on a documentary or something.

Shaun   I have.

Marti   What?

Shaun   Rung them.

Marti   Have yer? (**Shaun** *nods*.) So have I. See, we're all daft, aren't we.

Shaun   What did you ring 'em for?

Marti   Oh, this was years back. I got crabs and didn't know what to do.

Shaun   Did they tell you?

Marti   Oh, yeah. They even rang back a few days later to check they'd gone. When did you ring?

Shaun   Last night.

Marti   You shoulda rung me.

Shaun   You were out.

Marti   Well . . . d'you feel like going back to Liverpool?

Shaun   Gotta look after the business.

Marti   You could take a few days off surely.

Shaun   I'll be all right.

Marti   It might do you good to get back home.

Shaun   I am home.

George *enters. She impersonates Maggie Smith in* The Prime of Miss Jean Brodie.

George (*Scottish*)   I am a teacher. First, last and always. And you will never sack me. And I will never resign. (*Beat. Herself.*) Jean Brodie.

Marti   Oh, we're not playing that one any more. *He's* cutting someone's hair.

George   Really?

George *goes and sits down.* **Shaun** *gets up and starts walking around.*

Shaun   Not at this precise moment in time.

Marti   Oh, forgive me.

Shaun   Six o'clock.

Marti   Oh, six o'clock. He's cutting someone's hair at six o'clock.

Shaun   It's a French pleat actually.

George   Right.

Shaun   So in fact there's no cutting involved.

Marti   God, I was way off the mark there then.

George   Who's?

Shaun   You what?

George   Who's hair are you cutting?

Marti   He's just told you he's not cutting anybody's hair!

Shaun   This new bird's moved in upstairs.

George   Oh, Zoë.

Shaun   Nah ...

George (*to* **Marti**)   Zoë's an actress. From the television.

Shaun   Nah, I don't think ...

George   Not that that impresses me, I prefer a good book. But I bumped into her by the umbrella stand and she certainly seemed okay to goodish I'd say. And actors often get involved in causes, don't they?

Shaun   No, the girl that's moved in up there's a singer.

George   I specifically recall her saying she was an actress.

Shaun   And her name's not Zoë.

Marti   Maybe you've got *two* people living upstairs. My, this is an interesting conversation.

George   We've got artists on top of us/Shaun.

Shaun (*to* **Marti**)   Well, why don't you say something interesting then.

Marti   I only say interesting things in interesting company.

George   Malcolm was pretty interesting. I used to say to him, 'Malcolm you are so interesting.' He just used to laugh.

Pause. **George** *notices all is not well.* **Shaun** *wipes his eyes and sits back in the armchair again.* **Marti** *gets a hanky out of his pocket and passes it to* **Shaun**.

Marti   Blow your nose. (*Cockney.*) The poor boy's missing his bitch.

Shaun   Don't be vile.

George   Dear Shaun, now you know how the other half lives. When Malcolm and I, as was, kinda you know, split up, I was a wreck.

Shaun (*to* **George**)   We haven't split up.

George   Bedtime was the big killer. What's the point of a double bed when you're all on your own? Why have a ratio of four pillows to one head? That's why I got rid of the double bed and got the single futon. They're so practical. And it makes a facking good easy-chair for the daytime. You can really experiment with it.

Shaun   I've been out wit loads o' girls before. Mad ones from Liverpool. Moved down here wit one o' them. Suppose I've never been wit no one as brainy as Juliet before.

Marti   That girl from your Saturday job was brainy.

Shaun   But Juliet blew me mind.

Marti   She'd got fourteen on *Screen Test*.

Shaun   I suppose I just miss having someone to bounce ideas off really.

George   Hey, Shaun. I make a great intellectual trampoline.

Marti   What was her name?

Shaun   I forget.

George   Honestly, while Juliet's away... well ...

Marti   Tracey?

George   I'm only downstairs.

Shaun (*to* **Marti**)   No.

George   My door is always ajar.

Marti   She had red hair.

Shaun   Carmen.

George   There's always an extra vegeburger in my fridge of life for that unexpected pal.

Marti   She'd been on *Screen Test*. She showed us the video.

George   It's only fair. Juliet was a tower of strength to me when Malcolm and I, as was.

Shaun   It was Carmen.

Marti Was it? Who's Tracey?

Shaun Tracey worked in the pub.

Marti Did she?

Shaun Yes.

Marti Hadn't she been on *Screen Test*?

Shaun *Blockbusters*.

Marti That's it. That's who I meant. See? You always got brainy girlfriends.

Shaun Yeah but. Juliet's different. Brainy in a different way. Like ... Like ...

Marti The sex is better.

Shaun Yeah. No.

George Like you're in love. Right?

Shaun Nothing wrong with that, is there?

George It's ... the tops. Isn't it?

Marti (*to* **George**) Did you love him? Thingy?

Shaun Malcolm.

George Sure thing.

Marti Ah.

Shaun Are yer over it now?

George Oh, yes.

Marti Oh, good.

George I still ring him. Put on a silly voice. Pretend it's a wrong number. But that's just boredom really. Juliet was so good to me then, Marti, you know? She was fucking ... right there. Yeah? Now that's the sign of a true friend, don't you think?

Marti Fair play to her, she's a brick.

George (*to* **Shaun**) And if I could repay the compliment.

Shaun   But me and Juliet aren't splitting up. She's only gone for four weeks.

Marti   Yeah, well, George can keep an eye on yeh, Shaun. Can't you, George? Infidelity's in the genes in our/family.

Shaun   It's not in mine!

Marti   You'll keep an eye on him, won't you, George?

Shaun   I don't need looking after.

George   Actually, Shaun, I'm going out tonight if you fancy joining/me?

Marti   Where you/going?

Shaun   I don't think/so.

George   Oh, a departmental knees-up at a wine bar in Bow. The other English teachers have been haranging me to go for absolutely days.

Shaun   I'll stay in I think.

George   It won't be a late night. I'm going on a demo tomorrow in Welling so I'll have an early start. Shut the BNP. Hey, if you fancy coming to that.

Shaun   Well . . .

George   It's an important cause.

Shaun   I know it's an important cause.

George   I'm sure Juliet would jump at the chance/were she here.

Shaun   I know. It's just Marti's coming back here in the morning to chill out so I best stay in.

George   Oh. Going anywhere nice, Marti?

Marti   Just a fabulous bijou hole where they do a nice line in group sex in the bogatry.

Shaun   I hope you're careful.

Marti   God, I hope I am an' all. I can never remember. I'm that much off me face.

George   What . . . you actually have sex and stuff in those places?

Marti   Well, I don't pay an eight pound fifty entrance fee to do the cheque scene from *Mildred Pierce*.

Shaun   It's like a dark room.

Marti   We make it dark. First week we takes the lightbulb out and got stuck in. Second week they'd put a cage across the top o' the bogs so we couldn't reach the lightbulb. So this tranny takes her shoe off and jams the stiletto heel through the cage and smashes the bulb. Third week they'd put a perspex sheet across so the tranny gets a can o' black spray-paint out of her clutchbag and sprays it black. Instant darkness. Isn't she marvellous, George?

George   Cool.

Marti   I love that tranny. I'm meeting her there tonight.

Shaun   Have yer ever done it with her? Him?

Marti   Her. No. Sisters.

Shaun   What do they call her?

Marti   Fifi. Fifi Trixabelle La Bouche. Oh, Shaun, why don't you come out with us tonight? Ah, it's ages since we went out together, on our own.

Shaun   We wouldn't be on our own. Fifi Trixabelle My Hoop's gonna be there.

Marti   I've got six Es on me.

Shaun   I'm best off staying in.

Marti   Juliet'd love you going to a gay club. No temptation.

Shaun   Maybe another night.

Marti   Yeah?

Shaun   Yes.

George *gets up to go.*

Marti   Jesus, are you going the loo again?

George Sadly not. I promised myself some meditation before going out tonight so. Look, please don't think me rude rushing off like this but . . . if you do find that knitting pattern I lent Juliet . . . do come on down and knock on wood, so to speak. It's for a Javanese-style skull-cap. It's got a picture of a woman on the front, modelling one. A Javanese woman actually. It's just that I'm going to knit some as end-of-term presents for my kids.

Shaun Is it end of term soon?

George No, but there are thirty kids in my class so I want to get cracking on them a.s.a.p. Lovely to meet you, Marti.

Marti And you. A rare/honour.

George And I really appreciate the hospitality. I must repay the compliment sometime. Wednesday?

Shaun Er . . .

George That's my quietest night marking-wise. (*To* **Marti**.) I'm doing *Romeo and Juliet* with my Year Tens at the moment and we're really beginning to crack it.

Marti How clever of you.

George Wednesday then. I've got this fabulous new recipe. With aubergines. Bye.

Shaun See you/George.

Marti Trar,/doll.

George Miss you already!

George *exits.* **Shaun** *pours himself another drink.* **Marti** *gets up and goes around the room looking for something.*

Marti Good shuttance.

Shaun You can choose your girlfriend, but you can't choose who lives downstairs to you.

Marti You don't know anyone else.

Shaun I know loads o' people.

Marti *has found* **Shaun**'s *hair clippers.*

Marti Just coz you've cut their hair doesn't mean you've tested the bonds of friendship. (*Waggling the clippers in the air.*) Mow me lawn for me. I wanna look gorgeous tonight.

Shaun Take your jumper off. I've got loads o' mates.

Marti Name one.

Shaun (*tuts*) Connor.

Marti Now I don't want you laughing.

Shaun *gets a towel off the back of the door.* **Marti** *peels off his jumper. He's wearing a bondage harness.*

Shaun I'm past caring, me.

Marti *sits on the couch.* **Shaun** *plugs the clippers in and puts the towel round* **Marti**'s *shoulders. He then proceeds to go over his hair with a number two on the clippers.*

Marti Name another.

Shaun You.

Marti I'm your brother.

Shaun Laurence.

Marti Another. See? You can't.

Shaun I can.

Marti Well, go on then.

Shaun All Juliet's mates. You don't know them.

Marti When was the last time you seen Connor?

Shaun Couple o' weeks back.

Marti Laurence?

Shaun I dunno.

Marti Loner! It's a good job you've got me. It's people like you end up as serial killers.

Shaun Oh, shut up.

Marti I bet these walls are heaving with corpses.

Shaun   Only women and children. I'm very choosy about who I kill.

Marti   And then when you do let them in they're a waste of space.

Shaun   You being the prime example.

Marti   The prime example being that gang of skallies back home.

Shaun   There's nothing wrong with skallies.

Marti   Yes, but that particular bunch of skallies were a gang of twats.

Shaun   That was years/ago.

Marti   And you were one of/them.

Shaun   I don't see them any more.

Marti   You seen Jedda the last/time you were back.

Shaun   Jedda's all right really.

Marti   Tell that to his girlfriend.

Shaun   He doesn't see her any more.

Marti   She couldn't see him anyway with two black eyes. I'm surprised she could even find the baby half the time.

Shaun   Well, what about that gang of screaming queens you always had round the house?

Marti   They loved you.

Shaun   Me ma's wig went missing a few too many times for my liking.

Marti   At least they didn't go round beating people up coz they were bored.

Shaun   No, they just bitched people to death.

Marti   You're the one who ended up as a hairdresser, dear.

Shaun   You're never satisfied, are you?

Marti   (*sarcastic*)   No.

Shaun   Would you be happier me doing something more macho?

Marti   You? You're camper than a big van! Why d'you think the queens loved you so much? Maybe you haven't got a woman coming round for a French pleat. Maybe it's a fella. Oh, who is it? Is it someone I know? Is it someone near to me?

Shaun   Yes. It's Ricky.

Small pause. **Shaun** *stops clipping.*

Oh, I'm sorry, Marti, it just slipped out. Oh/I am sorry.

Marti   That was a bit below the . . .

Shaun   It's just . . .

Marti   Okay, you're sorry. Drop it.

Pause.

Shaun   Come here. It's not even.

Marti   (*looking in mirror*)   It's fine. It's fine.

Shaun   I'll just . . .

Marti   No.

There is a knock at the door. **Marti** *looks at his watch.*

Marti   It's six.

Shaun   Shit. (*To door.*) Hang on! (*Passes* **Marti** *his jumper.*) Put that on.

Marti   Oh, where's your sense of adventure?

Shaun   Barbados. Put it on, Mart.

Marti   Oh, you're determined to make me boring, you. Well, I refuse. I do. I simply refuse.

Shaun   Butch up or shut up, now which is it to be?

Another knock at the door.

Marti   I love a man who orders me about.

*Slowly **Marti** puts the jumper back on as **Shaun** opens the door to **Clarine**. She is dressed in a neon-blue seventies evening-dress and carries a guitar on a rainbow strap. She is speaking with a light, breathy, London accent.*

Clarine   Oright, darlin'? (*Laughs.*)

Shaun   Hiya, come in.

Clarine (*entering room, to* **Marti**)   Hiya.

Marti   Hiya. Fabulous frock!

Shaun   This is me brother Marti.

Clarine   Oh! Keep it in the family, yeah? Hello, babes, nice to meet you.

Shaun   This is . . .

Clarine   Clarine.

Marti   Like what they put in the swimming baths?

Shaun   D'you want a drink, Clarine?

Clarine   You're okay, darlin', don't wanna put you to any trouble.

Shaun   Ah, it's no trouble.

Clarine   Oh, okay then, a large one o' them'll do me fine thanks, love. Cor, got it nice in here, aint ya?

Marti (*passing her a Jack Daniels*)   Here you go, doll.

Clarine   Cheeky.

Shaun   Take a seat. French pleat.

Clarine (*giggles, sitting*)   You're a poet and you don't know. (*Remembers it's supposed to rhyme.*) It.

Marti   Can I have a look at your guitar, Clarine?

Clarine   Yeah, babes, you have a look at that, go on, you have a little play on that. Now . . .

Marti *takes the guitar from her. She is sitting on the couch.* **Shaun** *gets some Kirby grips out of a bag and starts messing with her hair, standing behind the sofa.*

Marti   When did you move in, Clarine?

Clarine   Oh, about three years ago now. I mean, days. I'm from Crouch End. Funny little place, init?

Shaun   Have you met George downstairs?

Clarine   No.

Shaun   Oh, she must've met your flatmate then.

Clarine   I haven't got a flatmate, darlin'. I'm on me own.

Marti   Have you seen *Mildred Pierce*?

Clarine   No.

Shaun   I wonder who she met then?

Clarine   I haven't met anybody apart from you, love. Maybe it was my mate who helped me move in. Maybe Mildred met her. She'll talk to anyone. It'll be her downfall.

Shaun   What's her name?

Clarine   Best Mate. (*Laughs.*)

Marti   I always wanted guitar lessons as a kid. Didn't I, Shaun? (**Shaun** *shrugs.*) Well, I did. But we were a bit strapped for cash in our family. I had piano lessons, for a while. Paid for them with me own pocket money. But the problem was, we didn't have a piano. So I used to have lessons on the table. Miss Burke, that was the piano teacher, she'd come round every Wednesday and draw the keys on the table in chalk and then we'd get cracking. I can still play 'Für Elise' even now. But after a certain stage she said it was pointless us carrying on. And me mother refused to buy us one. I mean, there was six kids in our family and they are pretty expensive, aren't they?

Clarine   Kids?

Marti   Pianos. I cried when she left the last time. Didn't I, Shaun?

Shaun   I wasn't born, was I?

Marti   Where d'you get it?

Clarine   The guitar? Oh, Jesus give me that. Yeah, wann'alf pleased.

Marti   Jesus?

Clarine   Jesus Christ. He's my best mate.

Marti   Kind of him, wasn't it? Generous.

Clarine   Well, when I say he give it me, he didn't actually give it me, he like, led me to it, if you like. I mean there I was groping around in the darkness for like, some sort of meaning to me life and a couple o' prayers later I'm in Hank's Music Store in Crouch End.

Marti   You're a Christian?

Clarine   I'm sorry but, I just love Jesus! (*Laughs.*)

Marti   So what, d'you play choruses on it?

Clarine   I only wish I could. See the only thing I can play is 'House of the Rising Sun'. But what I really wanna sing is 'Amazing Grace How Sweet the Sound'. I mean, I have prayed about, you know, acquiring the gift of playing by ear but. As of yet, no result. So, I have to make do with singing the words of 'Amazing Grace' to the tune of 'The House of the Rising Sun'.

Small pause.

And that's my act. Clarine Manger. Jesus was born in me! (*Laughs.*)

Marti   What, you just do the one number?

Clarine   And lead the people in prayer obviously. You've gotta have as many strings to your bow in the converting game. I'm down at the Kilburn Working Men's Club tonight. It's just my way of . . . spreading it about.

Shaun   Your hair's dead thick. This is gonna take ages.

Clarine   Oh, well. Must be a sign.

Small pause.

Marti. Can I just say, as a Christian, I feel it's right sad you
missed out on the gift of music. And that you were skint to your
last threepenny bit. And that your old girl couldn't summons up
enough love to buy you even a second-hand joanna. And well,
I'd like to take this opportunity to share with you both my gift.
And my joy, at having the Christ-child within me. By singin'.

Marti *hands her back the guitar quite guardedly.*

Clarine   No prizes for guessing the song though. D'you know
what I mean?

She strums a very long introduction of two chords.

Clarine   Usually I'd let the spirit move me and I'd be led in
some sort of choreographic format. But as I'm sitting down, I'll
skip that bit.

She continues with her intro. **Shaun** *is fixing her hair. Just as* **Marti**
*loses interest she begins to sing. She has a cookie, bar-room voice. She sings to
the tune of 'House of the Rising Sun'.*

Clarine (*sings*) Amazing Grace
                How sweet the sound
                That saved a wretch like me.
                I once was lost
                But now am found.
                Was blind but now can see.

*After a verse the lights fade. An instrumental version of 'House of the
Rising Sun' leads into the next scene.*

Scene Two

The next morning. **Shaun** *is in bed. The key goes in the door.* **Marti**
enters with coat and hat on accompanied by **Dean**. **Dean** *is dressed up as
Fifi Trixabelle La Bouche, glamorous sex kitten. His feminine get-up is
convincing, but he has the voice of a navvie. He carries with him a sports bag
and a lollipop-shaped Anti-Nazi League placard.*

Marti   Should I fly the kettle on?

Dean   Has he got any sounds?

Marti *exits to kitchen.* **Dean** *goes over to the stereo and switches it on.*
Morrissey is playing. **Shaun** *wakes up.*

Shaun   Aright?

Dean   Oright? You aint got nothing better than this, have you?

Shaun   What?

Dean   I'm Dean.

Shaun   Aright.

Dean   You Marti's brother?

Shaun   Yeah.

Dean   Thought you was. You aint got anything with a better
beat?

Marti *comes back in.*

Marti   Ah, sorry, doll, did we's wake yer?

Shaun   Yeah.

Dean   Ah, man, did we wake you up?

Shaun   Yeah.

Dean   Go back to sleep.

Marti   Shaun. Have you got anything else bar herbal tea bags?

Shaun   No.

Dean (*to* **Marti**)   Ah, man, listen to his accent. That accent is
like, like literature. Books. The voice and that. Ah, man.

Marti   Isn't Fifi marvellous, Shaun?

Dean   Party on, d'you know what I mean?

Shaun   I'm gonna try and kip.

Marti   Ignore us, Shaun. We'll be quiet as church mice. Deaf
and dumb church mice. In a very quiet church. In a very quiet
town.

Dean   Eastbourne.

Shaun *lies back down and pulls the pillow over his head.* **Marti** *and* **Dean** *sit in the armchairs.* **Dean** *is still holding onto his placard.* **Shaun** *sits up.*

Shaun   Where d'you get that banner?

Dean   Downstairs.

Shaun   You soft get, that's George's.

Dean   I love this banner.

Shaun   Marti, put it back it's not funny.

Marti   No, I know. It's not funny that.

Marti *takes the placard off* **Dean**. **Dean** *looks around himself.* **Shaun** *lies back down.*

Dean   Nice pad.

Marti   Shares it with his missis.

Dean   Straight?

Marti   As a dye.

Dean   What colour?

Marti   Haemorrhoid-blue.

Marti *exits with the placard to go downstairs.*

Dean   Where is she?

Shaun (*not lifting head up*)   Barbados.

Dean   When did you realise you were straight?

Shaun   I dunno.

Dean   Right.

Pause.

Dean   Ere, mate. You got a bath or a shower or somin'? I gotta be in work by ten.

Shaun   Down the corridor. Second on your right.

Dean   Did you never fancy blokes?

Shaun   No.

Dean   Right.

*Pause. Then **Dean** gets his sports bag and goes to the door. He stands at the door looking at **Shaun** who is trying to sleep.*

Dean   I'm gon'ave a shower.

*He exits and closes the door behind him. Knock on door. **Shaun** drags himself out of bed, in only boxer shorts and a frown, and opens the door. It's* **Dean***.*

Dean   You got a towel?

Shaun   In the bathroom. The red one's mine.

Dean   Can I use it?

Shaun   Yeah.

Dean   Ah, cheers, mate.

Dean *goes.* **Shaun** *shuts the door and gets back into bed. Knock at door.* **Shaun** *gets up again and opens it.* **Dean** *again.*

Dean   You got any shampoo?

Shaun   In the bathroom. Wash and go.

Dean   Soap?

Shaun   Yeah.

Dean   Eye make-up remover?

Shaun   Er, try the cabinet above the sink.

Dean   Cheers, mate.

Dean *goes.* **Shaun** *closes the door. On second thoughts he opens it and leaves it open. He gets into bed.* **Marti** *comes in with two lollipop-shaped Anti-Nazi League placards, leaving the front door open. He goes and sits down.*

Marti   Is that girl downstairs a lollipop lady?

Shaun *sits up.*

Shaun   Marti! Put them back!!

Shaun *angrily lies down and pulls the duvet over him.* **Marti** *however just sits there enjoying his placards. Presently* **Clarine** *comes in. She has changed her clothes. She wears brilliant-white tights, white Scholls, purple skirt, green top, red hair-grips. She goes and turns the telly on and sits down on the sofa.* **Shaun** *puts the pillow over his head. She gets the remote control and turns the volume up til it is deafeningly loud.* **Marti** *watches her incomprehensibly.* **Shaun** *sits up.*

Shaun   Oh, for fuck's sake, Marti!!

He sees it is **Clarine**.

Clarine   I like it loud coz I'm deaf in one ear.

She is now speaking with a Rochdale accent. **Shaun** *looks dumbfounded.*

Ask Miss Flaherty if you don't believe me.

Shaun   Clarine? D'you mind turning it down, girl?

Clarine   Ah, *Lost in Space* is on in a minute.

Shaun   Clarine?!!

Clarine   I wear goggles.

Shaun *gets out of bed and goes over to the telly and turns the sound down.* **Clarine** *looks at his semi-naked form in horror.*

Clarine   Mrs Flaherty! Mrs Flaherty! There's a man wi' no clothes on!!

He turns the music centre off.

Shaun   Clarine . . .

Clarine   I wear goggles.

Shaun   What's to do wit yer voice?

Clarine   Don't tell 'em. You know what they're like.

Marti   Who?

Clarine   They'll put me in isolation.

Shaun   Eh?

Shaun *is flummoxed.* **Clarine** *gets up and puts the telly back on.* **Shaun** *looks to* **Marti**.

Clarine   I wanna watch me programme.

Shaun *sighs. He still hasn't woken up properly yet. He goes off to the kitchen.* **Clarine** *looks around the room.*

Clarine   Do they let you sleep in here?

Marti   Who?

Shaun *comes to the kitchen door pulling on a T-shirt.*

Shaun   Where d'you think yer are?

Clarine   Do they?

Shaun   This is my flat.

Clarine   Is it?

He goes back to the kitchen. **Clarine** *looks round her again. She starts to cry.* **Shaun** *comes back in.*

Marti   Took too many drugs?

Clarine   I think I'm in the wrong place.

Shaun   Your flat's upstairs.

Clarine   Where am I?

Marti   Fifteen Rupert Street.

Clarine   Rupert Street? That's where I'm going.

Shaun   No, love, that's where yer are.

Clarine   I know you two.

Shaun   I'm Shaun. I done your hair last night. This is Marti, you know Marti.

Clarine   I get dandruff, do you?

Shaun   No.

Clarine   Why?

Shaun   I use Wash and Go.

Clarine   Why?

Marti   So he doesn't get dandruff.

Clarine Why?

Pause. This is freaking **Marti** *out. He looks extremely suspicious.*

Shaun Last night you had a cockney accent.

Pause.

Clarine Me mam's name's Elsie. She lives in Belle View Heights. Will you take me there?

Marti Take her there, Shaun, go on.

Shaun What's your name?

Clarine She's got a bloke called Phil. He works for Hargreaves.

Shaun But what's your name?

Clarine Lucky.

Shaun Yeah?

Clarine He were our dog.

Shaun Your name.

Clarine Joyriders got him.

Pause.

Marti I'm twatted.

Clarine Is that a Welsh name?

Pause.

Shaun D'you wanna go back to your flat?

Clarine Belle View Heights?

Shaun No. Upstairs.

Clarine I wet the bed. Promise you won't tell. You know what they're like. (*Looks at telly.*) Ah, look, *Lost in Space*! Can I have t'sound up?

Shaun Not today.

Clarine Oh. Oh, okay then.

Clarine *watches telly.* **Shaun** *goes into the kitchen.*

Clarine This int *Lost in Space*, it's *Aap Kah Hak*!

She gets up and goes to the door, not to leave but to feel secure. **Shaun** *returns with a cup of tea.*

Shaun I've got yer a tea here.

Small pause.

It's herbal.

Small pause.

Clarine.

Pause.

Shaun It's not Clarine, is it? Is it Zoë?

Clarine Zoë Wanamaker.

Shaun Is that your name?

Clarine I'm in *Love Hurts*.

Marti Have some tea.

Clarine I'm gorgeous.

Pause. He then walks over to her and gives her the tea.

Clarine Will you take me back to Belle View Heights?

Shaun D'you know where it is? Is it in Manchester?

Clarine *shakes her head.*

London?

Shakes her head.

Is your mum there?

Clarine It doesn't matter. I cut me finger before. I thought I'd got a stone in the sole of me shoe but it was glass and I tried to pull it out. Look.

Marti Ooh, that sounds nasty. Doesn't that sound nasty?

She shows them her finger.

Clarine I'm in Rupert Street, aren't I?

Marti Yeah.

Clarine Fifteen. Top flat. I best be getting back, me mam'll wonder where I've got to.

Shaun What's your name?

Clarine Me mam's calling me.

Shaun Look, there's a launderette down the road. You turn left out of here and it's by the lights. If you wanna wash your sheets.

Clarine Right.

Shaun *smiles at her. She goes, taking her tea with her.* **Shaun** *sits on the right armchair.*

Marti Is she barmy?

Shaun Dunno.

Marti Is she tripping?

Shaun Maybe she is on drugs.

Marti D'you think she's got any left? Oh, go up and ask her for me.

Shaun You go to bed.

Marti Can I take me lollipops?

Shaun Nah, I'll take them down in a minute.

Marti Fair enough.

Marti *gets into bed.*

Shaun Crash eh?

Marti Okay, I'll crash.

Dean *comes in with a red towel wrapped round his waist and carrying his sports bag.*

Dean Cor, my mouth feels like the bottom of a birdcage. Had a cockatoo in there last night.

Dean *starts to dress with clothes from the bag. Gradually he puts on a McDonald's uniform and cap.*

Shaun   D'y'ever watch a programme called *Love Hurts*?

Dean   These trousers. Bit tight round the crotch.

Shaun   Do yeh?

Dean   No. Man and woman together? Turns my stomach.

Shaun   Was there someone in it called Zoë?

Marti   Zoë Wanamaker.

Shaun   Is she pretty?

Dean   Well, you'd probably think so, seeing as how you're into pussy. And she's got a certain feline wotsit to her.

Clarine *appears at the doorway holding bedsheets in her hands.*

Shaun   Clarine. The launderette's downstairs. Out the front door and turn left. It's by the traffic lights.

Marti *looks up.*

Clarine   Right.

Clarine *goes.*

Shaun   D'you work in McDonald's yeah?

Marti   Night night. (*Settles down.*)

Dean   Yeah. Got a problem with that?

Shaun   No. But a mate o' me girlfriends. He went in McDonald's. Or it mighta been Kentucky Fried Chicken. Anyway, he asked for a chicken burger with no mayonnaise.

Dean   That's simple enough to do, you just miss the mayonnaise out.

Shaun   But he when he bit into it, he got a gobful of really sour mayonnaise.

Dean   Mistakes happen. It's a stressful job.

Shaun   Anyway, turned out it wasn't mayonnaise. The chicken had a cyst. And he'd bit into it.

Dean   Wouldn've been McDonald's.

Shaun I think it was.

Dean It weren't McDonald's.

Shaun Maybe I'm getting mixed up.

Dean And maybe your mate's a lying little toe-rag. It weren't McDonald's. Impossible.

Shaun I'll bow to your better judgement.

Dean You veggie?

Shaun Vegan.

Dean D'you know what gets me about vegetarians? What vegetarians seem to forget is . . . if it weren't for meat, right, there'd be millions more unemployed. You take a look at the news. We got, what, three million unemployed?

Shaun More or less.

Dean Yeah, well, if you vegetarians got off your fat arses and ate a bit o' meat instead o' being a bunch o'no-hope ponces, you'd be putting people in work. So I think you better think again before you start ramming paranoia down people's throats.

Shaun I don't impose my views on anyone.

Dean Good. Coz no cunt'd listen to you. This country's fed up of people like you. Do this, do that. You're a bunch o' champion wankers. No offence.

Pause.

We should go out for a pint with your missis away.

Shaun Yeah?

Dean *moves over to the bed.*

Dean I don't mind straight places. High Holborn (*Shaking* **Marti**.) McDonald's, you can reach me there. (*To* **Marti**.) I'm getting off, Marti. Oright?

Marti Sweet boy.

Dean Gonna go for a pint with your kid brother this week.

Marti Didn't we have a great time tonight eh?

Dean   Blinding. (*To* **Shaun**.) Later, boy. (*To* **Marti**.) See you, mate.

Marti   See yeh, doll.

Shaun   See yeh.

Exit **Dean**.

Shaun   Marti, don't go to sleep just yet.

Marti   I've gotta watch these drugs.

Shaun   You had a buzz, yeah?

Marti   You would tell me if it was getting out of hand, wouldn't you?

Shaun   I'm always telling you.

Marti   I was the Belle of the Ball in them bogs last night.

Shaun   Marti, I'm a bit worried about Clarine.

Marti   God help me if they ever found out I was so big in stretch covers.

Shaun   Marti.

Marti   Let's never fall out again. I know I'm on E but. Let's never fall out again. I'm glad we're mates now.

Shaun   Okay.

Marti   Promise.

Shaun   Aren't you worried about Clarine?

Marti   Promise?

Shaun   I promise.

There is a knock on the (open) door and **George** *pops her head round, then comes in.*

George   Not interrupting anything, am I? I was just . . . well, I'm going to Welling. Hi, Marti. And I wondered . . .

Marti   Hiya!

George   . . . if you'd seen . . . oh, there they are.

She gets the placards.

For the demo.

Shaun   I'm sorry, George. Marti's mate brought them up.

George   Oh, that's okay. Just thought I'd check and see if you'd changed your mind.

Shaun   No.

Marti   Them banners are gorgeous.

George   Made them myself from a special kit.

Shaun   Sound.

George   But you don't fancy it?

Shaun   I'm a bit knackered.

George   Right, well, I'll go and fight facism alone then. Have a good time last night, Marti?

Marti   Heavenly.

George   Great. See you later then.

Marti   See yeh.

George   Ciao Shaun. Take care. Looking forward to Wednesday.

George *exits with her placards.*

Marti   Wednesday?

Shaun   Marti, I think we need to talk about Clarine.

The lights fade. Patsy Cline's 'Come On In (And Make Yourself At Home)' plays us into the next scene.

Scene Three

A few days later. **Shaun** *is sitting on the couch with a glass of red wine. Another glass of red wine sits on the coffee-table, along with a stack of plates.* **George** *stands wiping a plate with a tea towel, looking out of the window. She looks to* **Shaun**, *but he's in his own little world. She searches for conversation.*

George   Did you know these windows are reinforced?

Shaun   No.

George   Well, they are. Redlich had them all reinforced triply about a year ago. All the large ones. In case of break-ins.

Shaun   Yeah?

George   He didn't however reinforce the kitchen windows. Now if you were a sneak-thief intent on burgling this place, which window would you go for? I know which one I would, the kitchen. It's much smaller. Much less mess. Typical.

Shaun   What?

George   Our capitalist bloody landlord.

Marti *comes in from work, suit and brief-case. He chucks the brief-case on the bed and sits in the right armchair. He holds a bottle of white wine.*

Marti   Hiya, girls.

George   Marti, hi.

Shaun   All right?

George   Dinner won't be long. You look tired.

Marti   You'd look tired if you'd been up the Ideal fucking Homes exhibition trying to sell the delights of stretch covers. Still I managed a lunch-time drink in the Coleherne where I was besieged by a plethora of angelic skally trade. Managed to club one into submission and drag it back kicking and screaming to the exhibition centre. Did I fuck. (*Passes* **Shaun** *the wine.*) Cabernet Sauvignon, get it opened.

Shaun   Tar.

George *is putting the plate on the coffee-table.*

George   Now. Cutlery.

Shaun (*getting up*)   I'll do it.

George   You sit down. Relax. It's about time someone pampered you.

Shaun   I can get the cutlery for God's sake.

Shaun *takes the bottle into the kitchen.* **George** *is admiring the stack of plates.*

George   Juliet has such great taste in plates. D'you think she got them from Africa?

Shaun (*off*)   I got them!

George (*to* **Marti**)   They're so ethnicy.

Shaun (*off*)   From Brick Lane market!

George   Temper temper! (*Laughs.*) Sometimes he reminds me so much of Malcolm it's untrue.

Shaun (*off*)   I'm not a bit like Malcolm!

George   Well. No. It's just. He had great taste in plates too. He used to say, 'George, I know they only get covered in food. But hey, a plate's a plate.'

Marti   How long were you going with him for?

George   Three weeks and a morning. (*Beat.*) But the emotional intensity was on a par with at least a six or seven monther. Juliet agreed.

Shaun *enters with knives and forks and a glass of wine for* **Marti** *and two open bottles of wine on a tray. He puts the tray on the table, then passes* **Marti** *his glass.*

Shaun   There.

Marti   Ooh, we didn't do City and Guilds in Hostess Skills, did we?

Shaun   I'm not the hostess. She is.

George I just thought it'd be a nice treat for you. To have someone cook for you. A house meal. And have people round. And you not to have to lift a finger. And you not to have to even leave your own flat.

Marti He's just got things on his mind, that's all.

George The cooker?

Shaun What? No.

George That is the landlord's responsibility.

Shaun Have you got an atlas?

George Yes.

Shaun Can I borrow it?

George I don't mind cooking it downstairs. It's no problem. Actually, don't you think, while I'm checking the food and grabbing that atlas, it'd be a good idea to ring Redlich and tell him about your Smeg?

Marti I beg your . . .

George Cooker. Smeg Cooker. I know that's what Juliet would do.

Shaun Yeah, I know that's what Juliet would do, but I'm not her, am I?

George Is there a problem with you and Juliet?

Shaun No!

George Oh. Oh good. Hey I'm really looking forward to having a chat with Zoë. Aren't you?

Shaun Er . . .

George (*heading for the door*) I can imagine we're all going to bond furiously.

Marti Haven't you told her?

Shaun George, I don't think her name is Zoë really.

George You don't?

Shaun   No. In fact I know it isn't.

George   You have been doing your homework. Stage name? Great!

George *exits.* **Marti** *bursts out laughing.*

Marti   You kill me, you do!

Shaun   Leave it out, will yeh?

Shaun *reaches for the phone. He gets a number out of his Filofax and dials it. It's a long number.*

Marti   Why the fuck didn't you tell George?

Shaun   Because I'm not in the mood for all this if you must know.

Marti   Who you ringing?

Shaun   Never you mind.

Marti   What d'you want an atlas for?

Shaun   What d'you think? (*On phone.*) Hello? Hello, can I speak to Juliet, please? (*Pause.*) Juliet Ransome? (*Pause.*) Oh. (*Pause.*) Shaun. (*Pause.*) Bye. (*He puts the phone down.*)

Marti   Why don't you just tell us all to piss off? It'd only be putting into words what your body language is screaming.

Shaun   All right then. Go on, piss off.

Marti   Not on your life. I wouldn't miss this for the world.

Shaun   See? What's the point?

Marti   The point is people are trying to help you.

Shaun   And I'm just trying to sort me head out.

Marti   It's just a few people. A few hours. Some good cooking and a bottle o'wine. By the time you slip into bed tonight believe me, your head will be sorted.

Clarine *enters in her evening-dress from the first scene. She's still speaking in her Rochdale accent.*

Clarine   Hiya.

Marti   Hiya, love. Er. Why don't you sit down and. Can you drink?

Clarine   White wine.

Marti *pours her a drink.*

Clarine   I hear things are afoot in Kilimanjaro. It wouldn't surprise me if we were all raped in our beds.

Shaun   Listen, girl. (**Clarine** *sits down on the sofa beside him.*) You know George?

Clarine   George?

Shaun   She thinks you're Zoë Wanaker.

Clarine   I'm not though.

Shaun   Yeah. I know that.

Clarine   It's Wanamaker, not Wanaker. (*Tuts.*) As in, 'I wanna make 'er happy, but I can't.'

Marti   But you're not. You're not her.

Shaun   And you told her you were.

Marti   And we think you should tell her you're not.

Shaun   Or d'you want us to tell her?

Marti (*to* **Shaun**)   *You* to tell her!

Clarine   Can't *she* tell her?

Shaun   Who?

Marti (*to* **Shaun**)   You'll have to.

Clarine   I believe there are grave misgivings in Poulton-le-Fylde. Leaves on the track, it's the road to ruin.

Shaun   We've got to decide on a name for you. Just for tonight.

Clarine   I can't tell you me name, it's not allowed.

Marti   Well, can you make one up?

Clarine   Can I?

Shaun   Yeah.

Clarine   Really?

Marti   Yes!

Clarine   Oh, there's so many to choose from. Juliet!

Marti   No. Not Juliet.

Shaun   My other half's called Juliet.

Clarine   You?

Shaun   Me girlfriend.

Marti   What's your favourite name?

Clarine   Shaun.

Marti   No, that's his name.

Clarine   It's my favourite name.

Shaun   Yeah, but it's a lad's name.

Clarine   Well, she's called George.

Marti   What about Clarine?

Clarine   We don't speak.

Shaun   Oh, come on.

Marti   Yeah, hurry up or I'll make one up for you.

Shaun   A name!

Clarine   Grace.

Shaun   Sound.

Clarine   Amazing Grace!

Marti   Well, Grace it is then.

Clarine   Just keep reminding me in case I forget.

Marti *gets up and hands* **Clarine** *her wine. He strolls round the room.*

Clarine   Thank you.

Marti   I take it Juliet still hasn't rung. (**Shaun** *shakes his head.*)
Well, maybe she's skint.

Shaun   What d'you know about anything?

Marti   Well, many's the time I've been away and wanted to ring fellas but me wallet's been empty.

Shaun   What, fellas like Ricky? Rich Ricky from Rain Hill?

Marti *puts his foot on the arm of* **Shaun**'s *chair. He's wearing Doc Martens.*

Marti   You see that? That's steel toe-capped that is. And d'you know what? If you don't shut up about . . . Ricky . . . you're gonna have a lovely impression of this steel toe-cap . . . just . . . (*Runs his fingers over* **Shaun**'s *forehead then pokes him.*) there.

Shaun   I'm shitting meself.

Clarine   I've done/that.

Marti   Oh, I would be if I/was you.

Clarine   Not at a/party, mind.

Shaun   If she is skint, there's such a thing as reversing the charges.

Marti   She's only been gone a week. Give her a chance.

Clarine   I like parties.

Shaun *gets up and goes to the kitchen.*

Marti   We all like parties. (*Sits back in right armchair.*) Except the Conservative one.

George *enters with atlas.*

George   I'll second that. (*Puts atlas on table.*) Five minutes foodwise, okay, everybody? Zoë! Hi! So glad you could make it! (*Kisses her on each cheek.*) Well, that's the way you thespians do it, isn't it?

Clarine   Mm.

George   What an amazing dress!

Marti   Er, which school is it you teach at again, George?

George   Crown Street Comp. Turn left at Toys 'R' Us and it's staring you straight in the face. So, Zoë, tell me, been on the telly lately?

Clarine No.

George Actually I have a terrible admission to make. I don't actually possess a TV. I mean, don't get me wrong, I'm not anti-TV. No way, I think it's great. I really do. It's just that you are looking at a total Bookworm with a capital B. And I just know, that if I had one, that'd be it. I'd be hooked. I'd watch everything. Even soaps. Actually . . .

Marti What is it you teach again, George?

George English.

Marti Oh, yeah. So that's as in, the language.

Goerge Yeah, that's right.

Marti That's great, yeah.

George (*to* **Clarine**)   I'm doing *Romeo and Juliet* with my Year Tens at the moment and I really think I'm finally getting somewhere. Great piece.

Marti Oh, he's fantastic that Shakespeare.

George Actually, I mean, don't tell anyone. It's not that I'm . . . oh, it sounds so silly. Two of my Year Eights have nominated me for the *Smash Hits* Teacher of the Year.

Marti Oh, brilliant, George. Oh, you must be made up.

George It's very embarrassing. Have you done much Shakespeare, Zoë?

Clarine No.

George Right. So. More contemporary stuff, yep?

Marti *shouts through to* **Shaun**.

Marti Shaun! George has been put up for Teacher of the Year!

George *Smash Hits*.

Shaun (*off*)   Brilliant!

George Don't tell anyone. (**Shaun** *comes to door*.) Well, you can tell Juliet, if she rings.

Shaun Could you, er, give us an 'and in the kitchen, doll?

Clarine   I can give you two. (*Gets up.*)

Marti (*raising his glass*)   Up yer bum and no babies.

Shaun (*to* **Clarine**)   Come 'ed.

Shaun *leads* **Clarine** *into the kitchen.*

George   She has got an amazing dress sense. She's so outrageous! I just wouldn't have the gall to wear something like that. D'you know what I mean? Hey, Marti?

Marti   What?

George   Cheers.

Marti   Cheers.

George   You know, you really remind me of my great mate, Pete. You've got exactly the same sense of humour. I must introduce you to him actually coz I think you'd probably get on really well. He goes to the L.A. D'you ever go there?

Marti   No, I think it's vile.

George   Right. I think he does too actually.

Marti   Well, it's pointless him going then, isn't it? Life's too short to surround yourself wit vileness.

Geroge   Right. Well, I think it's handy for him. Five-minute walk from his flat and stuff.

Marti   If there's one thing I despise in people it's laziness.

George   You wanna meet my Year Nines.

Marti   No thanks.

Shaun *and* **Clarine** *come back in.*

Shaun   George?

George   Aha?

Shaun   Can you just come in the kitchen a second?

George   Sure. (*Gets up. To* **Marti**.) Won't be long.

George *exits with* **Shaun**. **Clarine** *still standing. Pause.*

Clarine   D'you think she'll ask me to leave?

Marti   She's cooked yer a meal, hasn't she?

Clarine   I'm going.

Marti   Oh, don't go. Our Shaun's really on a downer at the moment. The more people here, the more it takes his mind of his girlfriend. Please. Just for him.

Clarine   I like him better than George. I only liked her coz she thought I was Zoë Wanamaker.

Marti   She only thought that because you told her.

Clarine   I need the toilet.

Clarine *exits.* **Marti** *lights up a cigarette.* **George** *returns with* **Shaun**.

Marti   She's gone the loo.

George   This is all rather . . .

Shaun   You weren't to know.

George   It's so sad. Erm. Dinner should be ready now, so . . .

George *exits via the main door to go down to her flat.*

Marti   What did she say?

Shaun   Why?

Marti   What did she say?

Shaun   Does it matter?

Marti   God, what's got into you?

Shaun   I've told her, all right. That's all that matters. (*He pours himself a drink, unnerved by* **Marti**'s *sudden silence.*) She didn't say/ nothing.

Marti   I don't wanna know now.

Shaun   I'm just sick of the third degree.

Marti   Oh, grow up.

Shaun   I'm sick of you.

Marti   Oh, the bitchy stakes are rising, I like it. Come on!

Shaun   Shut up.

Marti *launches into the girdle scene from* All About Eve, *playing Margo Channing (M), hoping* **Shaun** *will take the bait and do his Birdie impersonation.*

Marti (*M*)   You bought the new girdles a size smaller. I can feel it.

Shaun   Oh, God.

Marti (*more insistent*)   You bought the new girdles a size smaller. I can feel it.

Shaun   Oh, that's right, drag out Margo Channing. When the going gets tough resort to *All About Eve*.

Marti   You can't remember it.

Shaun   I don't want to remember/it.

Marti   You've forgotten/it.

Shaun   How could I forget/it?

Marti   You/have!

Shaun   The number of times you made me sit down and watch it over and over and over again till it was drilled into me skull. And every other scene. One day we were saying 'Hail Mary' at the end of school and I came out with the girdle scene from *All About Eve*.

Marti   You have forgotten it!

Shaun   You're not listening to me, Marti. Will you just shut up and listen to someone else for once in your life?

Marti   You/have.

Shaun   Oh, for God's sake.

Marti (*M*)   You bought the new girdles a size smaller. I can feel it.

Pause.

You bought the new girdles a size smaller. I can feel it.

Shaun *relents awkwardly, impersonating Birdie (B).*

Shaun *(B)*   Something maybe grew a size larger.

Marti *(M)*   When we get home you're going to get into one of those girdles and act for two and a half hours.

Shaun *(B)*   I couldn't get into the girdle in two and a half hours.

Pause.

Marti   We keep throwing you a bone, Shaun, trying to lift you out of this. George is doing it now, cooking you a meal. I'm trying me hardest. Snap out of it, darlin'.

Shaun *starts to cry.* **Marti** *stubs out his half-smoked cigarette.*

Marti   Oh, I can't do a thing right, can I?

Pause.

I promise I'll never make you do *All About Eve* again. From now on the names Margo Channing, Eve Harrington . . . whoever . . . they're all banned in this flat. Okay? *Mildred Pierce, Baby Jane,* banned. Are you listening to me?

Pause.

I done all them things, made you say . . . all them things . . . coz . . . well, coz I . . . coz you were me favourite brother. I practically brought you up. Where was me dad most nights? Down the boozer and quick mouthful of abuse when he got back. Not that you'd've known, you were in your bed by then . . .

Shaun   I knew.

Marti   You were only in bed coz I put you there. And where was me mam? Doing petty jobs like carrying boxes to keep us in grub and him in ale. Who spent half their life writing notes to your teachers, cooking you beefburgers, cleaning your bloody PE kit? And what did I get out of it? Christ, it was the biggest day of me life when I got that video knock off from Big Mary. We were the only house in the street wit one. Didn't mind bringing in your mates to show it off. Didn't mind bunking school to watch porn videos with them, did yeh?

Shaun   I'm not saying . . .

Marti   Don't you throw back in my face all I've done for you. You've done it once and I won't let it happen again. D'you hear me?

Shaun *tries to wipe his eyes as* **George** *enters. She sees he is upset.*

George   I just thought you should know. There are some very strange noises coming from your toilet.

Marti   I'll go and check.

Marti *exits.*

George   Dinner's ready. Smells good.

Shaun   I'll be all right in a minute.

Pause. The sight of **Shaun** *crying has moved* **George** *to modest tears.*

George   Last time I cooked this was for you-know-who.

Shaun   Take no notice of me.

George   Shaun. Do you mind if I . . .?

She goes to hug him.

Shaun   Why?

George   Well, if Juliet was upset.

Shaun   No, George, it's not . . .

George   I'm not trying to . . .

Shaun   What?

George   Hug?

Shaun *smiles. They hug. She is keener than him.*

George   Thanks.

She kisses him once on the lips. **Shaun** *is surprised.*

George   Sorry.

She returns to just hugging him. Just then, **Marti** *and* **Clarine** *enter.* **Marti** *coughs to announce their presence.*

Marti   She thought she was in a space capsule.

Clarine I forgot.

George If I don't get downstairs none of us is ever going to eat.

George exits. **Clarine** *sits on the couch.* **Marti** *eventually sits in the right armchair.*

Clarine How far away's Kidderminster?

Shaun I don't know.

Marti If you'd like us to go and leave you two to it, please say. Light a couple of joss-sticks, get Joni Mitchell on the CD, you'll be well away.

Shaun *laughs sarcastically.*

Marti You can do better than her.

Shaun I already have.

Clarine Is it near Birmingham? Kidderminster?

Shaun You've got it all wrong as per.

Clarine Where's Birmingham?

Shaun In the Midlands.

Marti I'm only saying.

Shaun All right lad.

Marti Don't call me lad you straight bastard. Call me girl, or doll, or love. Takes years to get this camp.

He goes in his pockets for something. Gets cigarettes out.

Clarine?

Clarine Zoë.

Shaun Grace!

Marti Oh, I don't care what your name is, d'you want one or not?

Clarine *shakes her head.* **Shaun** *is looking round the room for his ashtray.*

Marti (*to* **Clarine**)   No offence doll, but my brother's always been hopeless at finding the right people to surround himself with.

Shaun   Oh, and I suppose that Polish fella you used to knock about with was the ideal friend, was he?

Marti   I can't help it if I'm generous.

Shaun   He took you for every penny you had!

Marti   I can't help/being generous.

Shaun   What was his name?

Marti   I've grown up/since then.

Shaun   Maybe if I said I needed a fortnight in the sun to sort me head out you'd/come up with the readies.

Marti   I forked out . . . I forked out for that van of yours, didn't I? More fool/me.

Shaun   More fool me for accepting it. You remind me of it every five minutes.

Shaun *slams the ashtray he has found in* **Marti**'s *lap.*

Marti   Hey, watch the crown jewels. I'm sitting on a small fortune here.

Clarine   Have you ever been to Birmingham?

Shaun   He probably has. He's been everywhere.

Marti   Not by choice.

Clarine   What's it like?

Shaun   Yeah, what's Birmingham really like, Marti. I've often wondered.

Marti (*tuts*)   It's got a fabulous gay scene but I don't think much to its Bullring. You've got an atlas there. Why don't you show her where Birmingham is?

Clarine   I didn't really want Birmingham. I wanted Kidderminster.

Marti   Well, why have cotton when you can have silk?

Enter **George**, *followed by* **Dean**. **Dean** *is dressed to kill, in men's clothes.*

George   Look who I found skulking about in the lobby.

Marti *bursts out laughing.*

Dean   Oright?

Marti   You're timing's brilliant, Dean.

Shaun *nods a hello.*

George (*to* **Marti**)   Isn't it?! Grace, would you like to fetch an extra plate from the kitchen and get an extra glass? Dean's going to stay for dinner. You'll find them on the side.

George *exits.*

Clarine   Right.

Dean (*to* **Clarine**)   Cheers, mate.

Clarine   I'm Grace.

Dean   Right.

Clarine *exits to kitchen.*

Shaun   Did you know Marti was going to be here?

Marti   No, he didn't.

Dean   Thought we could go for that drink.

Shaun   Bit of a dinner party going on.

Dean   Don't let me stop you. (*Sits on couch.*)

Marti   You know my little brother's straight, don't you, Dean?

Dean (*to* **Marti**)   If you must know I come round coz I lost your number. Thought I could get it off of him.

Marti   I believe yeh. Thousands of highly intellectual people would be in two minds.

Clarine *enters with plate and glass.*

Clarine   I did it.

Marti   Oh, well done, girl. Give her a round of applause.

Marti *claps.* **Clarine** *puts the plate and glass on the table.* **Shaun** *fires an imaginary pistol at* **Marti**. **Clarine** *pours* **Dean** *a wine.*

Marti (*to* **Shaun**)   I'm not scared of you, yeh know.

Dean   Aint you got no lager?

Shaun   No.

Dean   You got a problem with me being here?

Shaun   No.

Dean   Well, put a smile on your face then, you miserable cunt.

Clarine (*horrified*)   That's not allowed.

Dean   What?

Clarine   The 'c' word. It's not allowed.

Dean   You some sort of feminist?

Clarine   I'm Grace.

Shaun (*to* **Clarine**, *passing her the atlas*)   Look. Kidderminster.

Dean   I understand that some women find the word cunt offensive. Personally the word don't offen me, but the thing does.

Clarine   Does that really say Kidderminster?

Shaun   Yeah.

Marti   You'll have to tell Shaun a few jokes, Dean. He hasn't been feeling to good.

Dean   Aint ya?

Shaun   Would you with a brother like that?

Enter **George**.

George   Now I need a big strong man to give me a hand upstairs with the hostess wagon. Marti? Would you do the honours?

Marti (*getting up, to* **Shaun**)   With friends like you, who needs enemas?

Shaun   You're not original, you know.

Marti   I know. I'm the two ends of Montgomery Clift, don't tell me.

Marti *and* **George** *exit.* **Dean** *proudly takes off his coat, brushes it down and rests it neatly on the back of the sofa.*

Dean (*to* **Shaun**)   How's life on your own?

Shaun   I'll hang that up for you.

Dean   Oh. Thank you very crutch.

Shaun *hangs* **Dean**'s *coat up on the back of the door.*

Dean   We gonna go out for that drink some time?

Shaun   I don't think so.

Dean   Scared I might pounce?

Shaun   No. (*Returning to seat. To* **Clarine**.) Dean works in McDonald's.

Dean   All work and no play makes Dean a very dull boy. I like playing. Enjoy the odd game.

Shaun   Yeah, and we all know which side you bat for an'all.

Dean   You got a problem with that?

Shaun   I was weaned on queenery.

Dean   Good. What you doing Friday night?

Shaun   Go out with Marti. He thinks you're marvellous.

Dean   I am.

Shaun   Modest an'all.

Dean   I don't blow me own trumpet. Not if I can get someone else to.

Clarine   Do you triple tongue?

Dean   Only the pink oboe. Party on, d'you know what I mean?

Just then **Marti** *shouts from downstairs.*

Marti (*off*)   Shaun?!!

Shaun   What?

Marti (*off*) Give us an'and wit this!!

Shaun Scuse me.

Dean You farted?

Shaun No.

Clarine *laughs as* **Shaun** *exits. Pause.*

Dean So. You're a mate o' Shaun's then, yeah?

Clarine Well, Shaun's my best friend, and Marti's my second best friend, but I don't like George coz she's a slut.

The phone rings.

Clarine That'll be the phone.

Dean You get it. Dare ya. It's better when a woman answers the phone.

They both stare at the phone.

Clarine Oright. (*Picks it up.*) Hello? (*Pause.*) Hiya mam. (*Beat.*) Yeah. (*Beat.*) No. (*Beat.*) Yeah. I know. What's the weather like your end? (*Pause. Then she puts the phone down.*) How did she know I were here?

Dean Musta tried your number and guessed you was here.

Clarine But I haven't got a phone.

Shaun *enters followed by* **Marti**, *then* **George** *who is pushing a hostess trolley.*

Shaun Who was that?

Clarine Oh, just me mum rang up for a gab. I told her I was at a function.

Shaun Your mam?!

Marti How did your mam know you were here?

Clarine I give her this number. Mmm, something smells nice.

Shaun Are you sure it was your mam?

Clarine I know me own mam when I speak to her, thank you, Shaun!

Shaun   But you don't even know who you are!

Dean   Do what?

Clarine   I do. But it's . . . top secret. I haven't to tell a soul!

Shaun   You/what?

Clarine   There's no point rowing with me/Shaun.

Marti   Yeah, come on, Shaun, sit down.

Shaun   Piss off, you, this is my flat.

Marti   And I'm your guardian angel, now park yer arse!

Dean   Hang on a minute . . .

Clarine   Anyway, George, happy birthday.

George (*phased*)   Thanks.

Dean (*to* **George**)   Oh. Happy birthday. Didn't/realise.

Marti   It's nobody's birthday, love. It's a house meal.

Shaun   House meal plus two.

George   I'll serve up, shall I?

As the conversation continues, **George** *ladles up the aubergine bake onto plates and passes them round. They end up eating off their knees.* **Marti** *is sitting in the right-hand chair,* **Shaun** *will be in the left.* **George**, **Clarine** *and* **Dean** *end up sitting on the couch between them.* **Shaun** *is still standing.*

Marti (*to* **Shaun**)   You invited me!

Dean   Don't give you too much heartache to see me, does it, Shaun?

Marti   Actually you didn't invite me, you begged me, now sit down. You've proved your point.

Shaun   Seen Ricky lately, Mart?

Clarine (*plate*)   What are they?

George   Aubergines.

Marti (*to* **Shaun**)   I'd have a job, wouldn't I?

Dean   Is there anything edible in this?

George   All nature's finest.

Dean   What no meat?

George   You remind me of my ex, Malcolm. He was forever bemoaning the state of my meat-free intake. The times he wailed on, 'Meat! Gimme Meat!'

Dean   Like a bit, did he?

George   Adored it.

Clarine   Was he handsome?

George   I thought so. Yes. He was handsome. Would you say he was handsome, Shaun?

Shaun   Who?

George   Malcolm.

Shaun   Beauty's in the eye of the beholder.

Marti   Mm, and some people are bog-eyed.

Shaun   Actually . . .

Marti   Oh, we're getting a lecture here, he used three syllables.

Shaun   I tell yeh who did look like Malcolm.

George   Who?

Shaun   Ricky.

Dean   Who's Ricky then?

Marti   No one.

Shaun   No one? But he was really special to you at one point.

Dean   Was he horny?

George   Well, if he was anything like Malcom he would have been. He was like a heat-seeking baboon.

Dean   Seeing anyone now?

George   No. I really value my independence.

Dean   (*to* **Clarine**)   You got anyone?

Clarine   Yeah.

George   Really? Oh, fantastic. Isn't that great, everybody? Grace has got a beau. Where did you meet him?

Clarine   He came visiting the last place I lived.

George   Really?

Clarine   He said I had nice hair.

George   You have got a really fine head of hair on you actually you know, Grace. Don't you think so, Shaun? Sort of . . . Hairdresser Heaven, yeah?

Shaun   It's just hair really, isn't it.

George   And does he have a name?

Clarine   Prince Charles.

Dean   What?

Clarine (*sheepish*)   Prince Charles.

Dean   Are you taking the piss?

Clarine   No.

Shaun   Dean.

Dean (*to* **Clarine**)   Are you fucking mental?

Pause.

George   I met this guy on a demo on Saturday. Asked for my phone number. On the pretext of sending me some SWP paraphernalia. But I don't know. How about you, Marti?

Marti   Sorry?

George   Is there a significant other in your life?

Marti   I had enough of that in me misspent youth. Two ran off with other women. One joined a monastery. The other had his hair permed. Mortal sin.

Shaun   And then of course there was Rich Ricky from Rain Hill. Our Marti, oh, you'll laugh when you hear this. Our Marti had a run of bad luck with fellas.

Marti   How would you know?

Shaun   If they weren't robbing him they were cheating on him. One blew three grand of his savings.

Dean   Who? I'll deck him for ya.

Shaun   And we started thinking. Maybe that's what he attracts. Maybe there's something in Marti that's . . . anyway. He proved us all wrong. Where were you at the time?

Marti   I dunno.

Shaun   Glasgow it was. Yeah, out of the blue there's a new man. Ricky. Swimming in money. Made his money in Quorn.

George   Excellent, the vegetarian alternative.

Shaun   Marti was getting whisked off abroad, holidays left, right and centre, we never saw a postcard mind, well, he was too busy having a good time. And did Ricky love him? Did Ricky love him?

Marti   Shaun, please . . .

Shaun   Yes. Ricky loved him.

Pause.

Shaun   Well, you can imagine, me mum and dad were dying to meet this Ricky. Pester pester pester. 'When's Ricky coming down?'

Marti   Me dad wasn't arsed, it was me 'arl girl.

Shaun   And as luck would have it Marti and Ricky were doing a whistle-stop tour to the North West. We could have an hour of their time. The big day came. Ricky seemed nervous. Did he seem nervous to you, Marti? Well, he seemed very nervous to me. And Ricky's got this suit on. Next. And unbeknownst to Marti, me mum had had central heating put in. Now she was very proud of her central heating, wasn't she, Marti?

Marti   Social climbing bitch.

Shaun   So in order to show it off, to show he never came from a bad home, she turns it up and makes Ricky take his jacket off.

And in order to show what a good host she was she made me hang it up in the wardrobe upstairs. Now I'm hanging it up and, okay, curiosity got the better of me and I thought . . . I want to see his American Express Gold Card. Coz Marti said he's got one.

George Wow.

Shaun So I have a little look in his inside pocket. No wallet. But I did find . . .

Pause.

A UB40. With the name HUGHIE GRAHAM on it. (*Starts to laugh.*)

George Right.

Dean I don't get it.

Shaun Oh, Dean. Marti had invented Ricky to make out he could manage the perfect relationship.

Marti I never. Ricky . . . Ricky couldn't come at the last minute so I brought me mate Hughie in his place. Well, is there anything wrong in trying to keep your pride?

Shaun Six months later Ricky was killed in an avalanche on a skiing holiday. The family sent Marti cards. (*Beat.*) I never. (*Pause. To* **Marti**.) I had to sit and watch me mother sobbing her heart out coz she was worried sick about how you were taking it.

Marti It near killed me. And you can sit there and joke about it.

A longer silence.

George Has there been anyone since?

Marti I wouldn't trust anyone who said they loved me.

Dean Hey, Marti. Any dirt to dig on Shaun?

George Yes! What don't we know from his sordid past, pre-Juliet?

Dean What was he like at sixteen? Was he a looker?

Pause.

George   Mm?

Marti   I don't know.

Pause. **Dean** *laughs.*

George   You don't know?

Marti   Don't laugh at me.

Shaun   She's not laughing at yeh, Marti.

Dean   No one's laughing at ya.

Clarine   Yes you were.

Marti *gets up and helps himself to a drink.*

Marti   When Shaun. When Shaun found out I was gay . . .

Shaun   Oh, Marti, this is/irrelevant.

Marti   They want to/know.

Shaun   It's totally/irrelevant!

Marti   An eye for an eye, you little twat! When Shaun found out I was gay . . .

George   Look, if this is going to cause/any uneasiness . . .

Marti   You have just asked me a question which I am now going to/answer.

Dean   Watch yourself,/Marti.

Shaun   I think they've probably guessed I didn't take an ad in the *Liverpool Echo* expressing my profound euphoria.

Marti   He threw a spanner at me. He was fixing his moped.

Shaun   It was a scrambler.

Marti   It was a Honda Express. A turquoise Honda Express. He threw a spanner at me . . . and then proceeded to beat ten different types of shite out of me. Sweet sixteen, and I was twenty-six. A toast.

Shaun   You're making a cunt outa yourself.

Marti   To brothers!

Shaun   The Honda Express was me mother's. I'd just fixed it for her.

Marti (*a toast*)   And to me mother, God love the bones of her!

Shaun   The bike I was fixing was my scrambler.

Marti   I didn't speak to him for years. Moved around the country. He was still in Liverpool. I'm sure he didn't mean it. Peer pressure (*American.*) and stuff. (*Himself.*) Well, he reckons it was. Fed up of me cajoling him into scenes from *Mildred Pierce, All About Eve* and worse. Well, I was asking for trouble, wasn't I?

Dean   All right, Marti, sit down.

Marti   I haven't started yet.

Dean   Don't work yourself up, man./You're working yourself . . .

Marti (*slapping* **Dean**)   Don't call me man!! I fucking hate that! Everyone calls each other MAN now. Even women. It's so fucking/American!

Shaun   But yer are a man!

Marti   I know what I am. I don't need you spelling it out.

Dean *stands and sits* **Marti** *down.*

Dean   Aye aye aye aye, easy, boy.

He sits back down.

Marti   So you can imagine how I felt when I bumped into him in a nightclub in Hammersmith two years back. A gay nightclub.

George   Right.

Marti   He was with her of course. It was then I discovered his political stance had swung somewhat from the right of Adolf Hitler to just a tad to the left of Kenny Livingstone. It was then I was allowed to be his big brother again. I haven't a clue what he was like at sixteen. I was nursing a few wounds in casualty.

Pause.

Clarine   Is there any salt?

George Here.

Shaun You nasty fucking twat.

Marti Well, at least we're getting some other emotion from you instead of self-pity. What's the atlas for? So you can trace her route?

Shaun At least I'm capable of love.

Marti If that's love, sitting in all day and being a burden to your mates you can stick love.

Shaun Yeah, well, at least I don't have to go sniffing round some minty fucking piss trough to find it.

Marti You think I'm looking for love in there? Do yeh? Are you that short-sighted? Get a pair o' glasses, love!

Shaun Well, what are you looking for? Sympathy? Coz that's the only reason anyone would wanna go near you.

Marti You'll never understand, will you.

Shaun Understand what, Mart?

Marti Me, dear, me.

Pause. The others are eating.

Shaun Well, who says I'd want to? Who's to say I haven't done all this for her benefit? To prove to Juliet I'm not the bastard I was.

Pause. No response from **Marti**, *it's really winded him.* **Shaun** *stands.*

Shaun Fancy that drink, Dean?

Dean (*beat*) Why not?

Shaun Come 'ed then. (*To* **George**.) I appreciate what you're doing for me and all that but, you know.

George That's cool.

Dean (*to* **Clarine**) See you. (*To* **Marti**.) Marti, mate, chill out.

Clarine Bye. Bye, Shaun.

Shaun   See yeh.

Dean *exits followed by* **Shaun**. **Clarine** *and* **George** *are still eating.* **Marti** *isn't touching his food.*

Marti   Sixteen bruises that lad gave me. One for every year that he hated me. I used to think I was lucky he never had a knife. Well, he's used it now.

George *goes to say something.*

Marti   And if I hear another word out of you about that gobshite Malcolm I'll rip your head off and shit down your neck.

George *says nothing. She is repulsed. She gets up and scrapes her dinner back into the compartment in the hostess trolley.*

George   Think I'll er, catch up on some marking.

George *exits.* **Clarine** *has finished her dinner. She looks at* **Marti**'s *full plate.*

Clarine   Are you gonna eat that? (**Marti** *shrugs.*) Give it here then.

She gets up and takes it off him. She returns to her seat and starts eating it. She smiles at him.

Nice party.

Blackout.

'*Big Mouth Strikes Again*' *by The Smiths plays.*

Act Two

Scene One
'It's Raining in My Heart' plays in the blackout.
*A week later. Late at night. It's pouring with rain outside. Empty flat. Key in the door. **Dean** comes in and sits on the bed. He's dressed as himself. Eventually **Marti** comes in fumbling in his pocket for a lighter. They're both a bit the worse for wear for drink. **Marti** puts the light on. They are both soaked to the skin. **Marti** puts the fire on and stands in front of it.*

Marti   D'you want something to put on?

Dean   You're all right.

Marti   You're soaked through.

Marti *goes in the chest of drawers and gets a selection of jogging bottoms and T-shirts which he drapes over the settee. He starts undressing.*

Dean   I can't wear his clothes.

Marti   He won't know. He won't be back for a week.

Dean   Did you see him in Liverpool?

Marti   Didn't hang around.

Dean   I hate Liverpool.

Marti   Been, have yeh?

Dean   What d'you call a Scouser in a suit?

Marti *(offering some jogging bottoms)*   Put these on. You'll catch pneumonia.

Dean   What *do* you call a Scouser in a suit?

Marti   I don't really care.

Dean   I can't wear his clothes. Aint right. Why d'you go back to Liverpool?

Marti   Why shouldn't I go back?

Dean   Guilty. That's what you call 'em. Guilty. What's it like?

Marti   What?

Dean   Liverpool!

Marti   I don't know.

Marti *changes into* **Shaun**'s *dressing-gown off the back of the door. He gets a kimono, Juliet's.*

Marti   D'you want this?

Dean   You walk down a street. Full of robbers and thieves. You get your car nicked, that's why you're walking. You bump into some git who reckons he knew the Beatles. You duff up some other git coz he aint got a Liverpool accent then you have a ride on the ferry. That's what it's like. That plant don't look too healthy.

Marti   Shit.

Marti *goes out to the landing.* **Dean** *gets undressed, apart from his jeans, and puts on Juliet's kimono.* **Marti** *returns with a kebab.*

Marti   Left it in the bog.

Dean   You wanna move that plant.

Marti   Do I?

Dean   It's too near the radiator. That's why it's dry.

Marti   You wanna go to Liverpool. Find out what it's really like.

Dean   I don't think I could compete with your salt-of-the-earth humour.

Marti   Ooh, you reckon you know it all you Southerners. Everyone's got a take on Liverpool, but nobody's really been.

Dean   This isn't casual by the way.

Marti   Since when were you green-fingered?

Dean   I water all the plants at work.

Dean *kicks his shoes off.* **Marti** *sits on the couch eating his kebab.*

Dean   I gotta say it.

Marti   Liverpool is the pool of life. That's what it means.

Dean   I've never touched you before.

Marti   You could have done in the club. You can't tell one from the other with the lights off.

Dean   I can.

Marti   (*kebab*)   D'you want any o' this?

Dean   Marti. That short for Martin? I can't think of you as a Martin.

Marti   David.

Dean   David?

Marti   Me second name's Caine. They used to call our Shaun Michael and me . . .

Dean   Marti. Caine.

Marti   It stuck.

Dean   He was really cut up when we went for that drink.

Marti   Was he?

Dean   No. But I reckon he was underneath it all.

Marti   I thought you fancied our Shaun?

Dean   I was just using him to get to you.

Marti   Piss off.

Dean   You shouldn't wear black, don't suit ya.

Marti   Did you know they make kebab meat out of crushed bones?

Dean   So?

Marti   You didn't, did you? He told me that.

Pause.

I'm not wearing black.

Dean   It just come to me.

Marti   Why shouldn't I?

Dean Blue's your colour.

Pause.

Funny things, beds.

Marti No, they're not.

Dean You sleep in them. You shag in them. And you make love in them.

Marti So there's a distinction is there?

Dean I'm through with it all, Marti, messing around.

Pause.

Come here.

Pause. **Marti** *goes and looks out of the window, eating his kebab.*

Marti.

Marti It's pissing down.

Dean I know.

Pause.

Marti I'm not very good at sex these days.

Dean Fair enough, we won't have sex.

Marti It's too messy. I don't like things that put me in touch with me own mortality.

Dean You do in the dark room.

Marti When I'm off me face.

Pause.

I wish it was different. I wish I was. When you're a teenager you try to be someone else. You spend your twenties discovering who you really are. And you spend your thirties getting used to it.

Dean I love you, man.

Marti No, you don't.

Dean You love me. You do, you told me the other week.

Marti When?

Dean   In the club. No, not in the club. After, in the cab. You held my hand all the way home and you told me you loved me.

Marti   I was off me face.

Dean *peels off his kimono. He stands there in his wet jeans and white vest starting at* **Marti**.

Marti   Oh, Dean. You're a sweet boy.

Dean   You gotta open yourself up to being loved.

Marti   I only fall in love with people I can never have. It's easier like that.

Dean   Why?

Marti   Less mess.

Dean *goes and switches the light off. They're now in total darkness.*

Dean   Does this help?

Marti *steps forwards and walks into the settee. He spills his kebab on it.*

Marti   Oh, fuckinell, switch it back on.

Dean *switches the light back on. We see the spilt kebab.*

Marti   Oh, God. I asked for extra chilli sauce.

Dean   Don't matter.

Marti   I can wash it.

Dean   Not now.

Marti   I know.

He goes and sits on the edge of the bed.

Is this some sort of fantasy of yours?

Dean   No.

Marti   Is it coz you've had a few?

Dean   No. I'm serious.

Marti   Make it just a fantasy.

Pause. Then **Dean** *switches the light off again. He unzips his jeans.*

Marti What's that smell?

Dean Fahrenheit. Go on.

Marti Oh, all right. Come over here.

Dean *moves over and stands before* **Marti***.*

Marti Your jeans are wet.

Dean I know. It's raining. Go on.

Marti Where is it?

Dean Here.

Marti Eh?

Dean*'s fly goes up. He puts the light back on.* **Marti***'s sitting on the bed.* **Dean** *doesn't know where to put himself.*

Marti Do it again and keep the lights on.

Dean S'all right.

Marti I don't mind.

Dean Nah, s'all right.

Marti Honestly.

Dean Gotta get back. Gotta feed my snake.

He starts putting his wet clothes on.

Marti You're gonna catch pneumonia.

Dean I'm all right.

Marti Stay.

Dean I can't.

Marti Dean.

Dean What?

Marti I prefer it when you're Fifi Trixabelle La Bouche.

Dean *finishes dressing.*

Marti Go and feed your snake eh?

Dean Later, Mart.

Marti Yeah.

*As **Dean** exits. **George** enters with a bottle of red wine and two glasses. She sort of bumps into him.*

George Oh, sorry.

Dean *exits with no comment.*

George I'm sorry. I heard footsteps. I thought Shaun was away.

Marti He is.

George Thought he'd made an early return.

Marti No.

George Right. I'll. Sorry.

Marti He should be back by the end of the week.

George Don't suppose you fancy a nightcap? I tried Grace but I couldn't get much sense out of her. Something about rats.

Marti Go on then.

George No, if . . .

Marti No, it's . . .

George Well, if you're sure.

*She sits on the sofa and pours two glasses of wine. **Marti** sits in the right armchair.*

George Shaun did say *you* were in Liverpool.

Marti The place we go to lick our wounds.

George Did you get bored?

Marti He turned up to lick his, so I come back down.

George Here. (*She hands him a glass.*)

Marti Tar.

George Cheers.

Marti Probably just what he needs, the home comforts.

George We can all do with those every now and again.

Marti   I was out round here tonight so I thought I'd stay over. I'd er, appreciate it if you, er, if you didn't tell him you seen me. If you didn't tell him I'd been.

George   If I don't that kebab will.

Marti   I'll wash it.

George   It's a bit odd, him going home. I'd have thought he'd want to look after the business.

Marti   I know. There's scores of grannies all over London whose blue rinses are fading away. What will they do without Curls on Wheels?

George   Find another stylist if they've got any sense.

Marti   But do I care?

George   Yes. I think you do.

Marti   Juliet'll kill him if she gets back and the business is rotten.

George   Do you think things are hunky-dory between them?

Marti   Don't you?

George   Well, four weeks seems an awfully long time to be away for a funeral.

Marti   Well, Christ, girl, if you had the choice between a sunny beach and Bromley-by-Bow, which would you choose?

George   True. I'm going camping next week.

Marti   Camp.

George   Daffyd's invited me.

Marti   Daffyd?

George   A certain knight in shining armour with the biggest SWP placard I've held in months.

Marti   Christ, George!! You didn't waste any time, did yeh?

George   It's not as romantic as it sounds. Though how wading through a muddy field in the Forest of Dean could ever be termed romantic is beyond me. No. He was already going with some SWP chums and he asked if I wanted to tag along. It's half-term next week, so.

Marti   You're grabbing life by the short and curlies.

George   Well, I'll have my own tent. Oh, I'm so looking forward to it, you know, Marti. Though I'll have bundles of moderating to plough through. We're reaching that time of the year where GCSE bells start ringing through the air.

Shaun *has entered during this last speech. He's soaked to the skin and carrying a sports bag. Pause. He stands there.*

Shaun   All right?

Marti   I was out with Dean. Couldn't get a cab.

Shaun   I've always said you could stay. I give you a key, didn't I?

Shaun *starts unpacking his sports bag on the bed.*

Marti   George heard me in here and thought you were back.

George   Glass of wine?

Shaun   No, tar.

Marti   It's got a lovely bouquet.

Shaun   You're all right.

George   I better go downstairs.

Marti   Right.

George (*to* **Marti**)   Finish this off. (*Leaves bottle.*)

Marti   Oh, tar. Night, love. Enjoy your tent.

George   Night, Shaun.

Shaun   Night.

George (*to* **Marti**)   Night.

George *exits, taking her glass of wine with her.* **Shaun** *still unpacking his bag.* **Marti** *gets up and starts tidying away the selection of jogging bottoms off the couch.*

Marti   You should put something else on. You'll catch your death.

Shaun   I'll just finish this.

Marti   How's mum?

Shaun   Fine.

Marti   Dad?

Shaun   Same as when you left 'em.

Marti   Look, I'll get out from under your feet . . .

Pause.

Shaun   Marti.

Marti   Mm?

Shaun   You don't have to get off.

Marti   No, I know what it's like when you wanna get a bit o' peace and quiet.

Shaun   Marti, why d'you think I went to Liverpool?

Marti   Homesick?

Shaun   I went to talk to you. Oh, listen I will have that drink.

Marti   I'll get yer a glass.

Shaun   Okay.

Marti *goes off to kitchen.* **Shaun** *gets a present out of the bag. It's a video in an Our Price bag. He puts it on the coffee-table. He removes the kebab from the couch and puts it in the bin. He starts stripping the stretch cover off the couch.* **Marti** *returns with a glass.*

Marti   Oh, I'm sorry about that.

Shaun   It's all right.

Marti   I was gonna wash it in the morning.

Shaun   I'll stick it in to soak overnight.

Shaun *exits to kitchen with the cover. We hear him running the taps to soak the cover.*

Marti   It's about time you washed it. I'm surprised it can't stand up on it's own.

Shaun (*off*)   I decided I'd do a big spring-clean as soon as I'd heard from Juliet.

Marti   Oh, right.

Shaun (*off*)   Better start tomorrow.

Marti   Did she ring?

Shaun (*off*)   I rang her. Me ma was going spare. 'You ringing that Barbados again?' I wasn't on for long. She said she'd sent us a letter so it should be here any day now.

Marti   Hence your early return.

Shaun (*coming back in*)   Curls on Wheels won't run itself. I made a few appointments while I was up there. I'm doing an old people's home in Greenwich all day tomorrow.

Marti   It's all go in the world of perming.

Shaun   And . . . I wanted to give you this.

Shaun *hands* **Marti** *the video in the bag.* **Marti** *gets it out.*

Marti   Oh, fabulous! The Nanny!

Shaun   Bette Davis.

Marti   Oh, Shaun.

Shaun   Thought it might give yer a few more lines.

Marti   On me face?

Shaun   To speak. I asked if they'd got anything with Joan Crawford in as well but . . .

Marti   Any fool knows they only did *Baby Jane* together.

Shaun   I forgot. The fella in Our Price gave me daggers when I asked. I think he might've been a queen.

Marti   Well, they were slated to do *Hush . . . Hush, Sweet Charlotte* together but Crawford did a few scenes then backed out, the bitch.

Shaun   I'm sorry, Marti.

Marti   I hate falling out with people. I don't wanna go through life not being able to speak to the people I care about. Whenever I meet someone new, or someone who shows an interest, mates, you know, not lovers or anything, I'm always full of this foreboding. It's like, I can't trust anything. It's like I'm waiting for them to catch me out. I'm always expecting things to go wrong. And then they do, they always do. I dunno, maybe me moon's in Uranus or something. Some bad planets colliding up there. That's how it feels at the moment.

Shaun   It won't last forever.

Marti   I hope you're right. I really do.

Shaun   You create your own reality.

Marti   Where d'you learn that? Back of a cornflakes packet?

Shaun (*shakes head*)   Off the woman I love. The woman I'm gonna keep. And from now on I'm gonna start acting like I deserve her and get me act together.

Marti   Positive thinking? I've heard about that, but I'm always too miserable to try it.

Shaun (*toast*)   To the future, kid.

Marti   You've changed your tune.

Shaun   Well, it was about time. Now stick that tape on.

Marti   Now?

Shaun *nods.* **Marti** *gets the tape out and puts it in the video.* **Shaun** *switches the light off and slips out of his wet clothes. He sticks some jogging bottoms on and a sweatshirt. They are lit now from the light from the screen.*

Shaun   D'you wanna stay with me till Juliet gets back?

Marti (*nods*)   All right. If you want.

Shaun   I'll cook us something nice for our tea tomorrow.

Marti   You're still quite new to me.

Pause.

Well, it worries me.

Shaun   Fast forward through this bit.

Marti *sits on the sofa with the remote control and fast forwards the video. He has a look at the cover and reads the blurb on the back.*

Marti (*reading*)   'The Fane family trusted Nanny, she helped them cope with the sudden death of their baby daughter. Young Joey didn't.'

Shaun   Wise man!

Marti   'He knew Nanny would do anything to remain Head of the Household. When the key suspects of murder are narrowed down to Nanny and the disturbed youngster, a frightening chain of events begins. Starring Bette Davis and Wendy Craig!'

They laugh. **Marti** *fires the remote at the telly. The video begins.* **Shaun** *has got changed and sits down in the right armchair. They are laughing. As the lights fade 'The Sunshine After The Rain' by Berri plays, leading us into the next scene.*

Scene Two

Marti'*s in on his own, chopping up a pineapple on the coffee-table. Berri is playing loudly on the stereo, and* **Marti** *is singing along to it. A clean stretch cover graces the couch. There is a knock at the door. He turns the volume down and opens the door to* **Clarine**. *She is wearing a T-shirt with the logo 'Barbados' on it. She is still speaking with a Rochdale accent.*

Clarine   Hiya.

Marti   Hiya, doll, is me music too loud?

Clarine   No, it's the rats.

Marti   You haven't got rats.

Clarine (*nods*)   Hoards of 'em.

Marti   Oh, God, you wanna get onto the council about that.

Clarine   I already have. They're sending someone round. (*Beat.*) Fruit salad. Very nice. Where's Shaun?

Marti Just popped the shop for a tub o'yoghurt. He's making a curry in there.

Clarine I like Shaun. He looks like Adam Faith, out of *Love Hurts*.

Marti (*laughs*) I didn't know you'd been to Barbados.

Clarine That's coz I haven't.

Marti Well, where d'you get the top?

Clarine Me mam give it me.

Marti Has she been?

Clarine Here?

Marti Barbados.

Clarine No. I don't think so, why?

Marti Well, coz o' your top.

Clarine Is that what it says?

Marti Yeah.

Clarine Barbados.

Pause. **Marti** *carries on chopping the pineapple.* **Clarine** *looks at her T-shirt, then puts a cushion on her knee to cover it up.*

Clarine I'm on me period.

Marti Goway.

Shaun *enters with shopping.*

Shaun Hiya.

Clarine Hiya, I'm on me period.

Shaun Yeah?

Clarine I've got tights on though.

Marti Oh, well, you're laughing then.

Clarine I've always liked tights.

Shaun (*handing money to* **Marti**) Here's your change. (*To* **Clarine**.) Can I get yer a coffee?

Clarine   No, I might have an accident.

Marti (*to* **Shaun**)   Tar.

Clarine (*to* **Marti**)   I like you living here.

Shaun *goes into kitchen.*

Marti   Well, it's not for long so make the most o'me. Then you'll meet Juliet.

Clarine   Is she pretty?

Marti   Juliet? She's gorgeous.

Shaun *comes to the kitchen door.*

Marti   She used to be a model but she helps Shaun out with the hairdressing now. They met at a hairdressing competition.

Clarine   Has she got lovely long blonde hair and blue eyes and legs that go on forever?

Shaun   No, she's mixed race.

Clarine   I was in a mixed race once.

Shaun   No. She's black.

Marti   As in the colour of skin.

Shaun   Her mum was white and her dad was black.

Marti   So that makes her mixed race.

Clarine   Egg and spoon.

Marti   But she's got too much up top to be a model. She's the brains of the business.

Shaun   Oh aye?

Clarine   They played a joke on me. Everyone else's was hard-boiled and mine was raw. Stacey McNamara tripped me up halfway and I got yolk down me nylons.

Pause.

Marti   She reckons she's got rats.

Shaun   Have yeh?

Clarine   Mm.

Marti   Have you seen these rats?

Clarine   I've heard them. Calling me names.

Shaun   I'm not being funny wit yer, Clarine, but, rats can't speak.

Clarine   These are a special breed. Don't call me Clarine. I don't call you Norman. They tell me to do things.

Marti   Have you got any tablets you should be taking?

Clarine   Can we have another party? I liked the last one.

Shaun   When Juliet gets back. We'll have one then. A big one. Coz she'll want to see all her mates.

Clarine *puts the cushion down, excited.*

Clarine   You'll want to have a party when you hear me news.

Shaun   Barbados?

Clarine   Yeah, it's nice, int it? Me mam gave me this.

Shaun   Has she been?

Clarine   Yeah.

Shaun   Goway. D'you wanna brew, Mart?

Marti   No thanks.

Shaun *exits to kitchen.*

Marti   If you wanna stay for something to eat, you know, Clarine, you're more than welcome.

Clarine   Sharon.

Marti   You what?

Clarine   That's me news. Today. I remembered me name.

Marti   Ah, excellent!

Clarine   Tar.

Marti   How did you remember?

Clarine   A leaflet came. And I read it. And it said Sharon. And that's when I remembered. And I asked someone in the launderette what the map on it was. And they said it was directions to the sorting office. So I went and handed the leaflet in and they gave me a parcel.

Marti   Who was it from?

Clarine   Me mam. But. Me mam's dead.

Pause.

Marti   What was in it?

Clarine   A T-shirt, a box of chocolates, two pairs of underpants, a photo of this girl, and a letter. But I couldn't read all of it, but I don't care coz it reminded me what my name is. Sharon.

Marti   Right. Oh, well, that's brilliant. Ah, I'm made up for you!

Shaun *appears at the door of the kitchen holding a photo.*

Shaun   Was this the girl?

Clarine   Eh?

Shaun   The photo in the parcel. Was that her?

He hands **Clarine** *the photo.*

Shaun   Well?

Marti   Shaun?

Shaun   Barbados?! Are you as daft as her?

Marti   .Shaun!!

Shaun   Shaun. Sharon. Sharon. Shaun. She can't read!

Clarine   I can read me own name.

Shaun   Where's this parcel? What've you done with it? Go and get it now!

Clarine   I can't.

Shaun   Just do it!

Clarine I threw it away. I don't want underpants.

Shaun Listen titforbrains, my bird is in Barbados. She said she'd sent us something. Now go and find it.

Clarine Bin men have been.

Shaun Y'what?!

Clarine Eh?

Marti Well, did you keep the letter?

Clarine I don't know.

Shaun Oh, I don't fucking believe this!

Marti Calm down, softtwat. Clarine. Sharon. Come upstairs wit me and we'll see if we can find anything.

Clarine It was from me mam, I know it was!

Shaun But you've just said your mam's dead!

Clarine Yeah, well, she could've sent it before she died or anything, couldn't she? Yeah!

Shaun You've only lived here for three weeks. How did she know your address!

Clarine It was for me. I know it was for me.

Marti Sharon, love, come on.

Shaun Sharon. Look at this girl here. (*Photo.*) You've seen her before, haven't you?

Clarine Yeah.

Shaun Thank you.

Clarine That's me mam that.

Shaun *is deflated.*

Marti Come on, love. We're going upstairs.

Clarine I'm not daft.

Clarine *exits.*

Marti Shaun, she can't help herself.

Shaun She can help herself to my property.

Marti She's sick, Shaun.

Shaun Well, so am I.

Marti *goes after* **Clarine**. *Left alone,* **Shaun** *dives for the phone and dials the international number again.*

Shaun Hello? Hello can I speak to Juliet please? (*Beat.*) Isn't she? (*Beat.*) Can you tell her Shaun rang? (*Pause.*) Have you got a number for there? (*Beat.*) Hello? (*Beat.*) Hello?

He puts the phone down. Immediately it rings again. He snaps it up.

Shaun Hello? (*Pause.*) No she's away at the moment. She'll be back in two weeks. Who's this? (*Pause.*) Andy? (*Pause.*) Shaun. I'm her boyfriend. (*Pause.*) Hello? Hello?

Marti *has entered. He holds a chocolate box.* **Shaun** *takes it and opens it. It is empty. He shakes it upside-down to show* **Marti**.

Shaun The greedy bitch!

Marti She said she didn't eat them.

Shaun And who did? A gang of Oxford don rats?

Marti Well, yeah, actually. (*Takes the box off him and puts it on the table.*) She'll balloon.

Shaun Why chocolates? We're supposed to be vegan. (*Cries.*)

Marti Oh, Shaun, what happened to all this positive thinking?

Shaun You know how much that letter means to me.

Marti Okay, okay.

Shaun I've spoken to her *once* since she's been away. I've just had some fella ringing up for her. I get one letter off her and *she's* fucking gone and nicked it on me. I hate living here.

Marti Oh, now stop it. Stop it! She's crying. You're crying. Maybe I feel like crying an' all.

Shaun I'm going up to look. You weren't up there long, you mighta missed something.

Marti   Shaun, she's got nothing in that flat bar a bare table, a mattress and a guitar. If she'd dropped a contact lens I'da been able to see it.

Shaun   Well, where are her clothes? She must have clothes.

Marti   Okay, there's a pile of dirty washing as well. Shaun, I want you to have Juliet's letter as much as you do. I looked.

Shaun   I'm gonna ring someone about that girl.

Marti   Well, try Virginia Bottomley for starters.

Shaun   Oh, you've got to bring politics into everything you.

Marti   Right, that's it. I'm phoning a cab. It's pointless me being here. I've got a nice easy flat in Stoke Newington. Nice neighbours. Artists, couriers. I can do without this.

Shaun   Someone wants to pull her up. You're not telling me she can get away with this. You don't seriously believe that, do yeh?

Marti   There's a pineapple, there's your knife. Sculpt it into the face of Juliet and give us all a break. (*Picks phone up. Dials a local number.*)

Shaun   Oh, you can't run out on me now.

Marti (*on phone*)   Can I have a cab, please? Yeah. 15 Rupert Street . . .

Shaun *cuts him off by slamming his hand on the phone.*

Marti   Well, that was rather childish, wasn't it?

Shaun *has frozen.* **Marti** *drops the phone and goes to the kitchen.*

Shaun   What you doing?

Marti   Checking the vindaloo! (*Exits.*)

Shaun*, left alone, kicks the couch. He chucks a cushion off it across the room. He looks for something else to throw. He gets the pineapple and hurls that backstage as well.* **Marti** *returns as he does this. He goes and retrieves the pineapple and then heads back to the kitchen again.* **Shaun** *sits down fuming. A tap runs in the kitchen, then is switched off.* **Marti** *returns with the pineapple and carries on preparing the fruit salad.* **Shaun** *lies on the bed and puts a pillow over his head.*

Marti   If you're tryina do an impersonation of me gran you're gonna need a rope and a chair. You tie the noose. I'll kick the chair away for yeh.

Shaun *hurls the pillow at* **Marti**. *He catches it.*

Marti   Can't you phone Juliet?

Shaun   She's not in, is she. She's gone to a barbecue.

Marti   Well, she'll be having a ball then. Can't you just enjoy the idea of that?

Shaun   What's she gonna eat at a barbie? She's vegan!

Marti   Well, don't they have Linda McCartney sausages out there?

Pause. Disheartened, **Marti** *throws his knife down on the coffee-table and buries his head in his hands. He looks up.*

Marti   It's been a crap life this. Maybe next time I'll come back as a prisoner of war. There's bound to be more laughs then. I want the class and campery of a Bette Davis movie and I feel like I'm stuck in an episode of *EastEnders*. Misery, misery, always misery. There's no let up. It's not easy oppression. I'm oppressed, you know.

Shaun   I'm depressed.

Marti   Yeah, well, I'm oppressed and depressed so there. And I'm recessed. And processed. And Beau Jeste. (**Shaun** *stifles a giggle.*) It's no laughing matter. Don't laugh at me, I'm a fool.

Shaun   You're no fool, Marti.

Marti   There's no fool like an old fool.

Shaun   You're not old though.

Marti   I'm thirty-three and I've finally come to realise what I am.

Shaun (*doing his 'Veda' from* Mildred Pierce)   A common frump whose father lived above a grocery store and whose mother . . .

Marti   A coward.

Shaun   Nah. I'm the coward. I'm the one who can't function just coz me bird's away.

Marti   I've spent a lifetime being defensive, being loud, camping it up. It's all armour. To cover up the real coward within.

Shaun   Noël Coward?

Marti   I'm being serious. Why is it the only time I'm not afraid is when I'm three Es under? I am. I'm a coward.

Shaun   Well, the right man comes along.

Marti   Don't you patronise me.

Shaun   I'm not. The right girl came along for me.

Marti   And what if he already did? And I was too scared to say Yes?

Shaun   He'll come back.

Marti   Yeah and he won't find me coz I'm always round here.

Shaun   Phone a cab then.

Marti   Have you seen what's on the telly tonight? *Stolen Life.* The man of my dreams would be a real Bette Davis freak. He's not gonna leave his house while that's on. And neither am I.

Shaun   I remember when I first looked at this ceiling like this. Thought I'd found me own little corner of Paradise. (*Sits up.*) What's *Stolen Life* like?

Marti (*nearly reaching orgasm*)   Bette Davis playing *twins*.

Shaun   We could go for a bevvy after.

Marti   I feel a mess today.

Shaun   Bollocks, you'll have loads of people coming up to yeh.

Marti   And saying 'Who's your mate?' Oh, why can't someone just walk through that door who's got half a brain and thinks Bette Davis is the best thing since sliced bread?

Clarine *enters with a piece of paper.*

Clarine   I've found it.

Pause.

It wasn't from her.

Shaun   What?

Clarine   It was from me mam.

Shaun   Let's see.

Clarine *hands* **Shaun** *the letter. He inspects it.*

Clarine (*sings*)   Every time we say goodbye
I cry a little.
Every time we say goodbye
I wonder why a little.
Why the Gods above me
Who must be in the know
Think so little of me
You decided to go.
I can hear a lark somewhere.

She stops.

(*Speaks.*)   My boyfriend's away at the moment. I understand.

Marti   Shaun didn't mean to shout at you, did you, Shaun?

Clarine   He shouts. He's in Northern Ireland. Visiting the troops. (*Beat.*) I'm stupid you know.

Shaun   No, you're not.

Clarine   I am. All that time forgetting me name.

Marti   It's easily done.

Clarine   It was on me UB40 all the time. Night.

Shaun   Night, Sharon.

She exits. She stands out on the landing. They are unaware that she's still there.

Marti   It's pathetic. She needs to be somewhere where people are going to say Yes, you are stupid. Your behaviour is seriously dodgy. Get a life. Remember who you really are.

Clarine *exits from view.*

Marti We could all do with a bit of that. I better check that curry hasn't evaporated. What's it say?

Shaun You're right, Marti. It is pathetic. (*Reads.*) Sharon. Squiggle squiggle squiggle. Mum. Kiss.

Marti *exits to the kitchen.* **Shaun** *looks at the letter. The lights fade. 'Every Time We Say Goodbye' plays, starting at the line 'I can hear a lark somewhere'.*

Scene Three

Later that night. **Marti** *and* **Dean** *enter supporting a very pissed* **Shaun**. **Shaun** *is singing 'American Pie'. Steeleye Span is floating up from downstairs.*

Shaun (*sings*)   Did you write the book of love?

Dean Come on.

Shaun And do you have faith in God above?

Marti Shaun!

Shaun If the Bible tells you so.

Marti D'you want your bed?

Shaun And do you believe in rock and roll
Can music save your mortal soul
And can you teach me how to dance real slow?

Marti (*to* **Dean**)   Oh, fuck him.

Marti *and* **Dean** *let go of* **Shaun** *and sit down.*

Shaun Well, I knew you were in love with him
Coz I saw you dancing in the gym.

Marti He's unrepentedly straight.

Shaun You both kicked off your shoes
And I did those rhythm and blues.

Marti Isn't this where we do a counter-attack of 'I Will Survive'?

Shaun *jumps on the bed and keeps on singing.* **Dean** *and* **Marti** *light up some fags.* **Marti** *goes towards the kitchen.*

Marti (*to* **Shaun**)   You're not impressing anyone! (*Exits.*)

Shaun   I was a lonely teenage bronkin' buck
With a pink carnation and a pick-up truck
But I knew that I was out of luck
The day the music died.
I started singing . . .

Dean (*joins in*)   Bye bye Miss American Pie
Drove my chevvy to the levy but the levy
was dry.

Marti (*entering with three cans of lager and joining in*)
Them good old boys were drinking
whisky and rye
Singing this'll be the day that I die.
This'll be the day that I die.

Marti *hands out the three cans, one each.*

Shaun (*speaks*)   You think all the good songs are fucking
'Secret Love' and torch songs and queer anthems. But everyone.
Everyone knows 'American Pie'.

Marti   We haven't all got it in for heterosexuals, you know.

Dean   Both my parents were.

Marti   And mine.

Dean   It's a conspiracy.

Shaun   D'you know what it is? Eh? D'you wanna know what it
really is?

Shaun *huddles them together, one either side.*

Shaun   It's . . . bollocks. (*Laughs heartily. Steps back from the
huddle.*) Ah Dean lad, d'you know him? (*Puts arm round* **Marti**.) I
love this man. And d'you know what? I fucking think the world
of him. You know when that Polish cunt fucked him around. I
was fucking spitting blood. Ah, I was though. No one. No one
messes my brother around. Ah, I was fuming, Marti. I really

was. (*Falls onto bed backwards by accident. Not onto his back, but sitting. To* **Dean**.) D'you know what I mean, lad?

Marti (*to* **Dean**)   He's talking to you.

Shaun   Dean. D'you know what I'm saying?

Dean   Yeah, mate.

Shaun *is trying unsuccessfully to get his trainers off.* **Marti** *goes and helps him.*

Marti   I think it was that last tequila slammer that did it.

Shaun   Ah, man. How many tequila slammers did we have?

Dean   I've got some whizz somewhere.

Shaun   About eight?

Dean   Wannabit?

Marti   I love it when I bump into you, Dean, you can always be sure of a wild time.

Shaun   Marti, Marti. (*American.*) You bought the new girdles a size smaller I can feel it.

Dean   Shaun?

Shaun   Something maybe grew a size . . . what?

Marti   He's asking if you want some speed.

Shaun (*dismissive wave of hand, carries on with* All About Eve)   When I get home I'm gonna . . . Marti!!

Marti   I'm having this, aren't I?

Marti *has some of the speed* **Dean** *has passed him.*

Shaun   Ah, well, fuck yeh then yeh bore.

Dean (*to* **Shaun**)   Sure you don't want none?

Shaun   I'm working in the morning.

Marti   You, y'drunken lush, are gonna have a hangover on you the size o' my nobbage in the morning. I don't see how a little bit o' whizz is gonna make much difference.

Dean Come on. Or are all straight bastards wimps?

Dean *dabs the speed round his gums.*

Shaun Have you seen *Reservoir Dogs*, Dean?

Dean Yeah.

Shaun Have yeh? It's brilliant, isn't it?

Dean Yeah.

Shaun It's fucking excellent.

Dean (*about the speed*) Shame it's not coke.

Marti Coke on the dole this.

Dean My snake's called Charlie.

Shaun Well, give it here then.

Dean I won't be able to get it up now. (*Passes* **Shaun** *the speed.*)

Marti Good.

Dean Listen.

Marti What?

Dean Downstairs. That music.

Marti God, it's loud enough, isn't it?

Shaun *is up off the bed, doing kung fu-ish kick-boxing around the room and talking to himself in an American Deputy Dawg voice.*

Shaun It's good shit, man! It's good shit!

Shaun *takes a run at the bed, jumps on it like he's in a kung fu film and going in for the kill. He lands and lies on his back and goes to sleep.*

Dean You're my mate. You know that, dontcha?

Marti I know.

Dean Yeah. Mate.

Marti Good. That's really good that. I do love you, Dean. As that old adage goes.

Dean I love you, mate. In a friendship way.

Marti   I know.

Dean   It's true, isn't it?

Marti   What?

Dean   Everything.

Marti   Right from the word go. Right from the moment you jammed your stiletto heel through the wire mesh up the top o'the bogs and broke that bulb.

Dean   Life's a train. And we're on that train. And some days it goes real fast right, and some days it goes real . . . slow. Yeah?

Marti   Yeah, like some days you can have a real Orient Express of a day, and the next your riding Ivor the Engine.

Dean   Ah, brilliant, what was the tune?

Marti   I forget.

Dean   Bang-on tune.

Marti   I know, yeah.

Dean   I'm surprised it weren't released on CD.

Marti   Maybe we should.

Dean   Ah, man! We would make seriously big money. Party on, d'you know what I mean?

There is a knock at the door. **Marti** *gets up.*

Marti   I know, yeah.

Dean   Yeah!

Marti *opens the door to* **George** *who holds a glass of red wine. She is wearing jeans and a waistcoat. No shoes.*

George   I heard you coming in. He's downstairs.

Marti   Is he?

George   Yeah.

Marti   Fab. Who?

George   Daffyd!! Had him over for dinner. He's staying over. Insisting I have the futon if you please.

Dean   I do, please. Half of Ilford can't be wrong.

George (*looking at* **Shaun**)   How *is* he?

Marti   He's asleep, God love him.

George   Did you take him out to drown his sorrows?

Marti   He had a bit of speed then fell straight asleep.

George   Juliet wrote and told me. I don't know what to say.

Marti   Told you what?

George   It's so sad, isn't it?

Marti   What?

George   That she'd written to him and done the evil deed. Did she use those words? Sorry, I've had two glasses of wine. Sounds so cold. Evil deed. I don't really believe anybody's evil. How did he take it?

Pause.

George   I know she's a great friend of mine, and I'm not being biased. But I don't think she's evil, do you? You know she doesn't hate him. You do know that, don't you? You know at one stage she downright worshipped the guy. Yeah? I'll show you the letter. Don't go away.

She goes to the door and shouts down the stairs.

George   Daffyd! Daffyd!! (*Turns back to* **Marti**.) He's a real Steeleye Span freak. (*Calls.*) Daffyd! Could you get me the letter that's in the pocket of my Gloria Vanderbilt jeans?!! (*Realises she's wearing them.*) Oh, scrap that! I've got them on!

She comes back into the room. She gets a letter out of her pocket. She reads a bit.

George (*reading*)   You probably already know by now, but I've finished with Shaun. It was a cowardly thing to do, I know, telling him by post. But it was the only way.

Marti *sits on the bed.*

George   Sorry. Haven't got my specs on.

Dean *gets up and takes the letter off her. He sits back down and reads.*

Dean   'He was stiffing me. Sorry, stifling. He was stifling me in the end and coming out here I felt such a release. Marti always said he was my bit of rough Scouse trade. Marti's more perceptive than he lets on. Sorry, Marti's Shaun's brother. A real case. Anyway, I hope Shaun's new single lifestyle doesn't cause you too much grief. If he plays his music too loud just give him a knock. He can be quite thoughtful when he's told to be. I just got sick of telling him. I've just read the new Jackie Collins. *Hollywood Kids*.'

Pause.

George   They seemed so good together. Anyway, Daffyd's simmering on a low light down there. It's about time I went in and really started cooking with gas.

Marti   He doesn't know, George, he never got the letter.

George   Shit me.

Dean (*to* **Marti**)   You gotta tell him.

Marti (*to* **George**)   You're Juliet's mate. You've got to tell him.

George   I'm up at seven to go to the Forest of Dean.

Dean   I haven't got a forest.

Marti   Oh, shut up, Dean.

Dean   Sorry, mate.

George   I'm truly sorry.

George *exits.*

Dean   Shit.

Pause.

What you gonna do?

Marti *jumps up, pulls the phone out of the wall then starts attacking the sofa. He claws at it with his hands and kicks it.* **Dean** *gets up to stop him. He pulls him off.* **Marti** *wrestles away and attacks it again.*

Dean Oi! Oi!

Dean *holds onto him.* **Marti** *pushes him off.* **Marti** *heads for the door.*

Dean Oi, where d'you think you're going?

Marti For a walk!

Dean Hang on.

Marti *exits.* **Dean** *follows with their two coats.* **Shaun** *is left alone in the room, lying on the bed. There is some sort of noise coming out of him, an animal-like groaning. It grows louder. He sits up. He moves over to the letter which* **Dean** *has left on the arm of the chair. He stands reading it. He breathes deeply through his nose. He finishes it. He doesn't cry. He moves over to the stereo. Very calmly he looks through some tapes. He selects one, puts it in the machine and rewinds it. He plays it. It is 'American Pie' by Don McClean. He kneels in front of the stereo and sings along, quietly at first, but getting louder. As he kneels, he folds the letter into an aeroplane shape. He stands up and starts to dance, the letter in his hand. He gets his lager and dances over to the window. He takes a big swig of his lager and opens the window. He throws the letter out of the window. He leaves the window open and goes and turns the music up full-blast. He dances round the room drinking and singing along with the song.*

Clarine *enters in bra and slip. She speaks with a Kidderminster accent.*

Clarine Turn it down! It's too loud! Turn it down!

He grabs her and dances her round the room, singing loudly to himself. This upsets her.

Shaun! I'm trying to get to sleep up there! Turn it down will you?

Marti *enters in the doorway with* **Dean**. **Shaun** *sees him and stops. He stares at* **Marti**. **Clarine** *rubs her arms where he's gripped her a bit too tightly.* **Shaun** *grabs* **Marti** *to dance. He dances for a bit then stops, hugs* **Marti** *to him and cries.* **Marti** *leads him to the bed and lies him down.* **Shaun** *pulls him down on the bed and holds onto him, still crying.* **Dean** *and* **Clarine** *both watch this, then* **Dean** *leads* **Clarine** *out, shutting the door behind them as the music fades.*

Scene Four

A few days later. **Shaun** *is packing away all his possessions into an assortment of suitcases. He discards some items in the room and keeps others. There's no pattern to the packing. Sometimes he'll go in the kitchen and return with things from there.* **Marti** *sits on the couch with a pen and paper.* **Shaun** *is dictating a letter to him.*

Shaun Dear Juliet,

How's Barbados? I hope your flight was turbulent and that all the air-hostesses were dykes and sexually harassed you. I hope the weather is really shite and that you get mugged at least seventeen point five times a day. I hope the funeral went disastrously and that there was some big cock-up and you ended up in the grave as well.

Marti How d'you spell disastrously?

Shaun Shut up. (*Continues.*) I just want you to know that I didn't enjoy a single second that I was with you. I ate kebabs behind your back. I was shagging George for six months. I faked every orgasm and since you've left have become a leading light in the British National Party.

Marti Oh, that's sick.

Shaun I said shut up. (*Continues.*) I was so delighted to hear that you'd finished with me that I threw a party and shagged loads of well tasty women. Linda Lusardi, the girl off the Peugeot adverts, Kate Moss and Björk.

Marti Björk?

Shaun Shut it. (*Continues.*) I forgot to mention that I am HIV positive.

Marti Ay!! Now I'm not playing any more. (*Throws pad down.*)

Shaun And as we never practised safe sex, you probably are as well by now.

Marti Even if you faked every orgasm?

Shaun I've never met anybody as ugly as you in my life, and if I ever do again I hope I don't take pity on them because I think it would have been better for both of us, and especially you, if I had taken a machete to your ugly face the day I met you. The grand you invested in Curls on Wheels I have spent on hiring a contract killer to slaughter all your family on Boxing Day . . . 1999. I hope you are ill. Lots of hate. Badbye. Shaun.

Marti And who says we people in Liverpool can't take a knock?

Shaun It's just a shame I don't know where she is.

Marti I think you're being stupid.

Shaun Marti, I can't send her that.

Marti No. This stupid idea of yours to move back to Liverpool. There's no room in me mam and dad's house. They'll drive you up the wall.

Shaun So far I have driven up that wall, across that ceiling and down the other side being here.

Marti But the business . . .

Shaun If it's the five hundred quid you're worried about then I'll pay you back.

Marti You can't afford that.

Shaun I can borrow it.

Marti Off who?

Shaun I'll send it to you.

Marti I'm not worried about the five hundred quid. I'm not a capitalist bastard, am I?

Shaun Aren't you? I dunno. You just seem a bit bothered about the bloody van.

Marti I don't give a shit about the van, Shaun.

Shaun Well, stop mithering me then.

Marti Moving back to Liverpool's a backward step. You wanna move forward. Onwards and upwards.

Shaun I'm not staying here.

Marti   Come and stay wit me.

Shaun   I just. I just need some time on me own to chill. Every street I walk down round here's got Juliet written all over it. I'm sick of heartache when I see . . . when I see the bench we sat on or the, or the bloody pizza place we went to. I'm doing meself in with it all. Anyway. I like Liverpool.

Marti   You left it soon enough.

Shaun   To go on some big adventure. To find me. Well, I didn't find me, I found her. Oh. It's not forever, is it. Might only be a few months. Or weeks. When London's knocking the shite and stuffing outa yer, where d'you go for a breather?

Marti   Brighton.

Shaun   You go back to your ma and da's, you know you do.

Marti   I'd hate to see you take such a big fall backwards coz of some snobby bitch.

Shaun   A week, a month, a year, it's neither here nor there. I'm doing it.

Marti   You can take the girl from Liverpool, but you can't take Liverpool from the girl.

Shaun   When you've split up with anyone in the past, what've you done eh? You moved on to a different city.

Marti   I didn't know you then.

Shaun   Well, it's true, isn't it?

Marti   I don't want to talk about it.

Shaun   Why not? I'll tell you why not, coz you know deep down I'm doing the right thing.

Marti   But you're stronger than me.

Shaun   Marti, we're from the same stock you and me. I'm not.

Marti   Go back to Liverpool. See if I care.

Shaun   You're . . . you're . . .

Marti   I said go back to Liverpool. With my consent.

Shaun   But, Marti, I don't need your consent. I'm not your boyfriend.

Marti (*American*)   Oh, really? I didn't know.

Shaun   Well, sometimes I feel that . . . oh, what's the point.

Shaun goes into the kitchen.

Marti   What have you felt?

Shaun (*off*)   Nothing.

Marti   That I'm in love wit yer?

Shaun (*off*)   Oh, forget I said anything, Marti. (*Returns with plates.*)

Marti   And what if I was?

Pause.

Shaun   Don't be daft.

Marti   I spent most of me life hating you. Why can't I spend the rest of it loving you?

Shaun   Shut up.

Marti   You were such a homophobic little bastard.

Shaun   No, I wasn't.

Marti   I know.

Shaun   Well, then.

Marti   I do. I know. That's my problem. D'yer ever feel you were blessed with the gift of insight? I do. And even as I lay there in the hospital, blood oozing from every orifice. I knew you didn't really mean it. It's only coz you were young. I knew it wasn't your fault, though it didn't help.

Shaun   I was a prick then and I've changed.

Marti   It didn't stop me hurting.

Shaun   Marti.

Marti   Shut up, will yer? I'm talking here. I never knew the real you.

Pause.

Shaun No one did. I was the hardknock coz I felt . . . I felt. Oh, you know the other day, when you said you'd built up the camp bit to protect you from the knocks? Well, that's what I did with me fists.

Marti And then Juliet's on the scene and suddenly you're Romeo. And I'm all right. Welcomed in with open arms. But I knew.

Shaun God, you know everything you, don't yer?

Marti I know you. I've known you since you were an egg. It was all her doing. You were nothing 'til you met her and now you're nothing again. And now I'm nothing.

Shaun Don't say that, Marti.

Marti All the time. I wanted yer all to meself. And now I've got it. And it's not what I want at all. I find it hard to love you. I find it so hard it fucks me up. The only men I've ever loved have been fellas, my fellas. I never loved me dad. I never loved you once you were older. I wasn't allowed.

Shaun But yer are now.

Marti Shaun, I can't love you.

Pause.

Shaun Now who's being homophobic? Can't love me coz I'm your own brother and you're a queen?

Marti I don't know any straight men.

Shaun You know me.

Marti You're our kid.

Pause.

Shaun The good thing about Juliet. She blew me brains away wit knowledge and understanding and tolerance . . .

Marti Oh, so I'm to be tolerated, am I?

Shaun   I'm not articulating this very . . . just . . . Credit me with some sense man. I'm not gonna drop everything we've got coz of her!

Pause.

What?

Marti   I'm not used to it.

Shaun   What?

Marti   Someone loving me.

Shaun *goes and sits on the arm of the sofa and cuddles* **Marti**. **Marti** *is crying.* **Shaun** *lifts his face up and wipes the tears off his face. He holds* **Marti**'*s hands.*

Marti   I do love yer, you know.

Shaun   Then stop fucking crying.

Marti *kisses him. It's half a snog. They have a snog for a split second.* **Marti** *pulls away.*

Marti   Jesus Christ, what've I done?

Shaun   It's all right, lad.

Shaun *stands.*

Shaun   I better get me stuff from the bathroom.

He exits through the main door. **Marti** *sits there gasping for breath. He looks around him panicking. He has difficulty sitting still. He gets up and goes to the window and batters it. He runs off to the kitchen and we hear a lot of banging about, drawers and doors. Then finally a quick smash of broken glass.*

Shaun *comes back in with a red towel.*

Shaun   It's pointless taking a half-empy bottle of Wash and Go back with me. Listen, lad, will you fly that kettle on while you're in there?

He lifts a suitcase onto the bed to close it. **Marti** *comes to the door of the kitchen holding his wrists, they're bleeding. He has slashed his wrists on the kitchen window. He stands there hysterically half laughing/half crying.* **Shaun** *hears and turns around. He is immobilised, staring at* **Marti**.

Marti I don't. I don't.

Marti *looks about him not knowing what to do. He goes to the window and pulls the blind down. He turns to* **Shaun**. **Shaun** *gets up and gets a cigarette. He holds it in his hand, trembling. There is a tap on the main door and* **Clarine** *enters. She is dressed as in the first scene and carrying her guitar. She speaks with a London accent.*

Clarine Hiya, darling.

Shaun *is staring at* **Marti**. *He lifts the cigarette to his mouth and lights it.* **Clarine** *looks around and sees* **Marti**. *She drops the London accent.*

Clarine Oh, my God. (*To* **Shaun**.) Have you phoned for help?

She gets no response. She goes to the phone and dials 999.

(*On phone.*) Ambulance. (*Beat.*) Yeah. Ambulance please. Fifteen Rupert Street. Middle flat. There's been an incident. (*Beat.*) An incident. Quickly please.

She puts the phone down. She throws the guitar down on the sofa and goes out to the kitchen.

Marti (*to* **Shaun**) Shut it, will yer? (*Beat.*) I said shut up.

Clarine *rushes back in with wet tea towels and ties them round* **Marti**'s *wrists.*

Clarine You're gonna be all right, love. You're gonna be okay.

Marti Yeah.

Clarine Isn't he, Shaun? You're gonna be just fine. There, there's nothing to worry about. Come on.

She leads him to the couch and sits down with him.

That's it. Everything's gonna be fine. I'm here. Shaun's here. Everything's gonna be okay.

Marti *is looking at the guitar and nodding to it. He is crying in pain now.* **Shaun** *sits on the bed smoking in a daze.* **Clarine** *picks up the guitar.*

Clarine Isn't it lovely?

Marti Yeah.

Clarine You like musical instruments, don't you?

Marti   Yeah.

Clarine   Ah, so do I! Listen. (*She strums a chord. He smiles. She strums again.*)

Marti   Yeah.

Clarine *strums an intro to 'House of the Rising Sun'.*

Marti   Yeah.

Clarine *starts to sing. As she does* **Marti** *sits back and leans his head back.* **Shaun** *continues to smoke.*

Clarine   Amazing Grace
How sweet the sound
That saved a wretch like me.
I once was lost
But now am found
Was blind and now can see.

The tea towels are now red with blood. The lights fade. As the blackout comes, 'Miss Chatelaine' by k. d. lang starts to play.